Presented To:

Larry + Donna Gruwell

From:

Abraham John

Date:

11/15/14

Thank you to work for partnering
with me to reach the world

11/26/14

THE THREE
MOST IMPORTANT
DECISIONS
OF YOUR LIFE

THE THREE
MOST IMPORTANT
DECISIONS
OF YOUR LIFE

Preparing a Generation
to Make History

ABRAHAM JOHN

The Three Most Important Decisions of Your Life
Preparing a Generation to Make History
Copyright © 2014 by Abraham John

Published by Abraham John
Maximum Impact Ministries
P.O. Box 3128, Syracuse, NY 13220

www.maximpact.org

email: mim@maximpact.org

(720) 560 4664

ISBN: 978-1-936578-37-5
LCCN: 2014913721
Printed and published in the U.S.A.

DEDICATION

This book is dedicated to our children Rachel, Joshua, and Renee, and at the Vision Center in India. You are growing up to be world changers and history makers for Christ and His Kingdom. You are the most extraordinary and amazing children in the world. Through you, God has taught me many things about life and blessed me in many ways; more than you will ever know. I pray that this book will be a great asset to your life and the generations to come.

www.visioncenterindia.org

ACKNOWLEDGMENTS

I would like to acknowledge the following persons for their valuable and sacrificial help in the fulfillment of this dream.

My wife Tahnya, who has done the preliminary editing and proofreading of this long manuscript. Besides doing almost everything with and for our children, you have stayed up many late nights to read through this book and offered valuable input. Though I may not say it enough or often, you are the best thing that has happened in my life so far.

Nathan Bliss, the prolific editor who has done a fast-track editing work and made this book more readable and attractive. Thank you for your sacrificial commitment to this work while working a full-time job.

Our new friend Mary Kate, who designed the cover for this book. Your creative mind is enviable.

John De Young, I have never in my life seen a person who is as resourceful and talented as you are. Thank you so much for flying all the way to Kerala to come and see me, and the work we do at the Vision Center. Our lives have not been the same since.

All my friends and leaders who took the time to read the manuscript and write an endorsement for this book. Your time and willingness is really appreciated.

And to the partners of Maximum Impact Ministries, whose prayers and selfless giving made this dream come true. You are my modern-day heroes of faith. Thank you.

All the glory, honor, strength, wisdom, power, blessing, and riches to my Lord Jesus Christ who has called me and entrusted me with this valuable revelation.

ENDORSEMENTS

Navigating through the intricacies of life with its complex configurations is challenging to say the least. The transitions of a child to a teen and eventually the emergence of an adult come with many life-altering complexities, which demand accurate decision-making. These times, which all will encounter, come with anxieties and fears. However, in Christ regardless of where you're at in life, we have access to a manual that provides precise information destined to impact the reader who's willing to follow the instructions.

Abraham John has done an excellent job in crafting out this discourse, which is a blueprint that will help you build in sequence with the Author of life. From the very preface of this book there's a sense of being set up to see truth on a much deeper level and encounter something new and fresh. I was tremendously blessed by the flow and content of this book, simple yet full of substance.

God's word encourages us to embrace wisdom as the principal thing, and in all our getting we are to get understanding. Within these pages wisdom and understanding are in abundance. I highly recommend this book, *The Three Most Important Decisions of Your Life: Preparing a Generation to Make History.*

Apostle Stephen A. Garner
Senior Leader, Rivers of Living Water Ministries Int'l, Chicago, Illinois USA

In this powerful book, Abraham John brilliantly unveils divine priorities, Kingdom principles and gives us practical applications. It's a deep and far-reaching study on life-changing decisions. The truths taught in this book can change a life and set a destiny on the right course: truly a blessing.

Dr. Joelle Suel
Lead Pastor, Glory to Glory Christian Center, Denver, CO USA

The Three Most Important Decisions of Your Life, written by my good friend and fellow minister Abraham John is of uttermost importance for every believer. We all are facing decisions in every area of our lives, but do we understand that every decision has a powerful effect on our lives? Every decision I take today will shape my future. Once the decision is taken, I cannot blame the circumstances or others, if the outcome is not what I wanted. Decisions - we face them, we have to take them and we have to live with the consequences they bring.

The Three Most Important Decisions of Your Life is a helpful workbook in the process of making/taking decisions. *I pray that Abraham John's* latest book will be a great blessing and encouragement to every believer.

Pastor Ivano Lai
Senior Pastor Pfimi Bern, Switzerland

As a businessman I cannot succeed without wisdom, understanding, and knowledge. In Abraham John's new book, *The Three Most Important Decisions of Your Life*, he introduces you to them, teaches you how to find them, and shows you how to build a successful life with them. Read this book and discover what very few people know but all truly successful people share. Abraham writes this book from first hand experience, and a life that is lived reflecting it.

David McDonald
President, Escalante Golf, Ft. Worth, Texas, USA

Abraham John has given us a life plan for living a biblically based successful life with God in *The Three Most Important Decisions of Your Life: Preparing a Generation to Make History*. You'll find a wealth of wisdom designed to order every aspect of your life in this book. I highly recommend it.

Os Hillman
President, Marketplace Leaders
Author, *Change Agent and TGIF Today God Is First* devotional.

Abraham, thank you for the time and energy that you have poured into this book. Readers, be ready to be challenged in many ways as you read this book on a perspective on God's Word that will anger some, challenge some, and open the eyes of many of those willing to read and study it for themselves. I thank

God for Abraham's courage to write and publish this book to challenge each of us in our thinking.

Ford Taylor
President, FSH/Transformational Leadership

Abraham John's latest book, *The Three Most Important Decisions of Your Life*, continues on the same path of excellent wisdom teaching as his previous books like *Keys to Passing Your Spiritual Tests*. Reverend John is a fresh voice for an ageless message that will challenge all generations. The results of our lives are largely the results of the decisions we make and knowing and understanding God's blueprint for our life is critical to our decision-making.

Pastor Reece Bowling
Orchard Road Christian Center, CO, USA

This timely book addresses the three most important decisions of life. I will call it a life manual, relevant for both Christians and non-Christians alike. Abraham took time here to understand the very mind of God for human success in every field of life and releases the basic golden keys to facing day-to-day challenges. I recommend this masterpiece to both Christians and non-Christians who desire a successful life here now and there after. Take time to read through, the information here will not only transform you, but will as well help you not repeat the mistakes of others.

Dr. Nelson Nnannah
Presiding Bishop, Soulwinners Int'l Churches, Nigeria, West Africa

CONTENTS

Preface   17

Introduction   19

PART I

Chapter 1: Three Friends You Need To Succeed In Life   27

Chapter 2: Which *God* Do You Believe In?   39

Chapter 3: Ingredients that Make a *God*   *51*

Chapter 4: God's Opinion Of You   61

PART II

Chapter 5: The Manual For Life On This Earth - Part 1   71

Chapter 6: The Manual For Life On This Earth - Part 2   83

Chapter 7: The Manual For Life On This Earth - Part 3   103

PART III

Chapter 8: The First Most Important Decision Of Your Life   117

Chapter 9: Seek God's Kingdom And His Righteousness   137

Chapter 10: The Law And Grace   155

Chapter 11: The Second Most Important Decision Of Your Life   183

Chapter 12: 6 Reasons God Created Man   197

Chapter 13: The Process Of Having Dominion   213

Chapter 14: 10 Keys To Discovering Your Purpose   239

Chapter 15: The Third Most Important Decision Of Your Life   249

Chapter 16: 14 Reasons Marriages Fail   275

PART IV

Chapter 17: The Process Of Making Good Decisions   289

Chapter 18: A Word To Parents   297

Chapter 19: Blessing The Four Stages Of Life   313

Chapter 20: The Season Of Total Restoration   323

PREFACE

I have heard parents say, "I wish babies came with a manual!" I have good news; babies do come with a manual! In fact, babies are the only products for which we get to read the manual before we have the product. That sounds like a good deal but it gets even better. No matter which country you live in, every baby born on this earth has the same manual because, through the centuries, the Manufacturer of babies has not changed! The same Manufacturer that produced babies five thousand years ago still produces them. The last I heard, He is not planning to switch the ownership of the company to anyone else or outsource production! He has not updated or changed the manual. The same manual that people used in earlier civilizations is still the same and is still valid. Life on this earth cannot get simpler than that.

But, there is a problem. Though the manual is available in almost every known language and it is only three chapters long, very few people understand its *language*. For this reason, most people do not read it. Some do not read it because they think it is too old. A few others do not read it because they think they know *better*. Moreover, the majority of those who do read it can't understand it because they do not have a relationship with the Manufacturer. One unique thing about this manual is that the relationship the reader has with the Manufacturer determines how well he or she understands it when they read. You need to know Him personally to know how and why He made you. Only the manufacturer knows the purpose of a product.

It is the most thorough manual ever written for a product. It is the most circulated and printed manual on the earth. Since it is a manual for human life, everyone needs a copy. In this book you will be introduced to that manual. The Three Most Important Decisions of Your Life are taken from that manual. They were written in it centuries ago. These decisions are not something new I just discovered, they are derived from old truths brought to light. Since the Manufacturer knows many will not read His original manual, He uses people like me to take excerpts like these and make it a little clearer to those who read it.

Everyone who reads and follows the instructions from this manual succeeds because it has the keys to success in any field of life, and solutions to every problem you will ever face on this earth. That is not an overstatement in any way. Finances, relationships, marriage, politics, sickness-you name it; whatever involves life on this earth, there are navigation instructions and solutions for your problems. It was written by the wisest Person in the universe. He has to be the wisest; otherwise, how can someone write one manual that is applicable for every single person on this earth? How does He know and understand each person's life situations and challenges? If He wrote it thousands of years ago, how did He know how life was going to be on earth in the 21st century? I told you, He is the wisest Person in the universe. He is the Author and the Source of all life and He is the Creator of you and me.

When we do not follow the manual of a product two things can occur. One, the product could malfunction and you may not even know it. Secondly, we may not be able to put to use the product's full potential. For example, most of us use a computer or smart phone, which have many different functions and apps that we do not know *how* to use. We just keep on using the basic programs and never demand the product's full potential. If we took the time to look around, we would see a malfunctioning world wherein most humans live below their potential. Our schools, marriages, churches, societies, and governments are all malfunctioning and people are not happy. What's the reason? We do not follow the manual for life on this earth!

The only problem man has on this earth is not reading this manual and/or following its instructions. I know this book will be a blessing to you regardless of which season of life you are in. After you read this book, share it and the wisdom you received from it with your friends and family. Get copies of this book and give them as gifts to people you know.

The purpose of this book is fourfold: 1) To raise up a new generation who will walk with God with all their heart for all their life. 2) To help the next generation not repeat the same mistakes we may have made in our own lives. 3) To help the current generation discover their purpose and solutions to life's intricate problems. 4) To open the eyes of the body of Christ to transition from a *consumer* mentality to a *producer* mentality, from an *escapist* (waiting to go to heaven) lifestyle to a *dominion* (living out our purpose here and now) lifestyle. May the LORD use this book to accomplish these. Amen.

INTRODUCTION

The Bible is a book about decisions. All trouble on this earth started with a wrong decision made by the first man, Adam. One single decision can alter your destiny for better or for worse. Life on this earth is very short. In fact, life is only long enough to make three major decisions. If you do not know that, your life will be half over by the time you figure out how to live. Before you discover the meaning of life, you will be heading toward the last season of your life. Life is very fragile. If we do not take the utmost care and precaution, life will slip away from us. You might have seen a sign on the top of a package that read, "Fragile, handle with care." That sticker should be placed on the front of all of us because life is very fragile.

Many live with the regret and pain of their decisions and choices. Sometimes, we can reverse their effects but, if it is a permanent choice, we cannot change it. Life is the sum of all of the decisions we make. Where you are in life right now is the result of all the decisions you made in the past. Some were wise and others were foolish. How do we know how to make wise choices?

I have seen people make important decisions in their life too casually. We live in a time where everything revolves around "having fun". Many people start doing things for fun, and later it bites them like a poisonous snake. All the fun runs out the window and they are left alone. All the friends they had while they were having fun have vanished.

We chart our course by our decisions. Each day we make hundreds of decisions. Some of them we are not aware of because they are part of our daily routine. You got out of bed this morning. That was a decision. For some it was easy and for others it was by force. From the moment we awaken until we go to bed again, we make decisions. It is an incredible capability God gave to human beings.

From the beginning of time, both the wise and foolish have been trying to figure out, "What is life"? Unfortunately, in the secular world, the wise and foolish have come to the same conclusions because it is impossible to understand the purpose of life without knowing the Author of life. As I said earlier, only the manufacturer knows the purpose of a product.

You might be just starting out in life, full of vigor and passion. You feel like there is nothing that can defeat or stop you. You may be somewhere in the middle. Perhaps you've tried different things and, so far, nothing has worked out the way you hoped. Now, you might be wondering what you should do with your life. You might be at the height of your success. Everything you dreamed and planned came to pass, but still you are not happy or satisfied—inside it feels like something is missing. You might be struggling with life because of all the bad choices you made and the consequences they brought in your life. You spend your days wishing you had one more chance to do it all over again. Or, you might be toward the end of your life, thinking you have been there and done it, wondering what is to come. You are tired and ready to go *home*. It does not matter what season of life you are in, you will benefit from this book.

I recently read an online article that talked about the ten things people regret the most. Another article said, "Ten things I wish my college professor had told me". I have heard that only three percent of people know exactly what they are supposed to do with their life. That means 97% of people you see do not know why they are here on this earth, Christians and non-Christians alike. They live day-to-day existences and are constantly in survival mode. That is really scary. How long will we pretend everything is okay?

It is interesting to notice that people talk more about movies, pets, games, and the things they bought at a store when they see each other than life's most important matters and seasons. Nobody wants to tell the truth. Everyone tries to hide behind some sort of mask. I do not know if it is because of pride, shame, ignorance, stupidity, or if they do not care at all. How can we not tell our children the mistakes we made so they do not have to go through the pain we went through? Why don't schools and colleges teach more about *real* life than subjects and things that do not impact our daily lives?

The Bible says one generation should declare the works of God to the next. God repeatedly told the people of Israel to tell their children what He did, and what they went through (Deuteronomy 4:9, 6:7). Sometimes He asked them to write it down, other times He told them to build a monument as a memorial to what He did for them. Unfortunately, we have left that job to a handful of preachers and to multimedia productions.

My children wanted to get a pet so I went to a pet store for the first time in my life. I was amazed to see that everything in that store was geared toward taking care of animals! There are pet hotels, groomers, trainers, doctors, spas, and everything else beyond imagination. I was wondering, "If they go through this much pain to take care of animals, how much more should we do to help men and women who are created in the image and likeness of God?" What would our children become if we paid them half of the attention and care we give to animals? I tell my family that if you are born a dog, you should be born in America!

More than fifty percent of marriages end up in divorce. Suicide is the third leading killer of teenagers in the United States (schoolhelpline.com). According to abortiontv.com, every day in the United States four thousand babies are murdered through abortion for the sake of convenience. That number is more than any terrorist group or dictator ever killed in the history of the world! What if they had taken the time before to get help? What if they realized the mistakes of thousands around them and asked for some valuable advice? As I mentioned before, people get more advice about which movie to watch and which car they should buy than regarding the most important decisions in life.

Somewhere, there is a blind spot in our hearts concerning these things because we do not see them until we are faced with them, or until it is too late. Is there a solution to this dilemma? Is there a way to know and receive wisdom before we make some of the costliest mistakes we could make? I believe there is. I want to tell you the truth; I pray you are willing to listen. This book might save you from a lot of unnecessary pain by helping you to make the wisest choices in life. It could even *save* your very life!

I wish there had been someone in my life willing to take the time and guide me through some of the decisions I made. I had a father and mother but they never opened up to share with me the realities of life. They never told me about any of the mistakes they made. They did not teach me about marriage or how to handle money. They provided food, shelter, clothing, and education, but how many of you know that is not enough to make it through life?

What I heard from friends, read in novels, and saw in movies was not real either. Everything was covered up under a religious mask and no one was willing to open up to tell the truth to the next generation. What I imagined to be true was far from reality. If I had known better, I would not have made some of the choices I made.

Some people are physically ill due to all the stress and pain that was caused by broken dreams. Others are hiding it under the costly make-up and clothes they wear. Still others have mastered hiding behind their performance or works. Believers hide behind their religious masks. Only a few are willing to open up to get the help they need, and they are on the road to recovery. I believe what God wants to do through this book is to share with you what to expect and how to navigate life.

Many are bitter toward God and others, casting blame for the mistakes they have made. "Why didn't God help me or stop this from happening? How come He didn't send anyone to tell me the truth?" That is the nature of fallen man. When something goes wrong, we tend to blame it on someone or something else. You might be asking those questions in your heart. No one can change what has already happened. We can better prepare for the future and help others not make the same mistakes. That is my intention, to help you with your life so that you will fulfill the purpose God has for you and, in turn, help others.

Time is getting late already. A wildfire of ignorance is raging and swallowing up many precious lives. Let us face the truth and proclaim it to the next generation. It does not matter how old you are, it's never too late to learn new ways of doing things in your life.

Life is only long enough to make three decisions. The life you experience will be the result of the consequences they bring. If one of those decisions is not made correctly, and in the right order, your life will encounter turbulence. Sometimes, it can even cause a fatal crash. If you have not made any of these decisions, it is important that you make them in the order that is mentioned in this book because that is the order designed by the Creator. Again, if you messed up the order, you will face some unnecessary challenges on the way. But, there is always hope. If you love God, He will make all things (everything that happened in your life) work out for your good (Romans 8:28).

May the Lord help you and give you the wisdom to make The Three Most Important Decisions of Your Life. And, may the next generation benefit from this even more than the present. All glory to God, who alone is wise.

3

PART I

CHAPTER 1
THREE FRIENDS YOU NEED
TO SUCCEED IN LIFE

CHAPTER 1: THREE FRIENDS YOU NEED TO SUCCEED IN LIFE

Since this book is about making the *Three Most Important Decisions of Your Life*, I would like to introduce you to three friends you need to meet in order to be successful on this earth. They are the best and most helpful friends I have. Someone was kind enough to introduce them to me, and my life has never been the same. You need their help to make right decisions. You need their help throughout your life. Before you make any major decision, please consult with them.

They are God's friends as well. They were with Him when He created the universe. Kings rule well with the help of these three friends, and the princes of this earth consult with them before they make a choice. If you love these friends, they will love you back and, if you honor them, they will bring you great honor. If you respect them, they will respect you. If you exalt them, they will bring promotion to your life. Everything you need in life is with these three guys. They have riches, honor, wealth, and long life and will teach you about anything you want to know. They have the answers to all of life's problems and tough questions. If you hang out with them, they will make you feel special. They will never put you down. They will bring you favor and introduce you to people of influence. They will teach you the secrets of life. They will help you find the purpose of your life, and teach you how to have a long, healthy life.

There is one distinction between all of your other friends and these three; they can tell whether or not you really love them. Unlike your other friends, you cannot fool them by pretending that you do. Just by looking at you and the way you live, others can tell if you have them as your friends. If you really love them, they will cause you to inherit great wealth and fill your house with pleasant riches.

But know this; if you do not love them and give them the place they deserve in your life, it will not go well with you. The earlier you make them your friends; the better your life will be. Seek and go after them before you seek money, sex, relationships, fame, or success. Make sure you have them before you venture out to do anything. Never quarrel or hate them. Never go anywhere without asking them to go with you. Take them with you and they will preserve your life. If they are with you, you will never be afraid because they will make you feel secure. They will keep you happy and lift you up when you fall. When you sleep, they will watch over you.

The Bible says that he who sins against them wrongs his own soul and that all those who hate them love death. It is that serious. I cannot emphasize enough how important it is that you make these guys your friends right away!

Now, you are curious to know these friends, aren't you? You might have a list of their possible names running through your head. Their names are Wisdom, Knowledge, and Understanding. The verse below reveals their roles in establishing this earth and the universe we live in.

> Proverbs 3:19-20, "The LORD by **wisdom** founded the earth, by **understanding** He established the heavens, by His **knowledge** the depths were broken up and the clouds drop down dew."

As I said earlier, they were with God when He founded the earth and established the heavens. The earth you and I stand on was founded by wisdom. Do you want to found, establish, and grow something? Then, you need these three friends. Do you want to make good decisions in your life? You need the help of these three.

The reason people say there is no God and the whole earth came out of an explosion is because true wisdom has not yet entered their heart. They are fooled by the reasoning of their mind. Since this book is about the Three Most Important Decisions of Your Life, I encourage you to make these three your friends as well. Hang out with them, and they will teach you incredible things that you do not know. They are as essential to life as the air we breathe and the water we drink. Without them you are destined to fail.

Now, you may be asking, "How does someone make wisdom, knowledge, and understanding their friends?" By loving them! Love them more than you love your pet, your favorite sports team, or your favorite movie. Respect them by your hunger to get to know them. Treat wisdom as your closest relative. The Bible says, "Treat wisdom as a sister, and make understanding your **closest friend**" (Proverbs 7:4) (NCV).

When you love God, you will automatically love wisdom. You cannot have one without the other because wisdom comes from Him (Proverbs 2:6). The more time you spend with God, the more you will discover and love His wisdom. The fear (reverential respect) of the LORD is the beginning of wisdom (Proverbs 9:10). All treasures of wisdom and knowledge are hid in Christ (Colossians 2:3).

If you really fear (reverential respect) God, it will show in your life through your love for wisdom. If you do not love wisdom, knowledge, and understanding, you have not known the real God of the Bible. He is the source of all wisdom. Study these three and find out everything you can about them. Cry out to God for them. Let me tell you that making wisdom, knowledge, and understanding your friends is a life-long process so the more you are hungry and search for them, the more you discover them.

If we are to understand the origin of the earth and the purpose of our life, we need to have these three friends. These are the three friends God used when He created this earth. He founded the earth by wisdom, established the heavens by understanding, and by His knowledge they are sustained. These are God's companions and without them He will not do anything.

God shows us how to do things by example. Whatever we do has to be founded on wisdom. Without wisdom you cannot found anything; it will fall. You cannot found your life on money or relationships (how many of you thought all your problems would be over if you just got married?) We think that way when we do not understand the wisdom and the order of God.

You may not trust what I am saying about these friends. Listen to what the Bible says about them in Proverbs 4:5-9, "Get wisdom! Get understanding! Do not forget, nor turn away from the words of my mouth. Do not forsake her, and she will preserve you; love her, and she will keep you. Wisdom *is* the principal thing; *therefore* get wisdom. And in all your getting, get understanding. Exalt her, and she will promote you; she will bring you honor, when you embrace her. She will place on your head an ornament of grace; a crown of glory she will deliver to you."

> Proverbs 3:13-18 says, "Happy *is* the man *who* finds wisdom, and the man *who* gains understanding; for her proceeds *are* better than the profits of silver, and her gain than fine gold.
>
> She *is* more precious than rubies, and all the things you may desire cannot compare with her. Length of days *is* in her right hand, in her left hand riches and honor. Her ways *are* ways of pleasantness, and all her paths *are* peace. She *is* a tree of life to those who take hold of her, and happy *are all* who retain her."

Whatever we do; wisdom must be the foundation. Our life must be built on the wisdom of God. A building is only as strong as its foundation. The foundation is the most important component of any structure. The reason many lives fall apart is because people do not apply the wisdom of God to found their life. They have given "the decorations" of life more priority than the foundation.

I found out that there is only one problem on this earth—a fundamental lack of wisdom. If God founded the earth by wisdom, everything that lives and operates on the earth should also be founded on wisdom. Without wisdom, nothing will function.

> The Bible says in Proverbs 3:16, "Length of days is in her right hand, and in her left hand riches and honor."

Wisdom has two hands. In her right hand there is long life and in her left hand are riches and honor. Wisdom brings riches, but riches may not bring wisdom. We all want to live healthy and long; what we need is the wisdom of God. We all want to have riches and honor. What is the solution? It is not getting another job, but getting the wisdom of God. If there are financial problems, it is not an unemployment problem or a recession problem; it's a wisdom problem.

If people are dying prematurely (unless you are martyred for Jesus), it means there is a wisdom problem, not a health problem. If the earth was founded by wisdom and the heavens by His understanding, what does it take to build a house or a family?

> Proverbs 24:3 says, "Through **wisdom** a house is built, and by **understanding** it is established, by **knowledge** the rooms are filled with precious and pleasant riches."

Houses and families cannot be built on money, or even love. Many people are losing their homes in America because they were not built (or bought) on wisdom. People do not consult with these friends before they buy their houses. Whatever we attempt, build, or buy without the help of these friends will fail.

In the above verses, God is narrowing it down to a family, the most important thing God established on the earth. From families come individuals. What does it take to build a life?

In the book of Daniel we see that God gave him knowledge, wisdom, and understanding, which was the secret to the success in his life. Daniel 1:17 says, "As for these four young men, God gave them **knowledge** and skill in all literature and **wisdom**; and Daniel had **understanding** in all visions and dreams."

Do you know why Jesus was successful in His life and fulfilled His purpose by the age of thirty- three? His life was founded on wisdom. Luke 2:52, "And Jesus increased in wisdom and stature, and in favor with God and men." What does it take to influence the world or to invent something new? Exodus 31:3, "And I have filled him [Bezalel] with the spirit of God, in **wisdom**, and in **understanding**, and in **knowledge**, and in all manner of workmanship."

We give more importance to the power of God and that is why we do not make much progress. I am all for the power of God. He has already given us the power but we do not know how to use it because we lack the wisdom of God.

Many marriages are falling apart because couples did not take time to found their marriage on the wisdom of God. Instead, they gave more importance to the ring, flowers, dress, and which color scheme to feature in their wedding ceremony, honeymoon, etc. I am not against any of those, but somewhere along the way they lost track of their priorities and made the least important the most important and vice versa.

If we study the Word in depth, we will see that God manifested His wisdom in His interaction with the earth and human beings more than He manifested His power. Any time the power of God manifested, His wisdom preceded. God is unlimited in His power and glory and He channels His power through His wisdom. He defeated the devil on the cross by revealing His wisdom. The preaching of the cross seems foolish but it reveals the power of God.

Electricity is power but to make use of that power we need to channel it through cables, wires, and switches. Otherwise, it will harm us. We have scores of equipment at home that function by electricity. Each has a different capacity, function, and purpose. The wisdom of managing electricity so that it will produce different results through different types of equipment is called electrical engineering. God has power but to manage and channel that power to benefit us in any area of our life we need to apply the wisdom of God. God taught Moses His ways and Israel his acts. His ways are His wisdom and His acts are His power.

What does the New Testament have to say about wisdom? Jesus said that whoever hears His sayings and does them is like a wise man that built his house on the rock (Matthew 7:24).

Jesus grew in wisdom and stature, which means maturity (or understanding), and favor with God and men (Luke 2:52). These were the foundation of His life; the power of God came later. I see people throughout the Church running after power because they think that power will solve all their problems. Without wisdom the power will not work. Many who get healed or delivered by the power of God go back into bondage because they lack wisdom and understanding about how to stay free.

31

Paul wrote to the Colossians, "Let the word of Christ dwell in you richly in all wisdom" (Colossians 3:16).

Ephesians 1:17-18, "That the God of our Lord Jesus Christ, the Father of glory, may give to you the spirit of wisdom and revelation in the knowledge of Him, the eyes of your understanding being enlightened…"

Moses laid his hands on Joshua and the spirit of wisdom came upon him. It takes wisdom to sustain the power of God.

Psalm 136:5, "By wisdom God made the heavens."

Ecclesiastes 9:16-18 says that wisdom is better than both strength and weapons of war.

Where do we find wisdom? The Word of God gives us wisdom. Knowledge of the Holy One is understanding. God stores up wisdom for those who are upright in heart (Proverbs 2:7).

In Christ Jesus, God has given us unlimited treasures of wisdom and knowledge. Colossians 2:3 says, "In whom are hidden all the treasures of wisdom and knowledge." Because we have access to all the treasures of wisdom and knowledge we should be the most productive and problem-solving people on the face of this earth.

Throughout the Bible we see these three friends mentioned and working together. When the true wisdom of God enters our heart, we want to build or make something. Wisdom is there to found something. Wisdom brings order and shape to those areas of your life where there is no shape or order. Again, there is only one problem on this earth and that is a wisdom problem.

"If any of you lacks wisdom, let him ask of God, who gives to all liberally and without reproach, and it will be given to him" (James 1:5).

The Bible says the fear of the Lord is the beginning of wisdom. One of the signs of the fear (respect and reverence) of God is a hunger for true wisdom. One of the signs of true wisdom is creating, making, or inventing things that were never made before.

WISDOM – FOUNDING

There are three steps to any enterprise, or endeavor of life. The first is to found it. Many people are excited to begin something but they do not follow up to finish it. Others start something but they do not know how to cause it to expand or grow. Wisdom is knowing *what* to do in your life, or in a specific situation. When you found something by wisdom you need another friend to establish it.

UNDERSTANDING – ESTABLISHING

Once you found or start something, you need understanding to establish it. To establish means to set the roots down so that you are ready for expansion. Understanding is knowing when and where to do something. There is an appointed time and place for every purpose under heaven.

KNOWLEDGE – FRUITFULNESS

The third step is knowing *how* to operate once you get established. It is God's design that you grow and expand. He created man to be fruitful and multiply. Jesus told the disciples that after they received the power of the Holy Spirit they would be witnesses for Him in Jerusalem, Judea, Samaria, and to the ends of the earth. It is God's desire that you grow and reach the uttermost parts of the earth. Your product, message, or whatever talent God has put in you, is not just to remain in the small corner of a tiny village. Go forth, multiply, and fill the earth in Jesus' name!

HOW DO WE FIND THESE FRIENDS?

The Bible compares these friends to treasure. How do we find treasure? If treasure was easy to find, it would not be called treasure. There were explorers who traveled around the globe searching for treasure. Many faced great dangers and others lost their precious lives on the way. They only dreamed about possessing those treasures. Others had to overcome great obstacles, endure hunger, and defeat enemies before they found the treasure they were looking for. But, once they found it, they realized that every sacrifice they made to obtain it was worth it.

Proverbs 2:3-7 says, "Yes, if you cry out for discernment, *and* lift up your voice for **understanding**, if you seek her as silver, and search for her as *for* hidden treasures; then you will understand the fear of the Lord, and find the **knowledge** of God. For the Lord gives **wisdom**; from His mouth *come* **knowledge** and **understanding**; He stores up sound **wisdom** for the upright; He is a shield to those who walk uprightly."

The Bible tells us to seek these friends as people seek hidden treasure. I once read a story about a treasure that was buried in the State of Colorado in the United States. Since I was in Colorado when I wrote this book, I thought it was interesting to mention.

In the 1700's, a French expedition of 300 men found a vast amount of gold on a mountain called Treasure Mountain. The treasure was worth more than 33 million US dollars. When they reached a place called Summitville, they set up camp and buried their loot. Their neighbors were Native American Indians and, at first, the relationship was friendly. However, one group provoked the other and a battle ensued. The gold was reburied and the French made a map to the new location.

However, through the battle with the natives, the weather, a second battle with the natives, and starvation, there was one sole survivor - a Frenchman named LeBlanc. He had two maps - one he gave to the French government, and one he kept for himself. There are many versions of what happened next. Some say there have been several unsuccessful expeditions to find the gold. Some say that the French government found it and kept it a secret. The truth of what happened has yet to be discovered.

The moral of the story is the sacrifice involved in finding a treasure. That is the reason many do not find wisdom, knowledge, and understanding, which are far more valuable than gold, silver, or any hidden treasures. But the good news is that the Bible says if you seek them, you are guaranteed to find them.

What I will be sharing in this book is what the Holy Spirit has taught me. This is not based on information learned from other books or materials of this world. As Paul said in 1 Corinthians 2:6-8 & 13, "However, we speak wisdom among those who are mature, yet not the wisdom of this age, nor of the rulers of this age, who are coming to nothing. But we speak the wisdom of God in a mystery, the hidden *wisdom* which God ordained before the ages for our glory. These things we also speak, not in words which man's wisdom teaches but which the Holy Spirit teaches, comparing spiritual things with spiritual."

So, before you go any further with this book, please take the time to make these new friends. You need them to benefit from this book and to succeed in making

The Three Most Important Decisions of Your Life. Tell wisdom, knowledge, and understanding that you would like to have them as your friends. They can hear you because they are spirits, not just information or ideas (Isaiah 11:2).

Please pray the following prayer:

> "May the God of our Lord Jesus Christ, the Father of glory, give to *me* the spirit of **wisdom** and revelation in the **knowledge** of Him, the eyes of *my* **understanding** being enlightened; that *I* may know what is the hope of His calling, what are the riches of the glory of His inheritance in *me*, and what *is* the exceeding greatness of His power toward *me* who believes, according to the working of His mighty power which He worked in Christ when He raised Him from the dead and seated *Him* at His right hand in the heavenly *places,* far above all principality and power and might and dominion, and every name that is named, not only in this age but also in that which is to come. And He put all *things* under His feet, and gave Him *to be* head over all *things* to *me* the church, which is His body, the fullness of Him who fills all in all. Amen. (Quoted from Ephesians 1:17-23 with the author's paraphrase).

CHAPTER 2
WHICH *GOD* DO YOU BELIEVE IN?

CHAPTER 2: WHICH *GOD* DO YOU BELIEVE IN?

Before we delve into learning about The Three Most Important Decisions of Your Life, we need to have the right perspective of God. Your perspective and belief about God will affect everything in life, especially the three major decisions you make. The life you are living now is the product of your belief system about God and yourself.

Do you know that you can create your own *god* and worship it all your life? Or a god someone else created, and never realize you were deceived or wrong? There are millions of gods and goddesses on this earth today. Most of them cannot even help themselves. Humans need to feed them, protect them, and carry them from one place to another. That is why there are fights and wars between people who worship different gods today. More people are killed for the sake of religion than any other cause. If they are gods, let them protect and take care of themselves and save your life for a better cause.

Another interesting thing I have noticed is that, if these religious beliefs are correct, people and nations who worship more than one god should be more blessed than people and nations that worship only on*e*. If two are better than one, they that worship them should receive double blessings. That is not what we see today. People and nations that worship more than one god are relatively poor and less productive than those who worship only one.

Do you know that hundreds and maybe thousands of the gods and goddesses that people worshiped in the previous centuries are no longer worshiped as gods today? They all went out of business or service, especially the ones worshiped in ancient Egypt and Greece. Also, there are hundreds of gods and goddesses being 'birthed' every year. I believe it takes about 250 years for a society to form a new deity.

You might say, "I am a Christian and go to church, how can I worship the wrong god? I want to tell you it is very possible you might be worshiping a god that was made by you, your denomination, personal experience, or your ancestors that has nothing to do with the God of the Bible. You might be a Jew or a believer

39

in any other religion, but make sure you are not deceived by your tradition, culture, or even ancestral practices.

I was a Christian and a Pentecostal, but I was worshiping and serving the wrong god for many years. To tell the truth, though we may be Christians we may have this emotional god that we made in our heart. That is one of the reasons for the divisions that are tearing apart the body of Christ. It is also one of the reasons we are not able to receive the love of God in our lives and share it with others.

If we say we all love and serve the same God, then we should all be united! Am I right? But, when we look around, we see different types of gods. There is a religious god, a punishing god, a traditional god, a distant god, a materialistic god, a charismatic god, a catholic god, an uncaring or unloving god, and many other types. When the body of Christ rids their hearts of these *gods* and receives a revelation of the Jesus revealed in the Gospels, we will be united in our faith.

The first thought that comes to your mind when you think of God is very important. If your concept of God is not what Jesus revealed in the four Gospels, it is a wrong concept. Jesus came to reveal the Father. He said, "As You, Father are in Me and I in You…" (John 17:21). "He who has seen Me has seen the Father" (John 14:9). So, if the concept of the Father we have is not what Jesus came to reveal, then we have a wrong concept of God the Father.

Why are there so many different denominations and sects among Christians? It is interesting to see how each believer has his, or her, own idea and concept of God. It seems like each of us believes in a different god. I want to share with you how this concept of God is formed in our life. Since no one has seen Him, the knowledge we received of God when we were children is based on someone else's experience or knowledge of Him. Our concept of God, and how our faith in Him was formed, has a lot to do with how we were raised. Unfortunately, most of the information we received about God was incorrect.

In His high priestly prayer in John 17, Jesus prayed that all believers in Him would become one as He and the Father are one. It will only happen when the concept of God that was made by our traditions and wrong interpretation of the Bible is exchanged for the concept Jesus came to reveal. It is time for us to read the Gospels again and adjust our thinking to line up with the New Testament. That process is called repentance.

Each of us may have a different concept and experience with God, and we view the world around us and live our life according to that experience. This concept could be far from the truth and may have nothing to do with the real God of the Bible. It could be the *god* of this world. How do we enter into a relationship with Someone we cannot see or know with our natural instinct or five senses?

On the other hand, God relates with each of His children differently. Each of us has different needs in our life. We cannot impose our personal experience of God on others and we need to be careful when we compare our experience of God with others, but the foundation has to be the same for everyone, universally. Then, it is up to each individual to decide how they will build upon it. When we all agree on the foundation rather than attempt to force individuals to have the same interpretation or revelation or experience we have, we will begin to see the unity that is mentioned in the Bible.

When a child is born into a Christian family, he hears about Jesus and prayer and worship in his home. He may not know what it is all about. There are some key factors that form the idea of God in us. Those factors determine the character and the quality of the god we hold in our heart. The real test comes when we read the Bible; specifically, when the god we believe in does not match the one that is mentioned in the Bible. God, as revealed in the Bible may be very different from what was actually formed in us by our background and childhood experience.

Another way to know the nature and the character of the god we believe in is when we are faced with challenges and opposition. When you are faced with challenges and are really frustrated, how you view God in your heart at that time reveals the god you really believe in and follow.

Each of us has an emotional god we have created in our life as a result of our imagination, education, experience, religious background, and upbringing. For most of us, that god was formed in our heart based on our childhood experience. I am talking here about Christians.

These are some of the oldest strongholds in our mind. I call them the "monster strongholds". Monster strongholds are strongholds by which the foundation of our life and mindset are formed. They could be about God or about our self. They dictate how we live and what we should or should not do. They become the "police" and the "judge" of our conscience. Many misinterpret the voice of a monster stronghold as the voice of God, or the Holy Spirit. They act as the dictator of our conscience and the judge of our actions. They are nothing more than voices of these monster strongholds that were formed in our mind early in life. If we do not detect them early enough, they can steal our life from us.

Each time we hear a new revelation or truth about God (and who we are) we temporarily get excited, but sooner or later these "monster strongholds" swallow them up so they will not have any lasting impact on our life. They will resist the truth, and any corresponding change, to keep a person where they were. For a new revelation or truth to make an impact on our thinking, we first need to rid those *monsters* from our mind.

Unless we intentionally demolish those concepts and recreate new ones in our heart with the truth of the Word of God, we will not be any better than those who worship idols. I have yet to see a Christian who did not have some kind of wrong concept in his or her heart about God. We all grew up in some kind of dysfunctional family. With a dysfunctional family comes dysfunctional theology. Do you see a person who is emotionally unstable? Behind him is a dysfunctional family, and the root of that 'dysfunction' could be a wrong theology inherited from their ancestors.

There are four key factors that play a major role in our life in forming our idea of God. Those four factors mixed with wrong experiences and scriptures that were taken out of context formed our theological concept of God. The reason some people are afraid of God, afraid to do God's will, afraid to trust in Him, and would rather remain in their mess, is because of these wrong concepts they have of Him. We are going to look at these factors individually and see how each of them has distorted our thinking to keep us from knowing the one true God.

One example of a person who had a wrong concept of God, which was created by wrong theology, is the woman at the well in Samaria in John chapter 4. The Gospel of John is a battle between the true God and the concepts people had about Him. Any miracle or teaching we see in it was a direct attack on how people thought about God during those days. We read in the first chapter, "He was in the world, and the world was made through Him, and the world did not know Him. He came to His own, and His own did not receive Him" (John 1:10-11). What a tragedy!

During Jesus' earthly ministry He traveled through a town called Samaria. There He met a woman at a well and asked her for water. Though the name of this woman is not mentioned, her life and experience is something relevant to millions of people today. That is an example of how God uses ordinary, "no-name" people to do extraordinary things. Jesus was a Jew and this woman was a Samaritan. There was no interaction between those races in those days. He broke the racial barrier and asked this Samaritan woman for water. In that culture and day, it was taboo to do so.

She was a very religious woman. Her concept of God was formed by four major elements. Her childhood upbringing (religious and cultural background), works (acceptance by God based on the good things we do), traditions (ways of doing things), and personal experience (mindset), led her to a particular place and form of worship. When we read the conversation she had with Jesus, there are certain factors that come to light about why her life was the way it was. Let us see from her story what flawed theology can do to a person's life.

> John 4:9 says, 'Then the woman of Samaria said to Him, "How is it that You, being a Jew, ask a drink from me, a Samaritan woman?" For Jews have no dealings with Samaritans."'

Her concept of God created in her a division between people based on their race: Separation between Jews and Samaritans. Jews believed they were superior to every other race and Samaritans were not willing to accept anything less. They said they were the true followers of the God of Israel because Jacob, their forefather, gave them that well. To this woman, when someone asked her for something, the first thing she considered was the race to which that person belonged. It was neither the need of the person asking nor a love for fellow humans. Does the concept you have of God divide people based on their race or caste?

Jesus said to this woman, "If you knew the **gift of God**, and who it is who says to you…" (John 4:10a). That means the Messiah that she had been waiting for and the whole world was waiting for, was standing in front of her but she did not recognize Him. That is the second thing wrong theological programming will do to us. It will either keep us talking about the glorious past or the future that is not here yet, but gives no hope for the present. We will miss out on everything that God has for us *now*. We are looking for something or someone based on the past experiences of others, but God will send something or someone who looks totally different. If we fail to recognize what God is doing right now, we can miss the season and the plan God has for us today, and many unfortunately did miss it!

Then, the woman said to Jesus, "Sir, You have nothing to draw with, and the well is deep. Where then do you get that living water?" (John 4:11). Whatever Jesus wanted to give her was a free gift, according to verse 10. In her mind, she believed that she had to earn it by her own works. Dear friend, do you know that salvation and the forgiveness of sin is a *free* gift? You do not need to do anything or go anywhere to receive it. You can receive it right where you are by believing in Jesus. You do not need to earn it by doing good works, nor do you keep it by being good. When you come to God asking, "What do I need to do?" you are asking the wrong question and you may not receive much. Instead, when you come to God, the right question to ask is, "Lord, what do I need to believe?"

Then, the woman said, "Are you greater than our father Jacob, who gave us the well, and drank from it himself, as well as his sons and his livestock?" (John 4:12). That reveals her religious tradition. The well became important because Jacob gave the well and might have drunk from it. Not only did he drink from it, but his donkeys, camels, and sons drank, too. That should make this well spiritually significant. To her, the God who created the water and the earth was not as important. A person and the well he dug out became more important than what God was doing. In any religious circle we notice that there are super heroes and "traditional wells" that people admire, sometimes they even put them in the place of God.

It could be something someone did hundreds of years ago that we still hold on to as a god, and dare not break the mold because we fear that the wrath of God will break out. I have seen these "spiritual wells" in every religious circle and in all major denominations.

Do you see how absurd traditions can become? I have seen them in my own church where I grew up. Someone did something a long time ago, for some reason it became a god, or became more important than God Himself and what He wants to do right now. Everyone who does not do it the same way is considered a heretic or backslider.

This woman believed that if she drank from that well she received some kind of spiritual solace. Though her lifestyle would have prevented her from drawing with the other women, this may be another reason she came out in the middle of the day under the scorching sun, thinking the more struggle she endured to get it, the more "blessings" she would receive.

Usually, people did not come to fetch water in the middle of the day. That is why Jesus offered her living water. This is what wrong theology does to us; it creates traditions and causes us to follow them blindly without ever thinking about why we do what we do. This woman was talking about water that would quench the thirst of her body, but she did not realize the thirst of her soul. Jesus was offering her the living water that would quench the thirst of her soul.

As it has always been with God, Jesus went straight to her heart and told her to go and call her husband. She said she did not have any husband. Jesus said her statement was true for she had had five husbands and was living with a man who was not her husband. When she saw that Jesus knew about her private life she tried to change the subject. We all have a past that we are afraid to face and wish it did not exist. It follows us like our own shadow. Only when we face our past in the light of God's truth will we be free to face our future and have a true relationship with Him so we can receive what He has for us today. We tried to have relationships that bring fulfillment; instead they brought hurt and wounds and now, as a result, we do not trust anyone. A proper relationship with God is the foundation for all other relationships on this earth, not the other way around.

She tried to change the subject by bringing out her religiosity and said, "Our fathers worshiped on this mountain, and you *Jews* say that in Jerusalem is the place where one ought to worship" (John 4:20). Like this woman, many of us hide our ugly past behind our religious mask (duty) or by not being religious at all. Our concept of God that was formed by culture, traditions, and religious and personal experiences always affects how we perceive God and can severely hinder our relationship with Him.

The Samaritans believed in a particular mountain where God must be worshiped. That is why today there are so many denominations (mountains) and religious groups (old wells), claiming to be the only "true one". Every cult and religious group on this earth has a trace of truth and a bit of God in it, but they were all formed by the above elements and personal experiences of someone. Most of them have been outdated for hundreds of years, but are still kept like glorified (petrified) mummies of Egypt.

Believe it or not, Jesus was not impressed by her religious tradition or by her form of worship. He did not care which mountain she worshiped on or how many times she climbed those religious hills. One of the astounding truths Jesus told her is in verse 22, when He said, **"You worship what you do not know..."** Bang! Can you believe her shock upon hearing that? All these years she believed she was worshiping the true God. But one encounter with Jesus made her realize that she was worshiping a *god* and practicing a religion out of ignorance. What seemed to her to be real and truthful for so long, Jesus destroyed in one shot, taking down the monstrous strongholds that formed her concept of God.

She had been worshiping something she did not know. Is that possible? Yes, very much so. You and I can be worshiping and serving a god that was formed by our religious traditions, culture, or even personal experience that may have very little to do with the real God. If we are worshiping the real God, then the evidence that the Bible says (love, joy, peace, power, health, and prosperity) would follow those who believe, will follow us. Otherwise, something has gone wrong somewhere.

Paul was another individual who thought he was worshiping and serving God with zeal and passion until, on the way to Damascus, he had an encounter that shattered his concepts *of* God and the mission he thought he was doing *for* God. He realized how wrong he was and was transformed into a new person. Unfortunately, the Pharisees and the religious sects were not willing to change and died with their erroneous concept of God.

Millions, or even billions, of people around the world today worship something they do not know personally, but they do it anyway because their ancestors did it. Many people internally do not like the god they worship, but do it because of fear or obligation (to their religion). They are afraid that if they do not do it, this *god* will strike them dead or cause some misfortune to happen to them. Some others have left churches and said in their pain and anger, "I don't want anything to do with this *god*."

If this woman lived in our day and someone asked her about her faith, she would have said, "I am a Christian," or "I am a Catholic," or even, "I am a Pentecostal or Charismatic." It is not their fault; it was not the fault of this woman either. She was just a by-product of her background. She did everything that others did because that was all she knew. She was religious. She had traditions. She believed in God and she thought she was serving Him, but the question is, "Which *God*?" The *god* she was serving did not seem to have any relation to the *real* God who was standing before her, nor did it have any affect on her personal life.

We can see such people all around us. The reason many do not want to go to church is because they do not like the *God* the Church presented to them. They did not like the *God* their parents lived out or represented to them. Most people believe in God; they even go to church or temple on Saturday or Sunday, on Christmas, or on a religious holiday—but in which *God* do they believe?

Those who have turned their back on God would never have done so if they knew the real Jesus! We need to discover the true Jesus apart from our traditions and past experience. Otherwise, we will be like the Jews and Samaritans who did not recognize Jesus the Messiah even though He lived among them. They gave more attention to their religious rituals, race, and traditions than helping and loving one another, and failed to see people through the eyes of God. It is happening in today's society. I do not want to miss out on God and what He has for me while I am busy doing religious things that have always been done. I also do not want the next generation to stumble on stones where I stumbled. Lord, help us.

There are so many versions of Jesus on this earth. There is a historical Jesus, who lives only in the pages of history. There is a religious Jesus, created by people who think He came to start a new religion. There is a secular Jesus, created by the people who want to follow their own lust and passions. There is a legalistic Jesus, created by those who adhere to the law. There is a Jewish Jesus, created by those who love the Jewish people. Jesus was Jewish in the flesh, not in the Spirit (Romans 1:3; 9:5; 2 Corinthians 5:16). There is a liberal Jesus, created by people who believe that anything and everything is okay. There is a Pentecostal and Charismatic Jesus. Which Jesus do you believe in and worship? The Jesus that is portrayed in the Gospels is none of the above.

Are any of the factors that hindered this dear woman from Samaria hindering you from knowing and having an intimate relationship with the true God that Jesus came to reveal? Are you happy with the god you believe in and serve? Are you serving him out of fear? Fear of punishment, fear of hell, etc? Take a moment and listen to what your heart says to you.

Each of us needs a personal encounter, like this woman had, with the real Jesus of the Gospels, apart from our traditions, and what we believe to be the truth. Unless we have that personal encounter, let me be honest with you, we all are influenced and controlled by some form of tradition, culture, or religious spirit. We can fight and argue all day and night about our traditions and rituals while people down the street are dying without Jesus.

CHAPTER 3
INGREDIENTS THAT MAKE
A *GOD*

CHAPTER 3: INGREDIENTS THAT MAKE A *GOD*

There are four major building blocks that form our concept of God. I am going to touch on these in the following lines. I am mentioning them to create a thirst in you for a real and true relationship with God. You might be looking for the living among the dead; it is time for you to come out from among the dead. We can find scriptures and philosophies to support almost anything we believe. That does not mean what we believe is the truth. What was true in the Old Testament (Torah) is not necessarily true in the New Testament. Only the Spirit of Truth can show us what we really need.

If there is only one God and one LORD, then all other gods and goddesses are made up by the imagination and traditions of people. It is like making pancakes in your kitchen; if you have the right ingredients, you can create your own god. I am going to share with you those ingredients in this chapter, and how the god you worship now might have been made.

1. EARTHLY PARENTS

One of the major factors that form the idea of God in our life is the life and character of our earthly father and mother. The real responsibility of earthly parents is to represent God to their children. There is nothing else that has deteriorated or become more distorted in our society than the role of earthly parents.

Your parents are the first "*god*" you see, feel, and experience. Their character and how they live affect the way you look at life. They are your provider, protector, sustainer, and they show you what life and love is. Your whole life depends on them. They are your source of life and what they do to you affects and marks you for the rest of your life.

The way we were treated by our parents when we were children has formed the god you and I have chosen to follow (or not to follow). Sometimes, parents teach their children about God and behave differently than what they taught. Though we might have heard sermons and read good books about God, the wiring that has taken place when we were children will not change on its own.

51

None of us had perfect parents, neither were our parents raised by perfect parents. We are not perfect parents either. The enemy of the human race knew one thing; if he could mess up the parents (especially fathers), he could easily mess up the perception in our heart of the nature and character of God. He has been increasingly successful in that for many generations.

All we experienced with our parents is deeply rooted and programmed in our mind and heart. If that is to be changed, we have to first identify what it is and replace it with the right information. As long as we do not identify these individually, they can never be replaced; not even by reading or hearing good messages. One of the great problems in life is to think we do not have any problems, or we consider what we feel and experience to be normal. There is only one thing that is supposed to be normal for us; that is what the Bible says about our lives.

If your father was the type of guy who was rude and angry and abusive to you, it will create in your mind a god who is cruel, ruthless, and merciless. If your earthly father was not loving, approving, or accepting, you will have a god who is unloving and unapproachable; someone that just barks out rules for you to follow. Your relationship with God will not be enjoyable; it will be based on your performance. You will be looking for a new rule to add to the list. At the end, you will become tired and weary in your heart.

If your earthly father never had any time for you and was always busy with his work or business, you will have a god that you feel has no time for you, or has no interest in your life. If your earthly father abused you physically, sexually, or emotionally, you will form a god that you can never completely trust.

If your earthly father was very strict and punished you often for the wrongs you did, you will form a tyrannical god who will come after you with a lightning rod whenever you do something wrong. If you grew up in a home where you never received forgiveness or mercy when you did something wrong, then the god you believe in will be a god who never forgives you or shows any mercy. You will also be ruthless to yourself (and others) when you (or they) make a mistake. You will not like yourself, and you will have problems loving or forgiving others. As an adult, you cannot give out something you did not receive yourself when you were a child.

If your earthly father was distant and never played with you or had any kind of fun while you were growing up, your Christian life will be boring and you will be very religious. Your religious expression will be based on following a set of rules and regulations. I found the following set of quotes by Dorothy Law Nolte. I would like you to meditate on these and see how your concept about God and yourself was formed when you were growing up.

"If children live with criticism, they learn to condemn.
If children live with hostility, they learn to fight.
If children live with ridicule, they learn to be shy.
If children live with shame, they learn to feel guilty.
If children live with tolerance, they learn to be patient.
If children live with encouragement, they learn confidence.
If children live with praise, they learn to appreciate.
If children live with fairness, they learn justice.
If children live with security, they learn to have faith.
If children live with approval, they learn to like themselves.
If children live with acceptance and friendship, they learn to find love in the world."

Consequently, if your parents were critical and never appreciated or accepted you, your concept of God will be as one who always condemns and is never happy with you. You will never be able to please that kind of a god. You will feel rejected by him. You will get caught up in the whirlwind of performance, perfectionism, and religious duties.

You will be self-critical about everything you do. You will be your own worst critic and judge. You will be haunted with thoughts like, "You could have done better, you could have given more, or, you should have…" You will have a fear of failure and a fear of other people and authority, and never accept yourself the way you are. If your parents had standards that you could never meet or, though you met them, they would change them the next moment, you will have a god to whose standards you are never able to measure up.

If your parents were hostile to you and never supported you, you will have a god who fights and loves war and destruction. You will be like James and John who said to Jesus, "Lord, do You want us to command fire to come down from heaven and consume them, just as Elijah did?" (Luke 9:54).

If children grow up with ridicule and sarcasm, their god will be one who will never be happy and they will feel shame and contempt about themselves. They will always try to be like someone else or look like someone else. They will have very low self-esteem and insecure feelings about themselves and their god.

If children grow up with shame, they will form a god who will make them feel guilty all of the time. As soon as they miss something or fail in something, it will take days or even weeks to get back to a normal relationship with this god.

The Bible says God is love, and it describes what love is in 1 Corinthians 13. Let me say this to you, if God is love and the definition of love is mentioned in 1 Corinthians 13, then if you have any concept of God or His character and nature that is contrary to what it says in 1 Corinthians 13, you have a wrong concept and need to change it.

"Love suffers long *and* is kind; love does not envy; love does not parade itself, is not puffed up; does not behave rudely, does not seek its own, is not provoked, thinks no evil; does not rejoice in iniquity, but rejoices in the truth; bears all things, believes all things, hopes all things, endures all things. Love never fails" (1 Corinthians 13:4-8a).

2. PERSONAL EXPERIENCES

The second factor that forms an emotional god is a person's own experience. We are not all born with a silver spoon in our mouth. Many of us grew up in homes where we had to struggle and only basic necessities were met. If we trusted our parents or someone in authority for something when we were children and that need was not met, then it formed a concept in our heart that God does not provide.

People go through all kinds of emotions when it comes to God and their relationship with Him. Some feel they cannot trust Him. Others feel He will not protect them, and still others feel He will not provide for them. Many feel He does not care about them, or that He is not a loving God. Some feel He is critical or are afraid of Him. They do not want to have anything to do with God. Others feel they have to follow certain rules and traditions to be accepted by Him.

They may feel they have to pray a certain number of hours at a certain time of the day or do something *for* Him to be loved *by* Him. Many feel they have been let down by God. Others feel they have to worship in a certain way to be accepted by Him. If you have any of these thoughts or feelings toward God, you need to go back to where it all began. It all started with a personal experience you had in your life that was stored in the place in your mind where you think about God. We all have these boxes in our brain where information about people and places is stored. We have a "God box" in our brain where information about God and knowledge about Him is kept. Many of these are wrong concepts. Our God is far from any of the things mentioned above.

We have read in the Old Testament stories about how God killed certain people or destroyed cities or nations. We think God is power and, if we do not walk the tightrope, He is going to strike us with lightning. Old Testament stories are not given to us to form our theological concept of God. They are given to us to show how He dealt with people and nations in different dispensations, and what happens if we do not repent and turn to Him. They are not the examples of how

He deals with His children now. If we want to know the truth about God, we need to listen to what He says about Himself. Exodus 34:5-7 says,

> "Now the LORD descended in the cloud and stood with him [Moses] there, and proclaimed the name of the LORD. And the LORD passed before him and proclaimed, "The LORD, the LORD God, merciful and gracious, longsuffering, and abounding in goodness and truth, keeping mercy for thousands, forgiving iniquity and transgression and sin, by no means clearing the guilty, visiting the iniquity of the fathers upon the children and the children's children to the third and the fourth generation."

We need to etch the above scripture deep in our heart and mind and think about it every time we think about God. You might wonder about the second part of the verse. Well, I have good news for you. Jesus died for our transgressions and was punished for our iniquities (Isaiah 53:5). No iniquity of your fathers has the authority now to cross the bloodline of Jesus. We need to cast down imaginations and feelings that rise up in our mind that are contrary to the above scripture.

3. SOCIAL AND ECONOMIC BACKGROUND

The third factor that forms our concept of God is our social and economic background. If it was a struggle to meet your needs when you were growing up, then you may have a god who is stingy and never wants you to have more than enough. If you grew up with lack and financial struggle, you will think God is not concerned about your finances, or about meeting your needs.

When you were little and you needed something but repeatedly heard, "No, we cannot afford that, it is too expensive," or, "We don't have any money," that can form a poverty mindset in you. When you become an adult and rehearse your childhood, you will form a god who is poor or who does not want you to have anything good in your life. Every time you go to buy something, you will hear that same voice in your head and will think it is God speaking to you.

When you go out and spend some money or buy something nice, suddenly a red light will go on in your conscience saying you can't spend your money on those things. Some people will think it is God who is telling them not to buy. It is not God, but their emotional god that was created in them by their parents. These voices come because our parents never spent any money on those things. I am not saying here you should go out and lavishly spend your money and God will not speak to you about it. Of course He will. I am speaking here against having a poverty mentality. If you grew up with plenty and abundance, then you will have a god who is generous and wants to meet all of your needs.

> Jesus said, "The thief does not come except to steal, and to kill, and to destroy" (John 10:10).

Our society is divided into different classes: The poor, the middle class, and the rich. Whichever class you grew up in will have an impact on your concept of God. If you look at society, it is difficult to move up from one class to another. I have seen the poor remain poor for generations while the middle class remain middle class for generations, with only a few exceptions to the rule. People who live in these three classes have different mindsets and outlooks on life. They speak differently, shop differently, and they give differently. Their lifestyle is different and how they relate to life and to others also varies. How they treat themselves and others is, often, dependent on the socioeconomic class in which they were raised.

For some rich people, money is their god and it is difficult for anything else to replace it. They will do things for God as long as they receive the praise and prestige from other people. Likewise, your particular race will have an impact on your concept of God. In many parts of the world, Jesus is considered a 'white man's god' and Christianity a religion of the West. Or, you might feel like an outcast because you belonged to a particular race or caste. These all form the wrong idea of God in our life. They need to be torn down and replaced.

4. CULTURAL AND RELIGIOUS TRADITIONS

The fourth element that forms the concept of God in our life is our cultural and religious tradition. In many countries, culture and religion are inextricably intertwined. When people think about their religion, they think about their culture. When they think about their culture, they think about their religion. Cultural values infiltrate their religious system and religious principles infiltrate culture, too. They both get mixed up and it is difficult to differentiate what is culture and what is religion.

Culture is formed by manners, customs, traditions, social & moral values, language, superstitions, geography, and race. These strongly influence the forming of the concept of the god we believe in. Some of the definitions of the word culture, according to Merriam Webster's dictionary, are as follows: a) The integrated pattern of human knowledge, belief, and behavior that depends upon the capacity for learning and transmitting knowledge to succeeding generations. b) The customary beliefs, social forms, and material traits of a racial, religious, or social group.

I grew up in India where the predominant religion is Hinduism, which is formed by a set of religious rituals, superstitions, and traditions. Everything a person does and thinks in India is somewhat religious. Every aspect of life is governed by religion. The culture is formed by religious practices and one cannot be separated from the other.

When people get converted from Hinduism, they tend to keep their mindset and most of them follow a very strict form of Christianity, almost to the degree of asceticism. It is very difficult for these converts to be free or to have any sense of freedom. The religious spirit is so strong on them they do not even recognize there is life beyond their perceived reality. Catholicism and other so-called Christian sects form a concept of God in the heart that is not biblical. You need to tear those concepts down and build a true theology based on the New Testament. Many of the things we do in church or as part of our spiritual life are nothing more than practices of our own culture and have little to do with God or the Bible.

It is not easy to tear down old practices and belief systems. God told Jeremiah that He had anointed him to root out, to tear down, to pull down and destroy, then to plant and build (Jeremiah 1:10). I believe God is talking about people's mindsets and spiritual strongholds. Jeremiah never physically pulled down any king from his throne. He did not wage physical war against any nation to destroy them. He did not root out any country in the physical sense. Jeremiah had to be engaged in spiritual warfare and that dealt with spiritual and cultural influences that were ruling nations at that time.

The Apostle Paul talked about the same concept in the New Testament. He said the weapons of our warfare are not carnal but they are mighty through God to the pulling down of strongholds (2 Corinthians 10:4).

Before we go any further, I want to make sure your relationship with God is built on the revelation of God that is revealed in the New Testament through Jesus Christ. By the grace of God, I had to change my theology because the *god* I used to serve was formed by the four factors I mentioned above.

Jesus said that He loves us with the same love with which the Father loves Him. That one scripture is enough to revolutionize our whole theology or '*theolugly*' (that is a word I made up for wrong theology).

> John 14:21, "He who has My commandments and keeps them, it is he who loves Me. And he who loves Me will be loved by My Father, and I will love him and manifest Myself to him."

John 15:9-10, "As the Father loved Me, I also have loved you; abide in My love. If you keep My commandments, you will abide in My love, just as I have kept My Father's commandments and abide in His love."

Many misunderstand the above verses. Where Jesus said to keep His commandments; they think He is talking about the Ten Commandments. He is not talking about the Ten Commandments here. He is talking about the commandments He gave to the disciples, especially the command to love one another (John 13:34; 15:12).

Ephesians 2:4-6, "But God, who is rich in mercy, because of His great love with which He loved us, even when we were dead in trespasses, made us alive together with Christ (by grace you have been saved), and raised us up together, and made us sit together in the heavenly places in Christ Jesus."

Every religion around the world is formed by the following common belief systems. They are: Origin of the earth and the purpose of creation, faith in god(s), rituals (what to do to keep that god happy), forms of worship, conduct toward fellow humans and nature, and life after death. Religious tradition has done a good job in many people's lives to create a god who is never happy with them, never pleased, and always condemning. As long as they follow all the rules, this god is appeased. But the moment they break one of those man-made rules, they feel judged and condemned.

What Jesus would not do or say to a person in the Gospels, He will not do or say to you now. Please read the Gospels again and again until you receive that in your spirit. He only rebuked His disciples for their unbelief, not for their wrong doings.

Find the scriptures from the New Testament that fit your specific situation. Root out the monster strongholds that keep you unproductive and replace them with the Word of God. You may be wondering why I am sharing about the concept of God in a book about decisions. As I said earlier, your concept of God will affect every aspect of your life, including and especially the area of decision-making.

CHAPTER 4
GOD'S OPINION OF YOU

CHAPTER 4: GOD'S OPINION OF YOU

In order to make good decisions, not only do we need the right concept of God in our heart, we need to know the concept God has about us, as well. Only when you are sure of what God thinks of you will you be free to make healthy choices for your life. Otherwise, instead of relying on God, you will make decisions out of fear or to please others. Many people do not like God because they think He is angry with them or does not accept them. I want to tell you up front that if anyone accepts you the way you are, it is God. I want to share with you what God thinks of you. First of all, I want you to know that when God speaks to one man it is for all of humanity. One man for all and all for one is God's principle.

Whatever He spoke to Adam in the beginning, today you and I experience the consequence of that Word. Whether it is a curse or a blessing, everyone born after that Word is released will have an equal opportunity to receive the result of that Word. He blessed Abraham and that blessing is still active for us through faith in Jesus Christ. The Bible says God doesn't show partiality nor is He a respecter of persons (Romans 2:11). He does not play favorites so the opportunity is open to anyone to receive His favor by doing His will.

In Jeremiah 29:11 we read,

> **"'For I know the thoughts that I think toward you,'**
> **says the LORD, 'thoughts of peace and not of evil,**
> **to give you a future and a hope.'"**

So, be assured in your heart and in your spirit right now that the thoughts that God thinks toward you are for peace and for life, not to destroy you. Any thought that comes to your mind that does not give you hope for your future, let me tell you; it is not from God. You need to renounce it and never again allow your mind to entertain it. It does not matter who said what or what you think about yourself. If you can change the way you are thinking about yourself and come into agreement with what God thinks of you, your life will change from that moment. The real battle is between your thoughts, ideas, concepts, and belief systems.

Otherwise, it does not matter what God thinks or says about you. Unless that makes an impact on your mind and you intentionally appropriate it in your life, it will not do you any good. Many are stuck in their mind and the way they live, and it is almost impossible for them to think anything beyond their immediate circumstances. For others, it is almost impossible to imagine anything beyond their current reality. Let's read another verse:

> "The LORD your God in your midst, The Mighty One, will save;
> He will rejoice over you with gladness, He will quiet *you* with His
> love, He will rejoice over you with singing" (Zephaniah 3:17).

Can you imagine God Almighty rejoicing over you with gladness? Can you imagine God quieting you with His love when you are afraid, or stressed out about something, just like a mother comforting her child with her love? Or are you worried about what God thinks of all the mistakes you have made in life? You might be thinking, "Sure, God does that kind of stuff for people who are perfect and always do the right thing." Do you know that there is no such person on this earth? Or you might say, "That is Old Testament and God will do it for the people of Israel because He loves them, but I am a Gentile." Let's see what the New Testament says about us. Please read the following verses.

> "But God, who is rich in mercy, because of His great love with
> which He loved us, even when we were dead in trespasses, made
> us alive together with Christ (by grace you have been saved)"
> (Ephesians 2:4-5).

For most of us, our tradition has done an excellent job of programming our mind and training us to think only within the boundaries of those man-made limits. When you try to do something beyond those limits, you almost feel in your conscience that you are breaking God's laws. In truth, you are only breaking the man-made boundaries you were trained in while you were growing up.

For example, in my culture it is disrespectful to sit with your legs crossed in front of someone who is older than you. God forbid if it is a woman! When I came to the West almost everyone sat with their legs crossed. Every time I sat before someone older than myself with my legs crossed, like a drill sergeant my conscience would prick in me a command, "Hey, put your legs down, now!" When that happens I have to retrain my conscience that it is only a 'holy cow' in my Indian culture and has nothing to do with respecting a person in a western culture.

To know and believe that the thoughts that God thinks toward you are for peace and to prosper you, some of you might need to break out of a cycle of negative thinking. You need to deliberately break the boundaries that have shaped your mindset. In the corporate world, this process is called a paradigm shift. The Bible calls it repentance. We tend to pay more attention to action than to what we believe, but right believing produces right actions; not vice versa.

Every person has a pattern of thinking based on his or her upbringing, personal experience, culture, and education. The truth is you can never go higher than you think. In a normal circumstance you will not attempt to do or believe anything beyond your current belief system. You will not attract blessing if you do not think in your heart that blessing is for you. Even if the blessing shows up, you will not accept it because in your mind you think that it is not for you.

There were individuals in the Bible whose thoughts toward themselves did not line up with how God thought about them. One was Gideon, who was afraid of his enemies and was hiding behind the threshing floor. He saw himself as a defeated and weak person who could not do much for God or people. God saw him as a mighty man of valor.

When the Angel of the LORD appeared to him, the Angel did not address Gideon as fearful or defeated, but exactly as God saw him. Dear child of God, are you afraid or do your circumstances terrify your heart? Please know that God is not looking at you that way. He is looking at your spirit, which was created in His image and likeness and is full of power, courage, and love.

Gideon had to change the way he thought about himself before he could go out and face the enemy. Because He believed God, Gideon acted upon his faith and God gave him a mighty victory. Unless you change the way you think, nothing else is going to change. God is waiting for you and He is only as big for you as you picture Him in your heart.

When God appointed Saul as the first king of Israel, he was not ready to take on that role. You might ask why God appointed someone who was not ready for such an important position. In God's sight he was ready, but Saul could not overcome his own insecurity and hid behind the sacks until the people had to go and bring him out. He was anointed, but his thoughts were not aligned with God's thoughts. Those thoughts destroyed him and God's plan for his life and family. God's plan was to keep him and his posterity after him as kings of Israel (1 Samuel 13:13-14), but what a loss! He was rejected by God and killed in battle, and his sons never became kings.

We see another story in the second book of Kings. In chapter seven, we read that Ben-Hadad, king of Syria, besieged Samaria and there was a great famine in the land. Everyone was afraid of the enemy and even ate human flesh for survival. No one dared to leave the city and face the enemy. But there were four lepers at the entrance of the gate of the city who decided to do something they had never done. They planned to go to the enemy's camp looking for food. They decided they were going to die if they sat there so why not at least die trying to do something worthwhile?

These lepers rose at twilight and walked toward the enemy's camp. When they reached the camp there was no one there, but they saw the horses, donkeys, and tents filled with plenty of food and substance (1 Kings 7:3-9). When these four lepers were walking, the LORD made it sound like the noise of chariots and horses. When the Syrians heard it, they became frightened and ran away in haste. That is the power of renewed thinking. God used those four lepers to save Israel from their enemies. I believe if anyone had decided to walk toward the enemy's camp, God would have done the same miracle through them.

It does not matter what God has promised you; unless you line up your thoughts with His thoughts and speak the same thing He speaks over you, you may not receive the fulfillment of those promises. The best example is the people of Israel when they came out of Egypt. God promised them a land that flowed with milk and honey, and they were excited about it. But they could not align their thoughts with what God said. Every time they opened their mouth, something negative came forth. Finally God said, "Say to them, 'As I live,' says the LORD, 'Just as you have spoken in My hearing, so I will do to you'" (Numbers 14:28).

Nothing, including your past and the devil, can stop you from fulfilling your destiny—nothing except your current beliefs and the words you speak. The Bible says you are what you think. You can never go beyond what you think possible. You are a victim of your own thoughts. For most people, their life is where it is, not because God has not promised them great things, but because they never thought it possible to have what God has promised them. They did not choose the blessing God gave them; instead, they chose what they *thought* could be theirs.

It is because their parents never had what God has promised, and their grandparents never had what God has promised. Their friends are happy with their life and where they are so why would they think that something all these people did not have, or could not achieve, would be possible for them? They feel they are not qualified to receive the best God has promised them. Dear friend, it is time for you to come out and explore what God prepared for you before the foundation of the earth.

**'But as it is written: "Eye has not seen, nor ear heard,
Nor have entered into the heart of man the things**

which God has prepared for those who love Him'"
(1 Corinthians 2:9).

The next verse says,

**"But God has revealed them to us through His Spirit.
For the Spirit searches all things, yes, the deep things
of God"** (1 Corinthians 2:10).

That means no one on this entire earth knows the kinds of blessings God has prepared for you. Then, why would you think that you could not have something that your parents did not have? Only the Holy Spirit knows what God has prepared for you. One of the works of the Holy Spirit is to reveal what God has for you, mainly your purpose. Once the Holy Spirit reveals that to you, you need to train your mind to think according to what is being revealed. What you see in your spirit is the destiny that God has prepared for you. Take action when He says something and see where God will take you!

For many, it is not because the Holy Spirit has not revealed anything to them, but because their mind is not disciplined to think in line with the Holy Spirit. They are almost scared to think anything new because they feel it is impossible to believe those dreams revealed by the Holy Spirit. The reason they are not able to think in a new way is because they have become too used to thinking the old way. For others, it is because what the Holy Spirit reveals does not make any sense to their natural mind. For them, if something does not fit into their logic, it is not acceptable.

Joseph was a teenager when God gave him his dreams. At the time, it didn't make any sense to think that his brothers and parents would ever bow down before him, but he believed it. Do you believe what the Holy Spirit has revealed to you? It might be huge and humanly impossible, but all you have to do is say 'yes' to the Holy Spirit. He will take care of the rest.

In the Bible God calls you and me His beloved many times. Beloved means the most loved person. But very few feel in their heart like they are God's beloved. Now, we are going to see how the concept we have of God became so twisted. How did the world become as it is today? How come we cannot think good thoughts about ourselves? Where and how did it all begin? Why do evil things happen to good people? In the following chapters, we are going to look at the manual the Manufacturer gave to us concerning our life on this earth.

3

PART II

CHAPTER 5
THE MANUAL FOR LIFE ON
THIS EARTH - PART 1

CHAPTER 5: THE MANUAL FOR LIFE ON THIS EARTH - PART 1

IN THE BEGINNING

As I mentioned earlier, every product of value comes with an operation manual. The manual God gave to us contains the Basic Instructions Before Leaving Earth (BIBLE). In the following pages I am going to expound on the first three chapters of the Bible, according to the grace that is given to me. Unless you understand these three chapters, your life on this earth will not go as God intended.

We do not understand the purpose of a thing when we do not know why it was made and who made it. The cause for all the problems we have on this earth is a lack of understanding of how it all began. I have found that the reason for the majority of the problems we go through in life is because we do not understand God's plan and purpose concerning that particular area of our life.

The reason we do not understand the purpose and plan of God is because we do not understand the first three chapters of the Bible. The solutions to *all* of the major problems we have in our lives and in our society are hidden in the first three chapters of Genesis. The rest of the Bible is the expansion of that revelation.

Every product of value comes with a manual. Human beings are the most valuable things ever created on this earth. Do you think the Creator thought of giving us a manual? I used to think that the whole Bible is given to us as a manual. Then, I understood that is not so. I tried to obey all the commandments in the Bible and it did not work out very well. I failed multiple times and was frustrated. Later, I understood that God gave only three chapters of the Bible as our manual, and in those three chapters everything we need to know about our life on this earth is mentioned. Wow! I could not wait to dig in! The rest of the Bible progresses from there and provides examples of how people tried to live out what came about in those first three chapters.

One day, I was driving my car and my wife was sitting in the passenger seat. All of a sudden, I noticed a warning sign on my dashboard. I thought it might go away after a while, but it did not. I had never seen this sign before. I knew the usual lights for gas, battery, oil, the engine, etc. I asked my wife if she knew what it was but she did not know either. The light looked like the face of a little demon with teeth sticking out! I began to rebuke this light to go away, but it did not. We came back home and the light was still there. The next morning, I started the car and the same light came on. Then, it dawned on me to take the manual and read it to find the reason the manufacturer put that light on the dashboard and what it was trying to communicate to me.

I found out that it is an indication of low air pressure in the tires. I got out of the car and walked around to see if all of the tires were okay. I noticed a large nail sticking out of the left rear tire. Thankfully, the tire stayed mostly inflated. I took the car to a repair place but they could not fix it because the nail was on the edge of the tire, and it needed to be replaced. To make matters worse, they said that since my car is an all-wheel drive I could not replace just one tire; all four tires needed to be replaced at the same time! Let me tell you, I was not happy.

The reason I am telling this story is to show you the importance of a manual. Here is another example. Perhaps you have had a similar experience to this: After buying something, you tried to put it together by following a manual but, toward the end of the process, you found that you missed one part and the whole thing needed to be taken apart and put together again. I had that experience too.

Have you ever wondered why life does not go the way most of us expect it to go? Why challenges and loss happen in our lives? Though the number of conveniences has increased and luxuries are better than ever before, the *quality of life* has gone down. Why? One of the main reasons this happens is because we do not read the manual for life on this earth. We try to outsmart other people by thinking we are better than others but, at the end, keep making the same mistakes they have made. Is there a solution?

Where do you look for help when life does not go the way you dreamed? Who do we ask for help when unexpected challenges show up in life? Do you know what to do when those warning signs show up in your body? Let me share with you some of what is included in the first three chapters of Genesis because everything you need to know is mentioned in those three chapters.

The reason most of the difficulties we experience in life occur is because we do not know how it all began. We do not understand the order of events that unfolded at the beginning of creation. When we understand and follow the protocols God set in motion on this earth, we will succeed in every area of life. Let me share with you how important the first three chapters of Genesis are.

The reason for your existence is mentioned in the first three chapters of Genesis.

Do you know your purpose and what you are supposed to do with your life? It is mentioned in the first three chapters of the Bible: God created man to have dominion over the earth. Each of us is created to master and to have dominion over a sphere of life, not over people. It is because we lost dominion over the earth that people are trying to dominate each other. I will explain this further later in the book.

The reason for all the mess that we see on the earth today is because of what happened in the third chapter of Genesis.

It does not take much to know that we are living in a messed-up world. We all try to blame it on others or the government of our country, but the root reason is because of what happened in the third chapter of Genesis. I will explain this more also in a later chapter.

All major management and leadership principles that exist in businesses and enterprises are mentioned in the first three chapters of the Bible.

Whether they realize it or not, all major inventors, businesses, and manufacturers on this earth use the principles that are mentioned in the first three chapters of the Bible as their foundation. I explain this in the 'Process of Having Dominion' chapter. I am writing a book called 'Laws that Govern Life' from the first three chapters of the Bible. God has shown me fifty laws so far!

The battle plan and strategy of the enemy, and his weapons, appear in these three chapters.

Are you tired of living a defeated life? Is there any area of your life in which you are struggling to overcome? The key is mentioned in these three chapters. The devil talked to the woman and she saw that the tree was good for food, pleasant to the eyes, and desirable to make one wise. She took the fruit and ate it. The woman sinned for three reasons. The first reason is because she saw that the tree was good for food (the lust of the flesh). The second was that she saw it was pleasant to the eyes (the lust of the eye). And, the third reason was that it was desirable to make one wise (the pride of life). Those are the three age-old weapons the enemy uses in every temptation against human beings.

The reason we are not able to reach this world is because we do not use the methods God used to establish the earth in the first three chapters of the Bible.

There are six methods God used in the book of Genesis to establish the earth. He used the same methods throughout the Bible to reach the world. I explain this also in the 'Process of Having Dominion' chapter.

Marriages are falling apart because people do not understand the first three chapters of the Bible. That is where it mentions the purpose of marriage, to whom, and why we should get married.

When we understand the Creator's purpose and method for marriage, we will have lasting relationships. When Jesus was questioned about divorce, He did not refer to the present culture. He said, "From the beginning it was not so" (Matthew 19:8). He referred to how marriage began.

People are stuck in religion and rituals because they do not understand the first three chapters of the Bible.

God did not start a religion. He wanted to have a relationship with each of us. He did not give a bunch of rules to Adam. He came down to the Garden of Eden to fellowship with Adam and Eve even after they sinned.

If you do not understand the first three chapters of the Bible, then you will not understand the rest of it. Jesus came to this earth because of what happened in the first three chapters of the Bible, to restore our relationship with our Heavenly Father.

Different denominations exist because people do not understand the first three chapters of the Bible.

When we all understand the foundational doctrines set forth in the book of Genesis, we will have unity among Christians. These chapters of Genesis contain the foundational doctrines that God established for everyone. When we believe and adhere to them, we will have unity in the body of Christ.

There is a caste system and racism on this earth because people do not understand the first three chapters of the Bible.

Life on this earth began with one man. God created one man; not a nation, or a particular race; He did not start with a community. We all came from that one man. Depending on which side of the equator you live, you may have a different skin color or language, but we all have the same father.

There are doctrinal differences and divisions in the Church because people do not understand the first three chapters of the Bible.

As I mentioned, the foundational doctrines everyone needs to obey are mentioned in the first three chapters of the Bible, which I cover in this chapter.

There are rich and poor on this earth because people do not understand the first three chapters of the Bible.

The poor on this earth are poor because they do not understand their purpose. Our provision is attached to our purpose, and our purpose is mentioned in the first three chapters of the Bible.

Jesus came to reinstate what God told us in the first three chapters of the Bible. Everything Jesus taught was from the first three chapters of the Bible. Everything He did was to restore what we lost in the third chapter of Genesis. Below are some of these.

Genesis Chapters 1-3	New Testament
God created man in His image and likeness (Genesis 1:26)	When we are born again we are recreated in the image and likeness of God (John 3:3; Colossians 3:10)
God blessed them and told them to be fruitful (Genesis 1:28)	Jesus blessed us and told us to bear fruit (Matthew 5:3-9; John 15:16)
God told man to subdue and take dominion over every creature He had made (Genesis 1:28)	Jesus told us to tread on serpents and scorpions and over all the power of the enemy (Luke 10:19)
God gave Adam the earth as his inheritance	Jesus said the meek shall inherit the earth (Matthew 5:5)
God put man in His Kingdom; the Garden	Jesus came to restore and give us the Kingdom (Luke 12:32; 22:29)
There was no sickness or curse in the Garden	Jesus came to die for our sickness and curse and gave us authority over all manner of sickness and disease (Matthew 8:16; 10:1)
God breathed into him His Spirit (Genesis 2:7)	Jesus breathed His Spirit on the disciples (John 21:22)
God gave them His Word (Genesis 2:16-17)	Jesus gave us His Word (John 17:8)
They were clothed with God's glory (Genesis 2:25)	Jesus said that He gave us His glory (John 17:22)

75

God instituted marriage (Genesis 2:22-24)	When Jesus referred to marriage He referred to the original marriage (Matthew 19:4,8)
God walked with man (Genesis 3:8)	Jesus walked with us and dwelt among us (John 1:14)
Adam had unlimited knowledge and wisdom (Genesis 2:19-20)	Jesus possesses the treasures of all wisdom and knowledge and He lives inside of us (Colossians 2:3)
Man had dominion over the earth (Genesis 1:26)	Jesus said all authority in heaven and on earth was given to Him. In turn, He gave that authority to us. He said whatever we loose on earth will be loosed in heaven and whatever we bind on earth will be bound in heaven (Matthew 16:19; Ephesians 1:22)
God told Adam everything in the Garden was freely his	Jesus said freely you have received, freely give (Matthew 10:18; Romans 8:32; 1 Cor. 2:12)
God gave Adam a woman	The Church is pictured as a woman
Adam was the son of God (Luke 3:38)	Whoever believes in Jesus becomes a child of God (John 1:12)
Genesis starts with, "In the beginning."	The Gospel of John starts with, "In the beginning."
God's will was done on earth as it was in heaven. There was no curse, sickness, poverty, or death in the Garden	Jesus taught us to pray the same (Matthew 6:10)
God did not ask Adam and Eve to sing to Him	Jesus never asked anyone to sing to Him
A river came out of Eden parted into four corners of the earth (Genesis 2:10-14)	Jesus said the rivers of living water will flow out of us to the uttermost parts of the earth (John 7:38; Acts 1:8)
God told them to multiply and fill the earth (Genesis 1:28)	Jesus said to go and make disciples of all nations (Matthew 28:19)

Every major doctrine of the Bible is hidden in these first three chapters. A doctrine in the Bible is a teaching or a principle to which we all need to adhere. Below are twenty of them.

1) THE DOCTRINE OF THE TRINITY

God revealed Himself in three Persons in the Bible: The Father, Son, and the Holy Spirit. It begins by introducing these three Persons.

76

Genesis 1:1-3 says, "In the beginning **God** created the heavens and the earth. The earth was without form, and void; and darkness *was* on the face of the deep. And the **Spirit of God** was hovering over the face of the waters. Then **God said [according to John 1, Jesus is the Word]**, "Let there be light"; and there was light."

In the above verse we see all three persons of the Trinity; God the Father, the Spirit of God who is the Holy Spirit, and when God speaks it is called the Word of God. Jesus is called the Word of God in the Bible. He is the Word that became flesh.

2) THE DOCTRINE OF LOVE

The Bible says that God is love. This may be the most important doctrine of the Bible in relation to human beings.

When God created the earth for human beings, He knew that man was going to sin and; consequently, betray Him. He knew the pain and the price He would have to pay to restore man. He knew that He had to send His only Son to die on the cross for all humanity. Knowing that, He still created us because of His great love. The Bible says there is no greater love than for someone to lay down his life for a friend. Jesus calls us friends, and He laid His life down for us.

3) THE DOCTRINE OF PRAYER

God introduced two kinds of prayer in the first three chapters of the Bible. Genesis 1:3 states that God said, "Let there be light." When it says, "God said," He was not just saying something; it was a command. We read in 2 Corinthians 4 that God commanded light to shine out of the darkness. Psalm 148:5 says, "...For He commanded and they were created." Commanding and speaking to our situations is one form of prayer. The next is when God came down to meet Adam and Eve every day. This is the highest form of prayer: fellowship and communion with God.

4) THE DOCTRINE OF REDEMPTION

After man disobeyed God and committed sin, God promised to redeem man from his sin. The first prophecy in the Bible is mentioned in Genesis 3:15. It says the seed of the woman will crush the head of the serpent.

5) THE DOCTRINE OF THE FORGIVENESS OF SINS

According to the Bible, a soul that sins must die because the wages of sin is death. And, there is no forgiveness of sins without the shedding of blood. Instead of killing Adam and Eve, God killed an animal and shed its blood for the forgiveness of their sins, showing them the pattern. That animal represented Jesus Christ, who is the Lamb of God that was slain before the foundation of the world.

6) THE DOCTRINE OF WORSHIP

Through the killing of an animal, God was teaching man about sacrifice and worship.

7) THE DOCTRINE OF ETERNAL LIFE

Man was not created to die. God designed us to live forever. He expected Adam and Eve to eat from the tree of life, which represents eternal life and also represents Jesus Christ.

8) THE DOCTRINE OF DEATH AND RESURRECTION

God told Adam, "The day that you eat from the tree of the knowledge of good and evil you shall surely die." Death means there is a resurrection. Spirit beings cannot be destroyed; if they die, they will resurrect.

9) THE DOCTRINE OF MARRIAGE AND FAMILY

When God created Adam, He saw that it was not good for man to be alone. He made a woman from the rib He took out of Adam and joined them together in marriage. God instituted marriage between an adult man and woman. That was the first family on earth.

10) THE DOCTRINE OF THE KINGDOM OF GOD

God created Adam and put him in the Garden, which was God's Kingdom. There was no sickness, curse, or poverty in the Garden. Man had everything he needed. God's will was done in the Garden as it was in heaven. Through sin, man lost the Garden and the Kingdom of God. Jesus came to give us back the Kingdom (Luke 12:32; 22:29).

11) THE DOCTRINE OF GIVING

God gave the Garden to man and said, "Of every tree of the garden you may freely eat..." God gave herbs, trees that produce seeds, and fruit for man's food. He gave the whole earth to man.

12) THE DOCTRINE OF SPIRITUAL WARFARE

God told man to subdue the earth and everything He created. Why does he need to subdue if there is no rebellion? God was telling man to expect intruders in the Garden and to keep them where they belong. When He gave Adam the Garden, He told him to till and guard it. Why did he have to guard it if there were no trespassers?

13) THE DOCTRINE OF SATAN OR THE ADVERSARY

We see in chapter three that Satan came into the Garden in the form of a serpent and began to talk to Eve. Serpent is one of the names of Satan that is mentioned in the Bible.

14) THE DOCTRINE OF SIN

Adam and Eve disobeyed God and sin entered them and the earth. Sin is a satanic operating system. The Bible says that because of one man's (the first man) disobedience, everyone became a sinner. So, all have sinned and fall short of the glory of God.

15) THE DOCTRINE OF BLESSING & CURSE

There are two things God blessed after He created them. First, He blessed the animals and the living creatures. The second is man. We need to follow God's example of blessing. We need to bless our family, our children, and one another. Many, instead of blessing, curse each other. God as Father blessed his son, Adam. If you are a parent, please make sure that you bless your children and do not curse them.

After creating man, God blessed them. In Matthew 5, Jesus began His preaching with blessing. Before He ascended to heaven, He blessed His disciples (Luke 24:50-51).

In Genesis chapter three, we also read about curses. Sin brought curse, poverty, sickness, and eventually, death to this earth.

16) THE DOCTRINE OF DISPENSATIONS

God divided the creation process into six days and on the seventh day He rested. The reason He did that was to show us there would be six dispensations on this earth. I will explain these dispensations later in this book.

We are going to walk in detail through the first three chapters of Genesis and see how it all began and why life is the way it is now on this earth. You will discover the reason for all the evil that is happening now. Who is responsible for what is happening on this earth? Where do we all come from? What is the purpose of man? What are we supposed to do with this earth? You will find the answers to all these questions in the following two chapters.

17) THE DOCTRINE OF WALKING IN THE SPIRIT/SPIRIT-FILLED LIVING

God created man to be led by his spirit. That is the only way we are supposed to live on this earth. Adam and Eve were full of the Holy Spirit. That was the reason they were able to commune with God who is a Spirit. They were led by their spirits until they fell.

18) THE DOCTRINE OF LOVING GOD WITH ALL OUR HEART, SOUL, AND STRENGTH

There were two trees in the Garden. God told man not to eat from the tree of the knowledge of good and evil. Man had to put God first in his life and love Him more than the blessings He gave to humanity. Instead, man chose the blessings over the One who blessed them.

19) THE DOCTRINE OF STEWARDSHIP

God gave the earth and the Garden to man to keep it and to guard it. The earth is the Lord's and the fullness thereof. But He gave the earth to man to take care of it. Whatever material things God gives to us are only temporary and we need to be a good steward of them.

20) THE DOCTRINE OF THE NAMES OF GOD

In Genesis 1, the name of God mentioned is Elohim. But from chapter 2:8 we read "the LORD God" or "Yehovah Elohim." Since then God has revealed Himself through different names in the Bible.

CHAPTER 6
THE MANUAL FOR LIFE ON
THIS EARTH - PART 2

CHAPTER 6: THE MANUAL FOR LIFE ON THIS EARTH - PART 2

Most of us are living and singing, "One day I am going to heaven, one day I am going to heaven." We are like the little girl who's Daddy told her that "one day" he is going to take her to the zoo. Every day she gets up singing, "This is the day my Daddy is going to take me to the zoo!" But, unfortunately, that day has not yet come.

We are like that little girl. Many of us do not know how life began on this earth or why God put us here. We just know bits and pieces and have been singing the song everyone else is singing. I want to tell you a fact that is scary; most people have no clue about why they are here. My humble attempt here is to give you a glimpse into our past so that you can have a strong foundation on which life can be built. Then you will be able to discover and fulfill your unique purpose on this earth.

Let me also share with you that some of the things I mention in this book may be contrary to popular belief. When we hear something new, our current mindset will not accept that easily, especially those concepts that impact what *we think* are the core beliefs of our faith. Our current knowledge about a subject, person, or a thing creates our reality. Our current reality is our boundary. It is difficult to even think there is something beyond that.

When I heard that I had to separate my relationship with God from the ministry I was doing, I first opposed the idea. I was angry because to me God and ministry were all intertwined and there was no way I could separate them. My concept was that if I do not do ministry, then God would not be happy with me. I grew up in India where culture and religion are mixed together. You cannot separate one from the other. It took me close to five years of struggle and fighting even to see a slight possibility of viewing God and ministry as two different entities.

So some of the things you will read in this book may not be culturally popular, but I can guarantee they are scripturally sound. We live in an upside-down world. For example, for years we have been saying, "We go to church on

Sunday morning." When we think of church we think of a building, but the Church is not a building. So, when we leave the building after a service we feel like church is over. People are the Church and we go to a facility to meet together. It is not easy to change an old way of thinking. Everyone knows we need change; we even talk about making changes, but few are willing to pay the price to bring or cause that change.

I believe change begins when we become the change that we would like to see in our society. For change to be possible, we first need to accept the fact that there is more than what we know now. Secondly, try to believe that there are different ways to do what we do and the way we do things now. As you know, the soldier who goes in front of the army takes more bullets. If you want to cause change, you may have to take some bullets. God created you to do something no one else has done before. When you receive the revelation of a truth, accept it and try to think differently.

CHAPTER 1 OF THE MANUAL

The manual begins by saying, "In the beginning God created the heavens and the earth."

When the Bible says, "In the beginning," it does not mean six thousand years ago. It could have been millions or billions of years ago. God existed prior to Him creating the heavens and the earth. He created the heavens for His throne and the earth as His footstool. The heavens and the earth were created at the same time, which was in the beginning. The earth we live on is as old as the heavens above us. How do I know that? When God began His six days of creation in Genesis 1:3 (actually, it was restoration), we see that the dark earth covered with water existed prior to that. We do not see God creating the earth or water during the six days of creation. How long has the earth existed? We do not know. We only know it has existed as long as the heavens. There is plenty of evidence in the science world that shows our planet earth is millions of years old. Many believe the earth was created during the six-day account of creation, but it was not. God only remodeled it and brought it back to order.

The above verse also teaches us three very important principles, which are imperative for life on this earth—the relationship between heaven and earth and the balance between the spiritual and natural realm. Heaven represents the spiritual, or unseen, and the earth represents the natural, or what is seen. Human beings are spiritual and natural at the same time. We need to know how to relate to both realms. Many people that I know are so 'heaven bound' they have no clue how the natural things work on this earth. Many others are so 'earth bound' they are not aware of the spirit world or their own spirit. God has put everything we need for our life on or in this earth. Wise people will know how to tap into those resources and their lives will prosper.

The second principle is that heaven is mentioned first and it is above the earth. We need to give priority to spiritual things. Life on this earth depends on, and is ruled by, heaven above us. That means we need to look at the earth and our life with heaven's perspective. When a person or society loses their spiritual perspective, life on this earth becomes meaningless and chaotic.

The third principle is that both the spiritual and natural worlds are governed by laws. When we discover those laws and operate our life accordingly, we will be successful on this earth. Genesis 1:2, "The earth was without form, and void; and darkness *was* on the face of the deep. And the Spirit of God was hovering over the face of the waters."

Something happened to the earth that existed prior to the six days of creation. Whatever God makes is perfect, but the earth written about in Genesis 1:2 is not perfect; rather, it is without form, void, and full of darkness. It looks like a flood took place somewhere in time. But the Spirit of God was hovering over the face of the waters.

THE SPIRIT OF GOD

Who is that? God is a Spirit. His Spirit is called the Spirit of God, or the Holy Spirit. God is present everywhere through His Spirit. God manifested Himself to us in three persons: God the Father (once you become His son or daughter you call Him Father), God the Son (Jesus Christ) who is the Word that became flesh, and the Holy Spirit. The first three verses of Genesis introduce us to the three Persons of the Godhead that we should know while we are on this earth. Theologians call this the Trinity, or Triune God.

> Genesis 1:3, 'Then God said, "Let there be light"; and there was light. And God saw the light, that *it was* good; and God divided the light from the darkness. God called the light Day, and the darkness He called Night. So the evening and the morning were the first day.'

All God needs to do to create something is speak. When God speaks, it is called the 'Word of God.' Jesus is called the Word of God. We will learn more about Him in the coming pages.

LET THERE BE LIGHT

Many people who did not believe in God, and even people from other religions, read the Bible to search for truth. They found that God created 'light' on the first day, but He created the sun, moon, and stars only on the fourth day. So, they claim the Bible's record of creation is wrong. This is because they do not understand what it says. The light God brought out on the first day is not the natural light we see with our eyes. It is the light that illuminates our heart and spirit, which leads us from darkness to light and from ignorance to wisdom. The light God called out on the first day is wisdom related to this earth. As we know, a ray of light has seven colors in it. God has seven Spirits, though the Holy Spirit is one. When you look at light you do not see seven colors, but when it passes through a prism, it comes out as seven different colors. Likewise, God revealed Himself in seven Spirits. They are the Spirit of the LORD, the Spirit of wisdom, the Spirit of knowledge, the Spirit of understanding, the Spirit of counsel, the Spirit of might, and the Spirit of the fear of the LORD. The Bible calls wisdom 'light' and ignorance 'darkness'.

The Bible says God founded the earth by wisdom, by understanding He established it, and by His knowledge the depths were broken up and the heavens pour down dew (Proverbs 3:19-20). The foundation of everything God does is wisdom. You need to make sure that you follow God's footsteps in your life. If you are to know God and His ways, you need to have wisdom, knowledge, and understanding. They are the keys that unlock the mysteries of life. So, on the first day God separated wisdom from ignorance. Again, the Bible says the fear of the LORD is the beginning of wisdom (Proverbs 9:10).

THE FIRST DAY OF CREATION

On the first day, God created light and divided the light from darkness. He called the light 'Day' and the darkness 'Night.'

THE SECOND DAY OF CREATION

Genesis 1:6-7, 'Then God said, "Let there be a firmament in the midst of the waters, and let it divide the waters from the waters." Thus God made the firmament, and divided the waters which *were* under the firmament from the waters which *were* above the firmament; and it was so. And God called the firmament Heaven. So the evening and the morning were the second day.'

On the second day, God made the firmament to divide the waters and called it heaven.

THE THIRD DAY OF CREATION

'Then God said, "Let the waters under the heavens be gathered together into one place, and let the dry *land* appear"; and it was so. And God called the dry *land* Earth, and the gathering together of the waters He called Seas. And God saw that *it was* good.'

'Then God said, "Let the earth bring forth grass, the herb *that* yields seed, *and* the fruit tree *that* yields fruit according to its kind, whose seed *is* in itself, on the earth"; and it was so. And the earth brought forth grass, the herb *that* yields seed according to its kind, and the tree *that* yields fruit, whose seed *is* in itself according to its kind. And God saw that *it was* good. So the evening and the morning were the third day.'

On the third day God made the dry land, ocean, and vegetation.

THE FOURTH DAY OF CREATION

'Then God said, "Let there be lights in the firmament of the heavens to divide the day from the night; and let them be for signs and seasons, and for days and years; and let them be for lights in the firmament of the heavens to give light on the earth"; and it was so. Then God made two great lights: the greater light to rule the day, and the lesser light to rule the night. *He made* the stars also. God set them in the firmament of the heavens to give light on the earth, and to rule over the day and over the night, and to divide the light from the darkness. And God saw that *it was* good. So the evening and the morning were the fourth day.'

On the fourth day God created the sun, moon, and stars.

THE FIFTH DAY OF CREATION

'Then God said, "Let the waters abound with an abundance of living creatures, and let birds fly above the earth across the face of the firmament of the heavens." So God created great sea creatures and every living thing that moves, with which the waters abounded, according to their kind, and every winged bird according to its kind. And God saw that *it was* good. And God blessed them, saying, "Be fruitful and multiply, and fill the waters in the seas, and let birds multiply on the earth." So the evening and the morning were the fifth day.'

On the fifth day God created creatures in the sea and the birds.

THE SIXTH DAY OF CREATION

'Then God said, "Let the earth bring forth the living creature according to its kind: cattle and creeping thing and beast of the earth, *each* according to its kind"; and it was so. And God made the beast of the earth according to its kind, cattle according to its kind, and everything that creeps on the earth according to its kind. And God saw that *it was* good.'

God created every living creature that is on the earth and in the sea. A monkey reproduces a monkey. Man reproduces man. Living creatures do not change their species over time, no matter how long they live on this earth. There is no scientific proof that shows that one species changes into another species; this is a concept derived from mythology and fiction. That is why God used the phrase, 'its own kind'.

'Then God said, "Let Us make man in Our image, according to Our likeness; let them have dominion over the fish of the sea, over the birds of the air, and over the cattle, over all the earth and over every creeping thing that creeps on the earth." So God created man in His *own* image; in the image of God He created him; male and female He created them. Then God blessed them, and God said to them, "Be fruitful and multiply; fill the earth and subdue it; have dominion over the fish of the sea, over the birds of the air, and over every living thing that moves on the earth."'

On the sixth day God created the animals and man.

THE CREATION OF MAN

God created us in His image and likeness. What does that mean? Humanity was created with qualities similar to what God possesses. Like Him, we are spirit beings. We can imagine, be creative, and make things. We have volition and freedom of choice. God created us male and female. From the word image comes imagination. A detailed account of how and why God made man and woman is in the next chapter.

THE PURPOSE OF MAN

After God created man, He blessed them and gave them dominion over all the earth and the things and creatures He made. That is your purpose my friend, to have dominion over this earth; but not people. He explains the steps to dominion in verse 28.

The first thing He said was to be *fruitful*. Every living thing God created multiplies or reproduces itself. God wants us to be fruitful. He put a 'seed' in our spirit. A seed is something that has unlimited potential to reproduce its own kind. That seed could be ability, talent, skill, passion, creativity, an idea, a product, an invention, or a dream. He wants you to focus your life on that seed, plant it, nurture it, and use it to solve a problem other people have on this earth. When you possess a quality that others do not have, they will pay to reap the benefits of what you have. That is your purpose. That is the key to your prosperity.

The second step to having dominion is to *multiply*. Once you know what you are supposed to be doing, your purpose and your product (fruit), you need to multiply it. To multiply means to mass-produce. If it is a book, or a song, you produce copies of that book or CD to reach the whole world.

The third step to having dominion is to *fill the earth*. Fill the earth means to distribute or market something so that others can benefit from it.

The fourth step to having dominion is to *subdue*. Subdue means to do what you do like no one else does, and bring that sphere of life under your subjection. That means you become an expert in that particular field and present it in a way that others need what you have to increase their quality of life on this earth. To subdue means to take authority over and master something. You are created to subdue and master an area of life on this earth.

The fifth step is *dominion*. When you subdue an area of life, you will have dominion. This is the secret of all prosperity and of fulfilling your purpose on this earth. Every successful business on this earth uses the above principle as their foundation for growth, whether they realize it or not. God set that in motion in the first chapter of the Bible. Whatever God does has the potential for growth.

GOD BLESSED US

Verse 28 says, "God blessed them," and, "God said to them." What does that mean? To bless means to speak well of, to empower, cause to prosper, give favor. To bless someone means to take from what you have and give it to him. God has not only given you a seed, but the blessing (everything you need) to bring forth that seed. God is a God who blesses and does not curse. There are curses and cursed people on this earth now but God is not the source of those.

Whenever you bless someone, you need to say something. Many people only say, "I bless you, or, "We bless you." That is not a complete blessing. You need to say how or what you are blessing them with. You see this throughout the Bible.

God created the whole earth for man. Unlimited wealth and resources are contained in this earth. Oil, precious stones, and metals are some of them. Man needs to subdue and extract these from the earth. Those who do will benefit from these resources; those who reject it remain poor. It takes wisdom, creativity, and hard work to succeed.

EVERYTHING WAS GOOD

God looked at all He created and saw that it was good. There was no evil or crooked thing on this earth. Everything was good. So, please stop blaming God for all evil and things that are not good. He made everything perfect.

LET "US" AND LET "THEM"

One of the age-old questions man has been asking is, "If God is good and powerful, then why does He let evil happen on this earth?" Or, "Why doesn't He intervene to stop a catastrophe or help people who are going through bad times?" One thing to notice very carefully is that when God created man He said, "Let *Us* make man." When it came to delegating the dominion and authority over the earth, He said, "Let *them*." God did not include Himself in the assignment of dominion. God created the earth for man and gave it to him as an inheritance. It is up to man to decide what he wants to do on this earth. God will not interfere with the affairs of man unless man asks Him. Until the creation of man, God directly did everything on this earth. After creating man, God did everything on this earth through human partnership. God will not violate His own Word. He is just and holy.

That is one of the reasons evil takes place on this earth and God does not intervene to stop it. Man was created with a will, to choose either to work *with* God or independently of Him.

> 'And God said, "See, I have given you every herb *that* yields seed which *is* on the face of all the earth, and every tree whose fruit yields seed; to you it shall be for food. Also, to every beast of the earth, to every bird of the air, and to everything that creeps on the earth, in which *there is* life, *I have given* every green herb for food"; and it was so. Then God saw everything that He had made, and indeed *it was* very good. So the evening and the morning were the sixth day' (Genesis 1:29-31).

WHY SUBDUE AND TAKE DOMINION OVER THE CREATURES?

God specifically told man to take dominion over the fish of the sea and over the fowl of the air, over the cattle and over every living thing that moves upon the earth (Genesis 1:28). Why would man need to subdue and take dominion over these creatures, and how were they in any way dangerous to man? The reason God told that to man is this: Satan and evil spirits were on this earth before God created Adam. They had access and permission to enter the earth realm and the animal kingdom before the fall of man.

As a loving Father, He was preparing Adam for a possible assault from the enemy, who would most likely use one of those four mediums. Since Satan and demons are spirit beings, they need a physical body to operate on this earth. They were not allowed to enter Adam and Eve, so they had to use either the fish of the sea, birds of the air, cattle of the earth, or the creeping things. Satan chose the serpent because it was more cunning than any other creature God had made on this earth. Even in our world today, in any culture, creatures from those four categories God told man to subdue are worshiped or considered gods.

God wanted Adam to subdue (make submit by force), any rebellion or attempt to usurp his authority. He was to put it out immediately. It was man's duty to keep them where they belonged. Unfortunately, Adam did not do it, but listened to the serpent and willfully disobeyed God.

MAN WAS A VEGETARIAN

God gave man herbs (vegetables & beans), fruit, seeds, and nuts for food in the beginning. Man did not start eating meat until after the flood with Noah.

Because of his diet, man lived longer and healthier in the first two thousand years on this earth.

CHAPTER 2 OF THE MANUAL

"Thus, the heavens and the earth, and all the host of them, were finished. And on the seventh day God ended His work which He had done, and He rested on the seventh day from all His work which He had done. Then God blessed the seventh day and sanctified it, because in it He rested from all His work which God had created and made" (Genesis 2:1-3).

WHY SIX DAYS OF CREATION?

God could have made everything in one day, but He divided the task into smaller segments and completed it in six days. He is showing us a principle of success. Any task you have, if you divide it into small segments and do one thing at a time and finish it before moving on to the next, you can easily accomplish. That is one of the secrets to achieving great things. The second reason God used six days and rested on the seventh is to show the seven dispensations that will unfold on this earth from the time of the creation of man until the reign of Christ on this earth. We are in the sixth dispensation right now (dispensation of grace), and there is one more left. In the seventh dispensation we will rest from our toil and the tears of this earth.

GOD RESTED ON THE SEVENTH DAY

God rested but not because He was tired. He illustrated a principle that we need to abide by on this earth. We need to rest one day per week. Rest is a necessity for healthy living. If you overwork your body, or a machine, it will soon break down.

This is how days, weeks, months, and years began. They were God's idea. The reason Sunday is a holiday in most countries is because they believe in the principle of rest.

HOW MAN IS DIFFERENT FROM THE ANIMALS

God *spoke* to the earth and animals and birds were created.

God *formed* man from the earth and breathed the breath of life into him.

God made man in His image and likeness.

Man has creativity; he can imagine and make something.

Man has a sense of God, or divinity, in him.

Man can speak (learn multiple languages) and change or create the atmosphere he wants.

Man has a spirit and can hear and relate to God.

Man has a sense of family and relationship.

Man has a sense of destiny and future (hope).

Man has faith and the ability to believe.

Man can choose right from wrong.

The enemy does not like human beings. From the beginning of time he has been trying to bring man down to the level of animals. If you look at our society today, the qualities mentioned above are becoming less and less apparent in humans. The future of the human race is at stake.

> "This *is* the history of the heavens and the earth when they were created, in the day that the LORD God made the earth and the heavens, before any plant of the field was in the earth and before any herb of the field had grown. For the LORD God had not caused it to rain on the earth, and *there was* no man to till the ground; but a mist went up from the earth and watered the whole face of the ground" (Genesis 2:4-6).

> "And the LORD God formed man *of* the dust of the ground, and breathed into his nostrils the breath of life; and man became a living being" (Genesis 2:7).

Our body was formed from the earth. Our flesh and bones are materials that come from the ground. When we die, those materials will return to the earth. We have something that is not derived from the earth, our spirit. God breathed His Spirit (the breath of life) into the nostrils of the man He made out of the dust and man became a living soul. That is the difference between man and animals. Animals have life but they do not have a spirit. A spirit is something that is not limited by space or time. We can imagine with our spirit and there is no limit to our imagination.

Our spirit is from God and because of that, without God, man cannot function on this earth. That is why every human being searches for God. It is a natural instinct; we know we are part of something bigger than ourselves. Animals do not look for God because they do not have the same capacity as we do to relate to Him.

93

ADAM

The first man created by God was called Adam. The Bible calls him the son of God (Luke 3:38). God is love, and He wanted a family to share His love and rule the earth. So, He created man in His image and likeness, and now all have the opportunity to become a child of God.

THE LORD GOD

In the first chapter of the Bible God addressed Himself as God. After creating man in the second chapter He adds a title to His name. He calls Himself the LORD God. There is a reason for it. Since he gave the dominion of the earth to man, He becomes the LORD of the earth and man. Lord means owner or someone who oversees. It is common in our day to call someone a landlord, which means that person owns a certain piece of land.

LIFE IN GOD'S GARDEN

"The LORD God planted a garden eastward in Eden, and there He put the man whom He had formed. And out of the ground the LORD God made every tree grow that is **pleasant to the sight** and **good for food**. The tree of life *was* also in the midst of the garden, and the tree of the knowledge of good and evil" (Genesis 2:8-9).

ATMOSPHERE FOR CREATIVITY

God not only created man, He also made a suitable place for him to live. He made a beautiful garden and put the man in it. The Bible says God made trees that are pleasant to the sight and good for food. He wanted Adam to be inspired by his environment, by what he saw, because your environment affects your mood and creativity. It is difficult to be productive and happy in a place where there is clutter and disorder. The first thing you need to do is create an atmosphere around you that inspires and motivates you. Even if you live in a hut or a small house, treat it like you are living in a palace and make it look its best. If you claim to be a child of God by any sense, the first sign of it should show in the place you live. One of the aesthetic qualities of people who are close to God is they love order, beauty, cleanliness, and excellence.

The next thing the above verse says is God provided man with good food. He gave them the best of the best. You know the old saying, "You are what you eat." What you eat affects your spirit, soul, and body. So make sure what you eat is good for your spirit, soul, and body, not just your mouth!

God is a good God, and He sustains and takes care of everything He created. It is His responsibility to provide for you. But, you first need to have a relationship with Him. Life on this earth was like life in heaven. God's will was done on this earth as it was in heaven. There is no sickness in heaven, and there was no sickness on earth. There is no evil in heaven and there was no evil on earth. God never intended for life on this earth to be any different than life in heaven.

> "Now a river went out of Eden to water the garden, and from there it parted and became four riverheads. The name of the first *is* Pishon; it *is* the one which skirts the whole land of Havilah, where *there is* gold. And the gold of that land *is* good. Bdellium and the onyx stone *are* there. The name of the second river *is* Gihon; it *is* the one which goes around the whole land of Cush. The name of the third river *is* Hiddekel; it *is* the one which goes toward the east of Assyria. The fourth river *is* the Euphrates" (Genesis 2:10-14).

Rivers show expansion and growth. God wanted man to multiply and fill the earth. He knew that man would require some resources. God was showing man the resources He has put in this earth for him. Precious stones and metals were deposited in this earth (by God) for man. It takes the creativity and wisdom of God to extract those precious things from the earth. God never expected man to be poor. He gave the whole earth to man. He is the one who said that gold and precious stones were good. He did not put them in this earth for the devil or for his children; He placed those resources there for us.

The name of the first river was Pishon, which in Hebrew means 'increase.' The second river was called Gihon, which means in Hebrew 'bursting forth.' The third river was called Hiddekel, which in Hebrew means 'rapid.' The fourth river was called Euphrates, which in Hebrew means 'fruitfulness.' That is what God expects from each of us.

Many people say that when God created us He did not give us a manual. Or, when a baby is born they do not come with a manual. What is more ridiculous than that? God spelled out every detail. He told us why He made us, what we are supposed to be doing, and what He is expecting from us. He is the Master Craftsman, and we are His workmanship. The problem is no one has taught us these things. The Bible tells us that to a natural man the things of the Spirit are foolishness!

'Then the LORD God took the man and put him in the garden of Eden to tend and keep it. And the Lord God commanded the man, saying, "Of every tree of the garden you may freely eat; but of the tree of the knowledge of good and evil you shall not eat, for in the day that you eat of it you shall surely die"' (Genesis 2:15-17).

RULES

Another reason some people do not like God is because they think all God cares about is giving rules and overseeing how we keep them. That is far from the truth. He gave man one rule in the beginning, because God wants man to honor Him and give Him the rightful place in his life. Even today, after you receive Christ and become His child and live in His kingdom, He wants you to keep only one rule. That is to love Him with all your heart, soul, mind, and strength.

THE GARDEN OF EDEN

Who said God does not provide for or care about our needs? God prepared a garden for man to live in. It was paradise on this earth. There is another name for the Garden of Eden, the Kingdom of God. It was like heaven on earth. There was no sickness, poverty, curse, or any other evil in the Garden. Man was in charge of it. God told him to guard and till it. Again, man did not do it. He allowed the enemy to enter the Garden. God wants man to live in His Kingdom. That was God's original plan and it has not changed.

THE TREE OF THE KNOWLEDGE OF GOOD AND EVIL

"And the Lord God commanded the man, saying, "Of every tree of the garden you may freely eat; but of the tree of the knowledge of good and evil you shall not eat, for in the day that you eat of it you shall surely die" Genesis 2:16-17.

Many people wonder, "If God is good and loving, why did He put the tree of the knowledge of good and evil in the Garden?" God gave man an opportunity to choose to love and trust Him more than anything else. Also, one thing to know about God is that He will test you and me. Life on this earth began with a test in the Garden, and man failed that test. If He had succeeded, he could have eaten from the Tree of Life and lived forever.

The tree of the knowledge of good and evil represents earthly knowledge, which is to know about good and evil. God did not create man to know good and evil or to live by choosing good and hating evil. We are spirit beings, and He wants us to be led by our spirit. He created us to live by love, and in love, with Him. Man chose the lowest quality of life, which is living by the knowledge of good and evil. Today there are Christians who live by the knowledge of good and evil. That means trying to live the Christian life by observing a bunch of rules and regulations. The law was given as the result of man choosing to know good and evil.

DEATH

God said that on the day man ate of the tree he would surely die. God never intended for man to die. Man was not created to die. He was created to live forever. The death He was talking about here was not physical death. God was talking about separation from Him, which is a kind of death that eventually brings physical death.

MALE AND FEMALE

> 'And the LORD God said, "*It is* not good that man should be alone; I will make him a helper comparable to him." Out of the ground the LORD God formed every beast of the field and every bird of the air, and brought *them* to Adam to see what he would call them. And whatever Adam called each living creature; that *was* its name. So Adam gave names to all cattle, to the birds of the air, and to every beast of the field. But for Adam there was not found a helper comparable to him'" (Genesis 2:18-20).

Why did God tell Adam to name the animals and creatures of the earth? We have seen that God gave the dominion over the earth to man, it was the right of man to name the creatures. When you name something, or someone, that shows you have authority over it or them.

Though God made man male and female, he was one person in the beginning. Both male and female qualities were contained in one individual. God said that it is not good for man to be alone, which means it is not good for him to be 'all in one'. He was like God. So, God brought all the creatures of the earth to see what Adam would call them and for him to find a helper and whatever he called them became their name. But he could not find a helper that was suitable for him.

> 'And the LORD God caused a deep sleep to fall on Adam, and he slept; and He took one of his ribs, and closed up the flesh in its place. Then the rib which the LORD God had taken from man He made into a woman, and He brought her to the man.

And Adam said: "This *is* now bone of my bones and flesh of my flesh; she shall be called Woman, because she was taken out of Man." Therefore a man shall leave his father and mother and be joined to his wife, and they shall become one flesh. And they were both naked, the man and his wife, and were not ashamed' (Genesis 2:21-25).

WHY EVE?

Man was created in the image and likeness of God. God is love and when you are love and you do not have anyone with whom to share that love, it is lonely and frustrating. God wanted a family so He created human beings in His image and likeness. Adam was alone in the Garden and he could not find a helper comparable to him. That means he could not find a creature that he could share with and who would understand him. God looked at man and said, "It is not good for man to be alone." He needed a companion who was at his level. So, God created a woman in his image and likeness and brought her to Adam.

MARRIAGE

Adam could not find a suitable mate among the animals. God caused a deep sleep to fall on him and He separated the female part (a rib) out of him and made a woman. Then, He brought her to Adam, who took her and called her woman because she was taken out of man. To join them together again, God instituted marriage on this earth. Marriage is the process of joining together a man and woman to become one flesh. God does not view them as two separate individuals, but one.

Marriage between a man and woman is God's idea. He did not take out of Adam another man. When a man and woman join together in marriage, they are no longer two, but one flesh, just like Adam and Eve were one flesh before God separated them. When they are married, again, they become one flesh. What a glorious idea! That is why the Bible says, "What God has joined together, let no man separate." What have we done to marriage these days?

GOD'S DIVINE ORDER

Do you know why life on this earth is not working well for many? Most are frustrated and disappointed. The reason is we do not understand God's order and we do not follow it. The Bible says that God made all things beautiful. That includes everything. Life on this earth is supposed to be beautiful. We understand from the first two chapters of the Bible that everything God does has an order.

The earth was out of order and chaotic, but God brought order and order brought beauty. When we follow His order, our life also will become beautiful.

What is God's divine order? In the first two chapters of Genesis, God mentions everything we need to know. This book is about those things. God did not give man a woman first. If you look at Adam's life, you will see that God set in motion a specific order we all need to follow. First, Adam had a relationship with God before he had a wife. Adam did not confront God and complain that he needed a wife. It was God who initiated the idea. Adam's relationship with God was so fulfilling that he did not think he needed anyone else. He was not insecure about himself. He was a fulfilled man before Eve ever came on the scene.

That is of utmost importance. We need to find fulfillment from our relationship with God, our Creator, before we can have a healthy relationship with others. When that relationship is not right, nothing else will go right. Life may seem to work for a while, at least until trouble comes. People on this earth do not take that seriously. They are trying to build a career, make money, find the right mate, succeed, and do many other things. For many, the result is a total mess!

The second major thing God gave to Adam was the Garden, and the responsibility to take care of it. Work: God created man to work. Taking care of the Garden, and protecting and expanding it, was Adam's work. That was his purpose. Once your relationship with God is in the right place, He will show you His purpose for your life: the work He created for you to accomplish on this earth. That is His responsibility. Adam did not sit around wondering what he should do with his life. God already prepared it for him and brought him to the right place at the right time.

One of the reasons you do not know your purpose yet is because your relationship with God is not in the place it is supposed to be. You may have problems trusting Him with your life. You might be afraid of Him. Whatever it is, just ask Him, and He will show you what needs to be done.

That is why the Bible says we are His workmanship, created in Christ Jesus for good works, which God ordained before the world began. Your life's purpose is pre-ordained by God. In fact, it was ordained before the world began. So, stop worrying about your life and what the purpose of it is. It was already prepared before you arrived on this earth. We just need to discover God's order, that's all.

The third major thing God gave to Adam was Eve. Once your relationship with God is in the right place, you are fulfilled and happy about yourself, and know what you are supposed to be doing with your life; then God will bring the right life-partner to you. You do not seek and try out different men and women like we try on clothes before we buy them. That is not God's idea. When we follow God's order, we will have peace and fulfillment.

This book is about choosing these three most important things in each human's life: Your relationship with God, your purpose, and your life partner. When you do things according to God's order, you will succeed. You may already have made a mess in your life. Do not worry about it because our God is a God of redemption. He can redeem you from your mistakes. All it takes is to come to Him, admit that you are sorry and made a mess, and ask Him to forgive you for what you did. He will begin to do a new work in your life. I can guarantee, it will not happen in a day or two. It is a process because it took you years to get where you are in life right now, and He does not reverse everything in one moment. He will do it one step at a time.

CHAPTER 7
THE MANUAL FOR LIFE ON
THIS EARTH - PART 3

CHAPTER 7: THE MANUAL FOR LIFE ON THIS EARTH - PART 3

CHAPTER 3 OF THE MANUAL

THE TEMPTATION AND FALL OF MAN

'Now the serpent was more cunning than any beast of the field which the LORD God had made. And he said to the woman, "Has God indeed said, 'You shall not eat of every tree of the garden?'"(Genesis 3:1).

THE SERPENT

As I explained earlier, the earth was inhabited by other spirit beings before God created man. Lucifer (an angel of God who became Satan) and his associates were living on this earth before us. They were not happy when God gave the earth to man. They plotted to deceive man and take over the earth. Satan and his spirits had permission to enter animals. To disguise himself, Satan entered a serpent and came to Eve. From that point on, Satan is also referred to as a snake, or serpent, in the Bible.

One way Satan operates is to question what God said in an attempt to create doubt about His Word in your heart. He will not come to you directly and tell you to do something wrong. He will appear as an innocent person or a thought and trap you in his net. Until the serpent came on the scene, there was no sickness, curse, poverty, or any other evil on this earth. Now we are going to see where it all began.

'And the woman said to the serpent, "We may eat the fruit of the trees of the garden; but of the fruit of the tree which *is* in the midst of the garden, God has said, 'You shall not eat it, nor shall you touch it, lest you die'" (Genesis 3:3).

103

'Then the serpent said to the woman, "You will not surely die. For God knows that in the day you eat of it your eyes will be opened, and you will be like God, knowing good and evil"' (Genesis 3:4-5).

'So when the woman saw that the tree *was* good for food, that it *was* pleasant to the eyes, and a tree desirable to make *one* wise, she took of its fruit and ate. She also gave to her husband with her, and he ate. Then the eyes of both of them were opened, and they knew that they *were* naked; and they sewed fig leaves together and made themselves coverings' (Genesis 3:6-7).

THE BANG!

The first man and woman chose to do something contrary to God's plan. They ate of the tree from which they were not supposed to eat. They chose the lowest quality of life, which is to live by knowing good from evil. The moment they ate the fruit, their relationship with God was broken. They died spiritually. They lost the glory of God. Every person who is on this earth who does not have a relationship with God is spiritually dead and lacks the glory of God.

SIN

The act of disobeying God is called sin. Living separated from God is living in sin. Any thought or act that is not pleasing to God is also sin.

From that point on, life on this earth began to spiral downward. Sin entered this planet. Sin is the nature of Satan. He comes to steal, kill, and destroy. Satan deceived mankind into giving up our right to have dominion on this earth. Deterioration and death also came to this earth. Every form of evil we see on this earth today came as a result of that first sin. This is where it began. Why do people kill each other? They act according to the nature of Satan. Why do they lie and steal? They are operating according to their sin nature. Why do earthquakes and wars happen on this earth? Satan wants to kill as many people as possible before they get a chance to have a relationship with God. The more people he can kill, the more souls he can potentially have with him in hell.

Why do some governments authorize abortion? It is because they act on behalf of Satan to kill innocent lives, so they will not be around to fulfill their destiny. Satan hates God and everything He does. He will try to inflict evil upon people and convince them it is God who does that. He is a liar and the father of all lies. If there is any lie spoken on this earth, it originated from Satan.

Man was separated from God, his life source. He did not know what to do. He made aprons out of fig leaves in an effort to cover his nakedness but he did not repent to God for his sin. Instead, he depended on himself to make up for it. From that point on, man's search for God began. People came up with all sorts of ideas and stories, many of which became the basis for modern religions. All religions began either with a search for God, or with an intense desire to please Him through human effort. God did not want man to do that. He had a better plan in mind.

WHAT DOES SIN DO?

The acronym for SIN is **S**atanic **I**nformation **N**etwork. When man sinned, knowledge and information that was not of God entered him. Since then, man has conceived some wrong perceptions. It changed how he viewed God, himself, and the world around him.

SIN AFFECTED MAN'S RELATIONSHIPS ON FIVE LEVELS

Man's relationship with God

Man's relationship with self

Man's relationship with man

Man's relationship with nature

Man's relationship with the animal kingdom

Though man had disobeyed Him, God, just as He always did, came as a loving Father to meet with Adam. This time, God also came to restore him. When God called Adam, he did not come. For the first time, a different kind of fear of God—a type of fear God never intended man to have—came into man. Until that day, he walked with God and was not afraid of His voice or His presence. But sin brought an unnatural fear of God and man hid from Him. Adam feared that God would not accept him. He thought God was calling to judge or punish him for what he did. That was not what God was thinking and that is not the reason He called him. God came to reconcile and restore the broken relationship.

Most people on this earth have a wrong perception of God. He is the most misunderstood Person in the universe. The reason they are not coming to Him is because they are afraid that He will judge or punish them. That is a misconception about God that sin brought into the hearts of people. The Bible says God calls the earth from the sunrise to its setting, but only a few are answering His call. He is calling His sons and daughters to come to Him; to leave every misunderstanding and wrong perception of Him; and come with your weaknesses, failures, and wounds. He will accept you, heal your heart, and restore your soul. Our own sins have distorted our heart's view of God. After Adam sinned, God's perception about him did not change. That is why He came to meet him. God has not changed a bit from who He was in Genesis 1. The Bible says, "I am the LORD and I do not change" (Malachi 3:6).

God created the earth and all that is in it for man, but man, because of the influence of evil, chose to rebel against Him.

> Psalm 50:1 says, "The Mighty One, God the LORD, has spoken and called the earth from the rising of the sun to its going down."

God is Love

As you travel this new journey in your life, the most important thing God wants you to know about Him is that He is Love. What is love? Many have tried to define love through the ages, but God, who is love, is the only Person who can tell us what it is. Here is what He says of Himself.

> "Love never gives up. Love cares more for others than for self [Message Bible]. Love is patient and kind. Love is not jealous or boastful or proud or rude. It does not demand its own way. It is not irritable, and it keeps no record of being wronged. It does not rejoice about injustice but rejoices whenever the truth wins out. Love never gives up, never loses faith, is always hopeful, and endures through every circumstance. Prophecy and speaking in unknown languages and special knowledge will become useless. But love will last forever!" (1 Cor. 13:4-8a (NLT).

In the above paragraph, wherever the passage mentions love, insert God there. If your perception of God is not what it says, then you have a wrong perception of Him and you need to change that.

> 'And they heard the sound of the LORD God walking in the garden in the cool of the day, and Adam and his wife hid themselves from the presence of the LORD God among the trees of the garden.
>
> Then the LORD God called to Adam and said to him, "Where *are* you?"

So he said, "I heard Your voice in the garden, and I was afraid because I was naked; and I hid myself."

'And He said, "Who told you that you *were* naked? Have you eaten from the tree of which I commanded you that you should not eat?"' (Genesis 3:8-11).

FEAR

One of the main reasons people do not come to God is fear. Man did not have that fear before he sinned. God does not want you to be afraid of Him. That is why He said 365 times in His Word, "Fear not." He knew that we would all experience and have to face fear in our lives. Certainly, He wants you to respect and honor Him. Whether we run to Him or run away from Him is based on the *kind* of fear we have of Him. But fear that causes you to run from Him when you do wrong is not the right kind of fear. Many people think God is angry with them and does not like them; that He is out to punish them. That is not God. He is after you to do you good. He loves you very much and wants you to run into His arms for help whenever you do something wrong.

"ADAM, WHERE ARE YOU?"

God used to meet with Adam in the evening. After man sinned, God came down seeking him. He wanted to meet with him and restore the relationship. But man was not willing. Instead, he hid from God and blamed God and his wife for his mistake. That is the nature of fallen men, when something goes wrong or when evil happens, they will always find someone to blame. Most of the time it will be God. God is a loving God and Father. He is merciful and kind. All Adam needed to do was come to God, admit what happened and ask God to forgive him. Because man chose his way, the devil (with the cooperation of man) for the next six thousand years brought sin, wars, and every kind of evil, and reigned on this earth.

God did not come down to blame Adam or to make him feel guilty for what he had done. He did not ask, "What have you done?" Instead, He asked, "Where are you?" It was a call based on relationship, not of one who has authority over another. He came down to reconcile with man, but man was not willing. That same God is calling you today to come to Him. Where are you?

'Then the man said, "The woman whom you gave *to be* with me, she gave me of the tree, and I ate."

And the LORD God said to the woman, "What *is* this you have done?"

The woman said, "The serpent deceived me, and I ate."

So the LORD God said to the serpent:

"Because you have done this, you *are* cursed more than all cattle, and more than every beast of the field; on your belly you shall go, and you shall eat dust all the days of your life."

PROPHECY

When God, or one of His servants, tells something that is going to take place in the future, it is called prophecy. Below is the first prophecy in the Bible.

"And I will put enmity between you and the woman, and between your seed and her Seed; He shall bruise your head, and you shall bruise His heel" (Genesis 3:12-15).

PLAN OF REDEMPTION

God did not plan to leave man in a sinful state forever. He planned to redeem man and restore him back to his original position and relationship. In order to do that, someone had to defeat Satan and his forces. Someone had to pay the penalty, which is shed blood, and die on behalf of man. The Bible says there is no remission of sins without the shedding of blood. God could have killed the man and destroyed everything but, because of His love, He chose to restore them.

Because of man's unwillingness to come to Him, God chose to come to man. Redemption means to buy back something that was lost. God paid the price to buy us back from the enemy and forgave our sins free of cost. Why? The Bible says, "God who is rich in mercy, because of His great love with which He loved us" (Ephesians 2:4).

Once God forgives you, He chooses not to remember the sins you committed because love does not keep any record of wrongs. There are no big sins or small sins before God. There is only sin. Once God forgives you, you can have the same relationship Adam had with Him before the fall. The good news is you cannot make any mistakes or commit sins that God will not forgive or that will cause Him to stop loving you. Once you receive the forgiveness of sin, you need to learn more about your new way of living, not how to avoid falling into guilt or condemnation.

TWO SEEDS

Since Satan took over the rule of this earth from man, two kinds of people were born on this earth. One is the seed of the woman and the second is the seed of the serpent. Though both are born through women, the spiritual influence behind and the destiny of both seeds is different. One is called the righteous seed and the other is called the seed of the wicked. The righteous seed does the will of God and the wicked seed does the will of their father the devil, which is to steal, kill, and destroy. There is enmity between these two seeds. The Bible calls people who are too religious a seed of the serpent as well. That is why John the Baptist and Jesus told the Pharisees that they were the children of the serpent, or the devil (John 8:44; Matthew 3:7; 23:33).

THE SEED OF THE WOMAN

God Himself decided to come to this earth in human form to live among us and die on the cross to pay for our sins so that you and I can have a relationship with Him. God said the Seed of the woman would crush the head of the serpent. Through the woman, whom the serpent deceived, God would bring another Adam (son) that would defeat him (crush his head means to strip someone of their authority).

Four thousand years later, when the fullness of time had come, God came to this earth in the form of a man born of a virgin. His name is Jesus, which means Savior.

SEVEN CURSES IN THE BOOK OF GENESIS

God pronounced seven curses in relation to man and woman in the third chapter of the book of Genesis.

TO THE WOMAN

1) Sorrow in conception and pain in childbirth. It affected her fruitfulness and multiplication.

2) Her desire shall be for her husband and he shall rule over her. Disunity in the family. Fighting for domination and position instead of fighting together to subdue and take dominion over the earth.

TO THE MAN

3) Cursed is the ground for your sake – Man lives by depending on the earth and what it produces.

4) In toil you shall eat of it – no more operating by the seed principle alone but by toil of our hands.

5) Both thorns and thistles it shall bring forth - The produce of the earth. Now it will produce weeds and plants that are unnecessary.

6) You shall eat the herb of the field – Food - what we eat is affected. The number one killer on earth is food.

7) In the sweat of your face you shall eat bread.

Every human being is affected by these curses, but I have good news for you. Jesus shed His blood in seven places to redeem us from each of these curses. When you come to Christ, He will redeem you from these curses and, once again, you will get to enjoy the blessings God gave to Adam.

SUFFERING

Suffering and pain began on this earth. It was not God's original plan or will. Sin brought suffering and death. Until we are redeemed from this physical body, we will experience suffering and pain on this earth because of the devil and evil men.

WHY CURSES?

If God is love and forgives, why then did He pronounce curses over the earth and humans? God operates according to spiritual laws. He is love and, at the same time, He is just and righteous. Man was not willing to admit his mistake. Instead, he tried to cover it (from God) and blame others for it. The Bible says Adam covered his sins (Job 31:33). Because man did not repent, God had to pronounce the punishment. Otherwise, He would not be a just God. Because He is love, He made a way to redeem us from those curses. Jesus became a curse for us. What a wonderful God we serve!

OUT OF THE GARDEN

'Also for Adam and his wife the LORD God made tunics of skin, and clothed them. Then the LORD God said, "Behold, the man has become like one of Us, to know good and evil. And now, lest he put out his hand and take also of the tree of life, and eat, and live forever"— therefore the LORD God sent him out of the garden of Eden to till the ground from which he was taken. So He drove out the man; and He placed cherubim at the east of the garden of Eden, and a flaming sword which turned every way, to guard the way to the tree of life' (Genesis 3:21-24).

Why did God remove Adam and Eve from the Garden? It is because there was another tree in the Garden, the tree of life. If you eat from the tree of life, you live forever. The tree of life represented Jesus Christ. God expected man to choose to eat from that tree first. Instead, influenced by the devil, man ate from the tree of the knowledge of good and evil. God knew man would next try to eat from the tree of life. If he did, he would remain in his sinful state forever. Then God would not be able to redeem him. Because He loved him, God had to remove Adam from the Garden so he would not eat from this tree.

God appointed a cherubim and flaming sword, which turned every way, to guard the way to the tree of life. God did not guard the Garden; He guarded the way to the tree of life. There is a two-fold meaning to this. One, God is saying you should not eat from it right now, and the second, the cherubim is showing the way to the tree of life, which means that there will come a time when man will be permitted to eat from it again.

> Once we are redeemed (by the blood of Jesus), we get to partake of the tree of life (Revelation 2:7).

CHERUBIM

Cherubim are a type of spirit-being that God created to serve Him. They fall into the category of angels.

RESULT OF THE FALL

Man lost everything God gave to him except his life and his wife. He lost God's Kingdom. He came out of the Garden empty handed. Sin, curse, sickness, poverty, and death began to operate on this earth. Satan began to use the children of Adam and Eve to accomplish his evil purposes and establish his kingdom. But, God always kept at least one righteous person on this earth to represent Him and His kingdom and to bring forth the Seed He promised in verse 15. There are two spiritual kingdoms operating on this earth now. Each person is under the influence of one of those kingdoms.

WHY JESUS HAD TO BE BORN AS THE SEED OF THE WOMAN: A MAN

It was man that was tempted and fell into sin. Therefore, a man needed to overcome temptation and sin.

It was from man the devil stole the authority over the earth. Therefore, a man needed to defeat the devil and take that authority back from him.

A man without sin needed to die in order to atone for Adam's sin. The problem was that no one could satisfactorily do it because everyone born after Adam was born in sin. It had to be someone without sin.

Only someone with a physical body can legally live and operate on the earth. God and the devil are both looking for a body to accomplish their will here. Jesus needed a body to live and operate on this earth and that is why He was born as a human. Now, we are called the body of Christ. Only man was given authority over the earth.

Jesus was born as a human being to redeem and restore man. The Bible says, "God so loved the world that He gave His only begotten son, and whosoever believes in Him shall not perish, but have everlasting life" (John 3:16).

Adam was the son of God (Luke 3:38). The Bible says that whoever believes in Jesus and receives Him, God gives the right to become a son of God (John 1:12).

Whoever believes in Jesus, God will forgive their sins and make them His children. They will have the original right and privilege Adam had before the fall. Only, now, it is even better than what Adam had. Because of Christ, you will not fall like Adam when you do something wrong. Jesus' blood is sufficient to forgive all our sins—past, present, and future. He ever lives to intercede for us. All we have to do is believe in Him and accept Him as our Lord and Savior.

Unfortunately, people have turned being a Christian into a religion with all sorts of rituals. For most of the world, Christianity became a religion like any other. People are confused and look at Jesus as one of the great religious leaders or simply as an historical figure that lived and died thousands of years ago.

Now that you know the original intent of God for life on this earth and the reason why life now is the way it is and the way back to our original intent, we are going to look at The Three Most Important Decisions of Your Life that will help us find our way back to God and to our purpose. Enjoy the journey!

PART III

CHAPTER 8
THE FIRST MOST
IMPORTANT DECISION OF
YOUR LIFE

CHAPTER 8: THE FIRST MOST IMPORTANT DECISION OF YOUR LIFE

DECIDING TO BELIEVE IN JESUS CHRIST – YOUR RELATIONSHIP WITH GOD

Now that you know where you came from, why you are here, why life on this earth is the way it is and what God provided for each of us through Jesus Christ, you are now ready to make the first, and foremost, of the three most important decisions you will ever make in this life. Even if you make the other two decisions right and miss this one, you will still be a loser at the end because the Bible asks, "For what profit is it to a man if he gains the whole world, and loses his own soul?" (Matthew 16:26). So, please make sure you get this right as you read further.

Of all the important decisions you need to make in your life, the foremost is to accept Jesus Christ as your Lord and Savior and believe that He is the Son of God and died for your sins. There are seven levels of relationship with God in the Bible. We decide which one we have. They are:

1) Creator and creation
2) Angry God and helpless creature
3) Master and servant
4) Judge and sinner
5) Father and child
6) Friend and friend
7) Bridegroom and bride

Right now you are experiencing one type of these relationships with God based on your spiritual maturity and the strongholds that formed the concept of God in you.

117

WHAT HAPPENS WHEN WE BELIEVE IN CHRIST?

God does not take into account what you did or where you were born. Once you believe in Jesus, you are forgiven (past, present, and future) and accepted into the family of God as one of His children. You cannot live as you used to anymore, for you are restored to your original purpose and relationship with God; just as Adam was before he sinned. God sent Jesus to die in our place so that we can be restored as the sons and daughters of God. He also came to restore and reveal the mystery of the Kingdom of God because we lost it when Adam fell into sin and was driven out of the Garden. God has a plan and purpose for your life. You need to discover that and fulfill it during the time you are on this earth. So, you may ask now, how do I believe in Jesus Christ? What am I supposed to do? Here is what He wants you to do.

> The Bible says in Romans 10:9-13, "…If you confess with your mouth the Lord Jesus and believe in your heart that God has raised Him from the dead, you will be saved. For with the heart one believes unto righteousness, and with the mouth confession is made unto salvation. For the Scripture says, "Whoever believes on Him will not be put to shame." For there is no distinction between Jew and Greek, for the same Lord over all is rich to all who call upon Him. For "whoever calls on the name of the Lord shall be saved.""

When you put your trust and faith in the Lord Jesus Christ, you are transferred from death to life, from hell to heaven, and from the kingdom of darkness to the Kingdom of God; you are no longer a slave but a son, taken from the dominion of sin to the free gift of righteousness. If you have never accepted Jesus Christ as your Lord, you can do it right now by praying from your heart this simple prayer:

> "Lord Jesus, I receive you as my Lord and Savior. I confess I am a sinner. I believe in my heart that you are the Son of God and died for my sins on the cross and that you were raised from the dead. With my heart I believe unto righteousness and with my mouth I make the confession unto salvation. Thank you for forgiving all my sins. Thank you for dying in my place. My life will never be the same from this moment forward. In Jesus' name I pray. Amen."

If you prayed that prayer sincerely, you are born again. Now you are a child of God. He is your Father; He is for you and not against you. Nothing can ever separate you from His love. There is so much to learn about this new life and you need the help of God and others. All the promises of the Bible are yours. Make sure you read it daily to find out what He has in store for you!

There are three phrases the Bible uses to describe our experience with God through Jesus. One is 'salvation', the second is 'redemption', and the third is 'born again'. Each is a different dimension of the work and benefit of the cross that is made available to a believer in Christ. In a nutshell, here is what those three phrases mean.

SALVATION

> Hebrews 2:3 says, "How shall we escape if we neglect so **great a salvation**, which at the first began to be spoken by the Lord, and was confirmed to us by those who heard *Him*?"

We often use those words frivolously or religiously. Very few take the time to understand the depth of them. Salvation is not changing churches or denominations. Salvation is not changing religions and becoming a 'Christian'. Salvation is not getting baptized or becoming a Pentecostal or Charismatic. Salvation is not changing how you worship, pray, or sing songs. If salvation is none of the above, then what is it?

If you are saved, you need to know what you are saved from. We were all slaves of sin and were under its dominion. When you believe in Jesus, you are saved from the dominion of sin. When you are saved from the dominion of sin, the devil (the father of sin) loses his grip on your life. The name Jesus means Savior; He saves people from their sins.

> Matthew 1:21 says, "And she shall bring forth a son, and thou shalt call his name Jesus: for he shall save his people from their sins."

When someone saves your life, he becomes your savior. Because Jesus saved you from sin and eternal destruction, He became your Savior. Because of sin we came under the bondage of the enemy. When God forgives your sins, you are *legally* free from all the power of the enemy. That is called deliverance and it is part of salvation. He no longer has any claim on your life (Colossians 1:13). He may not admit it, though, until we use and walk in the authority God gave us in Christ Jesus.

REDEMPTION

Ephesians 1:7 says, "In Him we have **redemption** through His blood, the forgiveness of sins, according to the riches of His grace."

119

Jesus did not come just to forgive our sins and take us to heaven when we die. When we are saved from the bondage of sin, God wants to restore everything we lost because of sin. Redemption means buying back or restoring something that was lost. First of all, we need to know what we lost when man committed sin. Man did not fall from heaven. We did not lose heaven. We lost relationship with God, our position that brought dominion over the earth. We lost the capacity of our spirit and mind (the ability to do extraordinary things) and the blessings God gave to us (His Kingdom). Those are the basic things we lost because of sin. Those are the foundational things God restores to us through redemption.

To redeem something there has to be a price paid. Jesus paid His own blood and bought you from the devil and his kingdom. When someone buys you he becomes your lord (owner). Jesus Christ becomes your Lord through redemption. Now you are not your own, you are here to do the will of Him who bought you (1 Corinthians 6:19-20). Through His blood, Jesus redeemed us from everything that came into our lives because of sin. Because of sin came curse, poverty, sickness, and death. When you are saved, you are free from those four deadly things. Jesus became sin so that you can become the righteousness of God (2 Corinthians 5:21). Jesus became a curse so that you can be free from every curse; including every generational curse (Galatians 3:13). Jesus became poor so that you can be free from poverty and become rich (2 Corinthians 8:9). Jesus was wounded and torn so that we can be healed (1 Peter 2:24). Jesus experienced death so that we can be free from the dominion of death (Hebrews 2:14-15).

BORN AGAIN

John 3:3 says, "Jesus answered and said to him, "Most assuredly, I say to you, unless one is **born again**, he cannot see the kingdom of God.""

Because we were born into sin and into the kingdom of darkness the first time we were born (our natural birth), God gave another opportunity for us to be born again (our spiritual birth). When you believe in Jesus, your spirit is born new and you are able to relate with God. Four main things happen when you are born again. First, you become a child of God born into God's family. He becomes your Heavenly Father. Secondly, as a result of the first, you become a new creation in Christ. Thirdly, you become a citizen of the Kingdom of God and, fourthly, you become a joint heir with Christ and receive an inheritance.

By our natural birth, we became the citizens of the country in which we were born. Not only that, you are an heir to your father's possessions just by being born into his family. By being born again, we become a citizen of the Kingdom of

Heaven (Philippians 3:20). Through Christ, we have peace with God. God is not angry with you. He wants to have a relationship with you. Adam was a son of God before the fall (Luke 3:38). Through Jesus, God gives us the authority to become a child of God (John 1:12). When you become a son or a daughter of God, you become an heir of God. That is where your blessings come from. Everything we lost because of sin God restored to us through Christ, plus more. Most believers do not tap into the resources that God has made available to them through Christ. The vast majority of them are only taught about going to heaven when they die.

WHAT HAPPENS WHEN YOU ARE BORN AGAIN?

When you are born again, you receive everything Christ has. The Bible says those who are joined with Christ are one spirit. If you are joined with Christ, your spirit and Christ's Spirit are one. They are not two different kinds. We have heard about the human spirit and the Holy Spirit, but once you are born again you are one spirit with Christ (1 Corinthians 6:17).

The Bible says if anyone is in Christ he is a new creature, old things are passed away, behold everything becomes new (1 Corinthians 5:17). When you are born again, you become a new creature. You were born once naturally, by your parents. When you were born, you became a new creature. You had not done anything wrong, and you did not have any memories of the past. You had a brand new life. That is exactly what happens when you are born again. God wipes clean everything of the past. You might not feel it in the natural, though some do. We receive it all by faith. You need to believe it in your heart. Whenever things of the old come up in your mind, you need to remind yourself they have no power over you. You are born again and you are in Christ.

What does it mean to become a new creature? When you are born again, you inherit everything Christ has: His Spirit, mind, and body; you become a part owner of everything He owns. When you were born by your mother, you inherited everything she and your father had. Likewise, when you are born again through Jesus, you inherit everything He and our Heavenly Father have. That is good news!

> 1 Corinthians 6:17 says, "But he who is joined to the Lord is **one spirit** *with Him.*"

What would Christ's Spirit do? We can do all things Christ can do.

Once you are born again, you have the same mind as Christ. 1 Corinthians 2:16 says, "For who has known the mind of the Lord that he may instruct Him? But **we have the mind of Christ.**"

121

What would Christ's mind think? That is why we are commanded to think on those things that are above (Philippians 4:8; Colossians 3:2). 'Above' here means who and what we have in Christ. We are seated with Christ in heavenly places. We are supposed to think on those things and make them a reality on this earth.

We are the body of Christ. 1 Corinthians 12:12-14 says, "For as the body is one and has many members, but all the members of that one body, being many, are one body, so also *is* Christ. For by one Spirit we were all baptized into one body—whether Jews or Greeks, whether slaves or free—and have all been made to drink into one Spirit. For in fact the body is not one member but many."

1 Corinthians 12:20 says, "But now indeed *there are* many members, yet one body."

1 Corinthians 12:27 says, "Now **you are the body of Christ**, and members individually."

Ephesians 5:29-32 says, "For no one ever hated his own flesh, but nourishes and cherishes it, just as the Lord *does* the church. **For we are members of His body, of His flesh and of His bones**. "For this reason a man shall leave his father and mother and be joined to his wife, and the two shall become one flesh." This is a great mystery, but I speak concerning Christ and the church."

The same way we received a spirit, soul (mind), and body when we were naturally born, we receive a new one (Christ's) when we are spiritually born. Some people look at children and say they look just like their mama, daddy, or another family member. Well, after we are born again, we should look at ourselves in the mirror and say we are just like our Daddy, God. Lord, help us. Do you see what I see, my friends?

WE BECOME A JOINT HEIR WITH CHRIST

When you are born again, God adopts you as His child. If you are a child, you are also an heir of God. An heir of what? Please read the following verses.

Romans 8:16-17a, "The Spirit Himself bears witness with our spirit that we are children of God, and if children, then heirs—heirs of God and **joint heirs with Christ**…" If we are joint heirs with Christ, we need to find out what Christ owns. The verses below show what Christ owns.

Luke 10:22 says, "All things have been delivered to Me [Christ] by My Father…"

John 13:3a says, "Jesus, knowing that the Father had given all things into His hands…"

John 16:15a says, "All things that the Father has are Mine [Christ's]…"

Hebrews 1:2 says, "Has in these last days spoken to us by *His* Son, whom **He has appointed heir of all things**, through whom also He made the worlds."

All of the above truths, and more, occur when you believe in Jesus Christ. It is up to each person to decide how much they appropriate into their life while on this earth. Unfortunately, there are many believers in Christ who do not believe in the full benefits of salvation.

THERE IS NO BLESSING IN HEAVEN WITH WHICH GOD HAS NOT YET BLESSED US

Ephesians 1:3 says, "Blessed *be* the God and Father of our Lord Jesus Christ, who has blessed us with **every** spiritual blessing in the heavenly *places* in Christ."

THERE IS NOTHING IN HEAVEN OR ON EARTH GOD HAS NOT YET GIVEN US

Genesis 9:3 says, "Every moving thing that lives shall be food for you. **I have given you all things,** even as the green herbs."

1 Corinthians 3:21-23 says, "Therefore let no one boast in men. **For all things are yours:** whether Paul or Apollos or Cephas, or **the world or life or death, or things present or things to come—all are yours.** And you *are* Christ's, and Christ *is* God's."

2 Peter 1:3-4 says, "As His divine power has **given to us all things** that *pertain* to life and godliness, through the knowledge of Him who called us by glory and virtue, by which have been given to us exceedingly great and precious promises, that through these you may be partakers of the divine nature, having escaped the corruption *that is* in the world through lust."

THERE IS NOTHING REMAINING FROM WHICH GOD DID NOT DELIVER US

Colossians 1:13-14 says, "**He (Jesus) has delivered** us from the power of darkness and conveyed *us* into the kingdom of the Son of His love, in whom we have redemption through His blood, the forgiveness of sins."

You have been set free from the kingdom of darkness and all its influences. When you believe that, you will discover the pathway to freedom from all bondages. Jesus said, "Nothing shall by any means hurt you" (Luke 10:19b).

THERE IS NOTHING LEFT FROM WHICH GOD DID NOT SET US FREE

John 8:36 says, "Therefore if the Son makes you free, you shall be free indeed." It is for freedom that Christ has set us free (Galatians 5:1). If there is any area of your life in which you feel you are not free, it is because you have not known that truth. When you know the truth, it shall make you free (John 8:32).

THERE IS NO SICKNESS FROM WHICH JESUS DID NOT YET HEAL US

1 Peter 2:24 says, "Who Himself bore our sins in His own body on the tree, that we, having died to sins, might live for righteousness—by whose stripes you were healed." Healing is part of salvation, not a special gift to some or a few. It is available to all those who believe.

THERE IS NO LAW JESUS LEFT HERE FOR US TO FULFILL BECAUSE HE FULFILLED IT ALL FOR US

Romans 8:3-4 says, "For what the law could not do in that it was weak through the flesh, **God *did*** by sending His own Son in the likeness of sinful flesh, on account of sin: He condemned sin in the flesh, that the **righteous requirement of the law might be fulfilled in us** who do not walk according to the flesh but according to the Spirit."

Matthew 5:17 says, "Do not think that I came to destroy the Law or the Prophets. I did not come to destroy but to fulfill."

Any passages you look at in the New Testament concerning our life on this earth are all past tense. There is no "going to," or "will be free," or "will bless."

YOUR HEART NEEDS TO BE ESTABLISHED IN THE GRACE OF GOD

Hebrews 13:9 says, "Be not carried about with diverse and strange doctrines. For it is a good thing that the heart be **established** with **grace;** not with meats, which have not profited them that have been occupied therein" (KJV).

Dear ones, it is time to believe what the Bible says, rather than what our grandpa did or said. Nothing can separate us from the love of God. There is nothing left for God to do for you. Stop waiting for Him to do something, instead start believing what He has already done for you and it will begin to manifest in your life.

Please meditate on the following scriptures that talk about your new identity in Christ. These describe what happened when you were born again through Christ.

God has made me equal with Christ (John 17:21-23).

I am made a partaker of Christ (Hebrews 2:11-12; 3:14).

I am a brother of Christ (Romans 8:29; Hebrews 2:11).

I am part of the body of Christ (1 Corinthians 12:20, 27).

I have the mind of Christ (1 Corinthians 2:16).

I have the Spirit of Christ (Romans 8:9; 1 Corinthians 6:17; 1 Peter 1:11).

I have the word of Christ (Colossians 3:16; John 17:8-14).

I have the glory of Christ (John 17:22).

All things of the Father have been given to Jesus and I am a co-heir with Christ (Luke 10:22; John 13:3; 16:15; Romans 8:17; Galatians 4:7).

I am a son of God (John 1:12; Romans 8:14).

I have been sent by the Father, as He sent Jesus (John 17:18).

I am seated with Christ in the heavenly places (John 17:24; Ephesians 2:7).

The Father loves me with the same love He loves Jesus with (John 17:23, 26).

As Jesus was on this earth so am I (1 John 4:17).

The Father loved me before the foundation of the world (John 17:24; Ephesians 1:4; 2 Timothy 1:9).

Jesus and I have the same God and Father (John 20:17).

Everything Jesus told us He heard from the Father (John 15:15).

We have the same wisdom and knowledge as Jesus (Colossians 2:3).

Just like the Father is in Jesus and Jesus is in the Father, Jesus is in us and we are in Him (John 14:11 & 20).

The above status has been made available to us, not based on anything we did or did not do, it was all purely by the grace of God and by His love for us in Christ Jesus. You are loved and blessed. He calls you beloved. Meditate on that until it becomes a part of your life and thinking. Make sure your righteousness is based on what Christ did for you and not on your works, and then you will be undefeatable. The gospel of the Kingdom is called good news. In a natural kingdom, the king goes out and leads the army to battle and wins the victory. Then, all of the citizens get to enjoy the freedom. In a democracy, the president or prime minister never goes out to war. Jesus is the King. He won the victory over our enemy, and over sin, and we get to enjoy the benefits for free.

WHAT DID GOD DO FOR US IN CHRIST JESUS?

When you were born again, the most extraordinary and miraculous thing took place! After you are born again you are not a poor sinner saved by grace. Believing that is equal to saying you are living under the law but believe in the grace of God. You cannot do that. The New Testament never calls a born-again believer a sinner. You are either a righteous person or a sinner; you cannot be both at the same time. We are the righteousness of God. It is blasphemy and a reproach to the blood of Jesus to call yourself a sinner. You are now a *saint* saved by grace. Please change your vocabulary first. You are either saved or you are not; there is no middle ground.

I see believers get 'saved' over again almost every Sunday morning; sometimes they call it recommitting their life to Jesus. I have three children, two girls and a boy. My children are wonderful and smart. When they reached two years old, they began to do things that displeased me as a father. They picked up things they were not supposed to. They put things into their mouth that were not edible. They pinched and took things away from each other. So, I had to discipline them. Just because they did things I told them not to, they never ceased to be my children. After they did something wrong and I disciplined them, they did not have to recommit to being my children. They became my children by birth and they will be mine forever.

When my children do something wrong, their position does not change, but they may not receive all the blessings and favor I want to give them. We become a son or a daughter of God not by filling out some papers. We become His children by birth, by new birth. When you do something wrong, you do not cease being His child. All you have to do is repent and ask Him to forgive you.

When you were born naturally, you were born as a baby only once. When you reached two or three years old, you began to do some naughty things and your parents disciplined you as a result. Sometimes we were spanked. When we made a mistake we felt bad, and we knew we were going to get in trouble. But, we did not go to our mother and say, "Mama, I am dead now because I pinched Jimmy, I need to go back into your womb and be born again. You need to give birth to me one more time!" Or, "I need to recommit my life as your son one more time, because I sinned." How many chances do you get to be born by your parents? Twenty? Or, just one? When you are born again you are born again once; you do not have to do it every Sunday morning. Once you are born as a son or daughter to your parents you are always a son or daughter. You may become a prodigal son or daughter, but your position never changes regardless of what you *do*.

That really sounds odd, doesn't it? But, that is what many Christians do in church. They make a mistake on Thursday and live with the guilt for the next three days. When they come to church on Sunday they repeat the sinner's prayer and ask Jesus to be born again… again. That is ridiculous! They live like that for fifty years and never come to the knowledge of the truth or receive the assurance of salvation. They are constantly hearing and learning but do not understand what they learn. Some people are living in the regrets of what they did twenty or thirty years ago. Come to Jesus, my friend, and receive His forgiveness and love.

When we do wrong God disciplines us, and His discipline is always for our good, not for our destruction. If, after you endure His discipline, your life has not gotten any better than before, it was not God behind that discipline. Either you self-imposed the discipline, and mistook it for God's discipline, or the devil took advantage of your guilt and ignorance and whipped you bad.

> Hebrews 12:9-11 says, "Furthermore, we have had human fathers who corrected *us,* and we paid *them* respect. Shall we not much more readily be in subjection to the Father of spirits and

live? For they indeed for a few days chastened *us* as seemed *best* to them, but He for *our* profit, that *we* may be partakers of His holiness. Now no chastening seems to be joyful for the present, but painful; nevertheless, **afterward it yields the peaceable fruit of righteousness to those who have been trained by it.**"

When you are born again (you do not get to do that more than once) everything you ever did, and your parents did, and as far back as our ancestor Adam did, was wiped clean from your account by the blood of Jesus. Believe it or not, that is the truth. Nothing has the authority or power to cross the blood of Jesus to get to you. You need to believe this and stop digging dead bones out of past generations. There is no mention of breaking generational curses in the New Testament. All you dear saints trying to break or cleanse generational curses from your life, I want to tell you the good news; this was done by the blood of Jesus. If someone could have broken you free from your sins and curses, then Jesus did not have to die on the cross. You do not need to turn over each dead leaf to see what your forefathers have done (no one can really find everything they did). If you do fall into that pattern, you are going back to works again and you will fall from grace. It is all done by faith in the finished work of the cross. Amen.

The blood of Jesus cleanses us from all sin. "Then," you may be asking, "What about the sins I commit after I am saved?" I am glad you asked because I asked the same question for twenty years and was mired in guilt and condemnation. God does not view our sins as 'before saved' and 'after saved'. He does not have a separate list. He is outside of time. When Jesus died for me, I had not yet committed any sin. All of my sins were in the future. The truth is that after you are saved, sin has no more dominion over you. You are dead to sin and you are no longer under the law, so when there is no law; sin is not imputed. You are a free man. Tell that guilt and condemnation to go away in Jesus' name!

Here is more good news! When God forgives you, He does not remember those sins anymore. That means any time you are reminded of your past sins, that is not God doing it. The devil will keep reminding you of your past sins in an effort to steal your confidence and effectiveness as a child of God. As long as he can keep you feeling guilty about your past sins, you are as good as a dead lion. What good is a dead lion? It looks the same, but cannot do anything and is no danger to anyone. Please read the following verses about the New Covenant.

Hebrews 8:12-13 says, "For I will be merciful to their unrighteousness, and their sins and their lawless deeds I will remember no more." In that He says, "A new *covenant*," He has made the first obsolete. Now what is becoming obsolete and growing old is ready to vanish away."

Hebrews 10:16-17 says, "This *is* the covenant that I will make with them after those days, says the Lord: I will put My laws into their hearts, and in their minds I will write them," *then He adds,* "Their sins and their lawless deeds I will remember no more."

Romans 5:13 says, "For until the law sin was in the world, but sin is not imputed when there is no law."

The Bible says, "…If the Son makes you free, you shall be free indeed" (John 8:36). As I said before, you are either free, or you are not free; you cannot be free in some areas and bound in others. We feel like that because of the misinformation we have believed in our heart. We heard that we have to do something, Jesus did not do it all, in some areas the devil still has a hold on us and we need to free ourselves later. So, you have to read some *good* Christian books and go to some *good* Christian conferences and counselors, and they will help you or set you free. The Bible does not say to free yourself. If we could, then Jesus did not have to die. If He wanted part of the job done by us or by anyone else, then he would have asked our help when He hung on the cross.

While on the cross Jesus did not say, "Listen guys, half of the work is done. I can only do this much. This is really unbearable. I did my best. I wish I could do more to help you but you need to take it from here. Now the rest is up to you folks. I need to go and see My Dad, okay? It is *kind of* done." Most people walk around looking for what they should do to be free or for someone who will set them free, never knowing that they are already free. That is what we subconsciously believe, and that is why we do not walk in freedom. That is not what He said. He said, "It is finished" not, "to be continued." Everything that was required for our freedom and forgiveness [total restoration] was paid in full. Hallelujah!

SALVATION AND REDEMPTION THROUGH CHRIST ARE ETERNAL

Salvation and redemption through religious works are temporary and partial. If you believe you are saved through being good, when you do something wrong you will feel you lost your salvation and will feel damned and condemned. That is called salvation by good works. People who receive this kind of salvation get saved every Sunday morning. That is not the kind of salvation Christ offers to anyone who comes to Him. Hebrews 5:9 says, "And having been perfected, He became the author of **eternal salvation** to all who obey Him."

Hebrews 9:11-12 says, "But Christ came *as* High Priest of the good things to come, with the greater and more perfect tabernacle not made with hands, that is, not of this creation. Not with the blood of goats and calves, but with His own blood He entered the Most Holy Place once for all, having obtained **eternal redemption**."

Hebrews 10:11-14 says, "And every priest stands ministering daily and offering repeatedly the same sacrifices, which can never take away sins. But this Man, after He had offered one sacrifice for sins forever, sat down at the right hand of God, from that time waiting till His enemies are made His footstool. For by one offering He has **perfected forever** those who are being sanctified."

Are you afraid that the devil will snatch you out of God's hand? Please keep reading.

John 10:27-29 says, "My sheep hear My voice, and I know them, and they follow Me. And I give them eternal life, and **they shall never perish; neither shall anyone snatch them out of My hand**. My Father, who has given *them* to Me, is greater than all; and **no one is able to snatch *them* out of My Father's hand**."

Now, there is room for punishment and judgment. It is for those who are going back to the law. If you go back to the law to try to obey its rules and regulations, you will be punished when you disobey. It is our choice whether we stay in grace or go back to the Old Covenant. There are many believers who go back; we will learn about it in a different chapter. Some mix the law and grace and never make any progress. It is like rowing a boat that is tied to a tree.

Your freedom was purchased on the cross two thousand years ago. That is total freedom, not partial. In every way man was kept in bondage, Jesus set us free, from generational curses, sin, the devil, poverty, law, sickness, etc. There is no mention of generational curses in the New Testament. Neither Jesus nor the disciples (apostles) broke anyone's generational curses before a person received salvation or healing. There was no counseling program in the New Testament Church, but there were apostolic doctrines, and believers had a relationship with the Wonderful Counselor. That is why we need counselors in our churches today, because we do not have apostolic teachings and doctrines. These counselors bring the truth of Christ to light. The majority of believers do not know what the New

Testament doctrines are. Instead, we have Jesus loves me this I know, Hell and brimstone teaching, or prosperity and motivational (money and success) teaching.

"Then," you might ask, "What about the devil? Doesn't he attack us still? What about witchcraft and voodoo and false religious powers? What if a witch doctor puts a curse on me and my family? Will that not affect me?" The answer is a big NO. Jesus said, "I give unto you power to tread on serpents and scorpions and over all the power of the enemy and **nothing shall by any means hurt you**" (Luke 10:19). **No weapon** formed against you shall prosper (Isaiah 54:17). Is that full or partial coverage? What do you think?

When we bought a used car, we also bought a three-year warranty with it. Actually, the dealer pushed us to buy it. It had different levels, silver, gold, and platinum, with different payments. We bought the platinum level and it covers almost everything, except the things that break! When something happened to our car, I called the company to see if they would pay for it. They said they would not. Then, I called the car insurance company and they also said no. I had to spend more than a thousand dollars to fix that problem. It seems like they exempted everything in their coverage that will break under normal circumstances. That is the way we think about salvation and what Christ did for us. We try to reason things out, listen to our friends, and listen to the devil then conclude, "Well, that was not covered on the cross. The blood of Jesus will not forgive that one, so I have to live with it on this earth till I die." NO!

When Jesus said that nothing shall by any means hurt you; it included witchcraft, false religions, voodoo in your neighborhood, and everything else you can imagine. It is a full and total coverage, bumper to bumper, top to bottom is covered; nothing is exempt.

1 John 5:18 says, "We know that whoever is born of God does not sin; but he who has been born of God keeps himself, and **the wicked one does not touch him.**"

The devil will try his best to use fear to cause you to doubt what God says about you. Once he pushes you off from your position of authority (your faith in His Word) you go on a downward spiral. Then, all of a sudden, you will be more focused on the devil and what he is doing than who you are in Christ. Once you agree with the devil on any level about anything contrary to what the Word says, you will be a victim of unbelief. Unbelief will open the door for every evil the devil has to offer and it will keep you out of your Promised Land.

The reason we feel we are bound in some areas is because we believe (agree with) some lies of the devil regarding that area of our life. The moment you break that agreement and receive the truth of the Word of God you will be free in that area. Once you are free you need to be steadfast and stand on that Word and keep your ground by fighting the good fight of faith.

You can decide the level of life you want to live as a Christian. Just like the different types of warranty coverage available for our car, it is up to us what to believe. What you believe has power over you and it determines what you receive from God. I heard that serpents and scorpions only operate at a low altitude; they cannot survive at a high altitude. The secret to living a victorious life in Christ is to go higher in God and go deeper into the truth of God's Word. The deeper you go in the Word; the higher you go in God, where the serpents and scorpions cannot reach you.

When you are free, you are free from sin, free from curses, free from the law, free from generational curses and sicknesses, failures, poverty, familiar sins, from this world, from Satan; you name it, your freedom has been purchased.

So, when you are born again you are not a partially born baby. You are a whole, new person. Everything old is dead and gone. That is why the Bible says, "If anyone is in Christ, he is a new creation, old things are passed away, behold everything becomes new" (2 Corinthians 5:17).

Did God save everything that pertains to our lives when we were saved? Or, did He only save our spirit man? That is what some believe and they bear all the sickness and infirmities in their body, thinking their body will be redeemed only at the Second Coming. That is not true. What will be redeemed at the Second Coming is not the sickness and infirmities of our body, but the mortality of our body. Right now you are redeemed from every sickness, disease, curse, and infirmity you can think of.

The Bible says that your body is sealed by the Holy Spirit for the day of redemption. If it is a piece of junk, the Holy Spirit would not seal it (Ephesians 1:13-14). Your body is also the temple of the Holy Spirit (1 Corinthians 6:19). The Bible says your spirit and body belong to God (1 Corinthians 6:20).

> Hebrews 7:25 says, "Therefore **He is also able to save to the uttermost** those who come to God through Him, since He always lives to make intercession for them."

Jesus is able to save to the uttermost. That means the farthest you can think of and to the least important area of your life; His salvation encompasses your whole life. The problem is most are not *in* Christ yet, they are still remaining *in* their natural parents, their nature, their personality, their way of thinking, etc. Their family history and lifestyle is controlling them. You need to say goodbye to everything you received through your natural birth then discover and think about what you received through your spiritual birth, the second birth through Christ. When you receive Christ, Christ becomes *in* you; when you receive the Holy Spirit, you become *in* Christ.

The ways you act, react, think, talk, look, and behave all came from your natural parents by birth. Your personality traits, your citizenship, caste, race, financial status, health, and color all came by your natural birth. When you are born again, you are dead to those things. You are not what you were when you were naturally born. You are born a second time. Most believers are more aware of what they received and what came to them by their natural birth than by their spiritual birth because that is the way we are trained to think; it is part of our subconscious. So, we try to analyze our spiritual birth based on that information and the experience we had through our natural birth. What is the result? Doubt, confusion, and frustration.

Unfortunately, many Christians are stuck in religion and works of the Old Testament Law. They do not have a full revelation of what God accomplished for them in Christ. They live based on their past and their natural birth. When we believe in Christ, we are born again (you are born new) and everything you were until that moment is dead and gone. Otherwise, you are not born again; you believe a vain philosophy. I will explain this more in the following pages.

CHAPTER 9
SEEK GOD'S KINGDOM
AND HIS RIGHTEOUSNESS

CHAPTER 9: SEEK GOD'S KINGDOM AND HIS RIGHTEOUSNESS

Now that you are saved (you have a Savior), redeemed (you have a Lord), and born again (you have a Father), what should you do next? The reason many believers do not experience the fullness of their new life in Christ and the benefits of salvation (the New Covenant) is two-fold. After being born again, most join a church and learn all the Christian cliché's and sing the songs that everybody else sings. No one tells them what really happened to them or what to do next. Most are told not to smoke, not to drink alcohol; do this and don't do that. Instead of the blessings they inherit a bunch of rules and regulations.

According to the Bible, after we are born again, there are two things we need to seek after before we do or learn anything else in life. They are the Kingdom of God and His righteousness. Jesus said, "Seek ye **first** the kingdom of God and His righteousness, and all these things shall be added unto you" (Matthew 6:33 KJV).

When Jesus (our Lord) says to seek something *first* we had better pay attention and do it first. When you are born again, you will be able to see (in your spirit) the Kingdom but will not enter it. Neither will you inherit it (John 3:3-5). Before we learn how to clap and sing all the contemporary songs, we need first to seek His Kingdom and His righteousness. Why do we need to seek God's Kingdom and His righteousness? When you were born, you became a citizen of your country. You grew up based on the system of your country and might have received an education and found a job to make a living.

When you were born again, you became a citizen of the Kingdom of God. It is your responsibility to seek and discover how this new country (system) operates and functions. The Kingdom of God works much differently than the country in which we are naturally born. The sooner you learn, the better your life will be as a Christian. In the Kingdom, your heavenly Father has some works for you to do, which He prepared before the foundation of the world. There is another name for those "works," which is "purpose." Purpose is the original intent for which something is made. When you do those works (walk in your purpose), the Kingdom of God will provide for you; that is the secret to your prosperity.

As we saw earlier, human life began in the Kingdom of God. Because of sin, we lost it and became part of a world system that works contrary to the Kingdom of God. Through Jesus, God restored His Kingdom back to us. When we talk about the Kingdom of God now, it is not made up of palaces, gardens, and thrones; it is an invisible kingdom. The Kingdom of God now is a way of functioning. It is a belief system or a system of operation that we should operate under, which differs from how the world around us functions and operates.

Only when we discover God's Kingdom will we be able to make the next most important decision of our life. That is what I share in the next chapter. When God made Adam, He gave him one rule. His relationship with God was not based on him keeping a bunch of rules; rather, it was based on love. God does not want anyone to come to Him based on their goodness or right living. God wants us to come to Him based on faith in Him and His love for us. That is why we need to understand His righteousness.

When we are born again, we are transferred from the kingdom of darkness into the Kingdom of God (Colossians 1:13). If you try to operate in the Kingdom of God based on your past experience or belief system, it will not work. It does not matter how hard you try.

Once we become a Christian, we need to learn as quickly as possible how the Kingdom of God operates. The more we learn it, the better our Christian life becomes. A Christian can operate according to any of the following systems. Just like a computer, we have different operating systems. Like windows, IOS, and other programs, our life operates by different systems that were installed when we were growing up. You operate and function on this earth based on that programming.

There are three operating systems on this earth. The first is the world system (kingdom of darkness, and this operates differently based on the country you are from), which works opposite the Kingdom of God. The second is the Law (rules and regulations, also called legalism), which is the foundation of all religion. The third is called the Word of Righteousness, by which the Kingdom of God operates (Hebrews 5:13).

The moment you put your faith in Jesus Christ and in the finished work of His cross, God declares you a righteous person. Jesus took your sin on the cross and gave you His righteousness as a gift. It was a divine exchange. From that moment on, God sees and treats you as a righteous person, not as a poor sinner saved by grace. You become His son or daughter not based on what you did or do, but solely based on what Christ did for you. The question is; how do we seek a kingdom? It is impossible for me to write it in detail since this book is not about the Kingdom of God. I am currently working on a Kingdom series!

The second part of seeking the Kingdom of God is to seek His righteousness. Seeking God's righteousness is as important as seeking His Kingdom. One will not work without the other. Even if you seek the Kingdom and see it, you cannot enter without receiving the righteousness of God. Most people do not benefit from the Kingdom because they walk in self-righteousness instead of the righteousness of God. Most do not realize they do this. I did not for a long time. If God tells us to seek His righteousness, that means there is another kind of righteousness out there that is not His. It is self-righteousness that comes through works. It is difficult for most humans to admit total helplessness; we all try to find some "goodness" in us.

I look around at believers in the Church. They are wounded, fearful, sick, anxious, and depressed-sometimes more than people in the world. They are not sure if God loves or even likes them. They are not sure that God accepts them. They are not sure they are saved or that God has forgiven their sins, so they 'get saved' again and again. They have a religious look but point their finger at each other. They have a form of godliness but no power.

They say that Jesus is their Lord, but have yet to surrender a thing to Him. They think they have because they sing "I Surrender All" once in a while, but they try to control their life along with everyone and everything around them. Sometimes, they even try to control God. Insecurity, self-pity, guilt, and condemnation are eating them up, so they are not confident in God.

I am not trying to point my finger at you; this was my story too. I was the most self-righteous person on the planet. I was as blind as a leech. I was a tongue-talking Christian but I judged and criticized everyone. I felt in the flesh that I was the most righteous person on earth, but in the spirit I was as weak as a dry leaf. The reason I judged and criticized others was because I was living under the law, and I did not like myself. Insecure people feel better when they criticize or talk about someone else's weakness or failure. The reason we talk about the weakness of others is it deflects our attention off of our own weaknesses.

When I received the revelation of the grace of God, I knew I had no right to judge anyone. I knew that, in the sight of God, I was equal to everyone else. In Christ, you and I have the same *amount* of righteousness imputed to us. I see how much the religious spirit has done to damage us; stealing every good thing God has given us to enjoy, and making our lives miserable. Everyone needs the law until they receive the revelation of the love and the grace of God; otherwise, this world would become rotten with sin.

Paul says in 1 Corinthians 15:10, "But by the grace of God I am what I am, and His grace toward me was not in vain; but I labored more abundantly than they all, yet not I, but the grace of God which was with me."

Most believers I see believe and act like God's love for them depends on what they do and how *spiritual* they are. They act like they earned their salvation by confessing *all* their sins, even to the minutest wrong, and feel that one mistake would ruin the whole thing and force them to start all over again from zero. They are in that cycle of being righteous one day and a sinner the next morning, feeling holy on Sunday and like a sinner the rest of the week. Most never grow beyond this. These people will not do a thing for God other than showing their cute face in church on Sunday morning and giving a *tip* once in a while.

We blame the world for the way they live and what they do because we are not happy with ourselves and don't like ourselves. We think that if the people in the world would just get their act together and come to church then all of our problems will be over. Well, we were those people in the world once, doing the same things they do, and we came to church. Did everything change overnight for us?

The religious spirit always causes people to blame someone else for their problems. They will not admit they are wrong; it is always the other person. "If they would just act right and get their life in order, then I would be fine." Or, "I am not happy because so and so is making my life miserable. They are not holy enough or living right." Let me tell you, that is a religious and controlling spirit. Pharisees were the best example of this. They could not see their own wrongs. They always pointed their finger at the sinners and at Jesus, while the plank was in their own eyes. One of the most important lessons I learned as a Christian, which also happens to be one of the most difficult to practice, is emotional responsibility: Taking responsibility for what I feel and how I act.

Self-righteous people end up being extremely religious and conservative, but they never become holy. They always wonder what they should do next to add another rite to their religious duty list. They will do prayer walks, hospital visitations, prison ministry, caring for the elderly, and anything else that will make them feel better. Their heart is miserable or they are irritated with themselves and others because, however much they do, it is never good enough. They always feel like they have to do more to make their God happy.

Self-righteous people believe in righteousness by the works they perform. In truth, they are still under the law. They will not admit it because one part of their head believes they are saved by grace, but they never understood what that

140

means. With the other part, they are trying to obey the law. Others are saved by grace, but they believe they can only remain saved by keeping the rules of the Old Testament. They go back to the law. Let me tell you, if you go back to the law, the curse of the law, which is poverty and sickness, will begin to manifest in your life. If any of these are operating in your life, it means you are not living in the grace of God but in the pseudo righteousness that comes by keeping rules and regulations.

Self-righteous people are very disciplined. If there is a prayer meeting at the church at 4 am, they are the first to be there. Then, they will tell ten other people that day about it so they will feel better and more spiritual than others. The people who hear them will feel bad because they are not spiritual enough. They feel guilty and lost because they do not pray at 4 am.

Self-righteous people have a set of rules and disciplines they observe, and they do anything they can to keep them because they feel God's love for them and the blessing they have is based on keeping those rules. If they break one, they will be out of God's favor that day or week, and have to repent and confess their sins once again. So, they take their 'list of sins' or their 'special prayer pill' (some call it confession) that hits the 'right spot' in God, and go through it again.

I used to be a spiritual Pharisee, extremely religious, unusually insecure, and with zero confidence in my faith in God. I appeared spiritual but, inwardly, I did not believe I was saved. I was living on the basis of righteousness by works. I used to hide or sometimes would not go to preach when people invited me because I did not feel spiritual or righteous enough. I am sharing this with you so that if you are stuck in that religious rut, you can be set free. There is nothing more miserable than getting stuck between the law and grace of God.

God tried to reach out to me many times, but I could not accept His offer because it did not look religious enough for me. Just like Jesus tried to reach out to the Pharisees, they refused His offer because they would not accept His lifestyle. For them, He was not spiritual enough, not holy enough. They were dead in their sins. I knew there was something wrong but was not quite sure what it was. So, I began my search to find out the problem and the solution. I read spiritual warfare books, deliverance books, generational curse books, and I attended seminars and conferences by so-called 'specialists', but found no answer. The result was more frustration.

I thought that if I could meet the most anointed person and if they would lay hands on me, I would be delivered and anointed, and then my ministry would explode. So, I fasted and prayed for God to connect me with the right person, a famous preacher so that I could launch 'my ministry' under their umbrella and influence. Well, God did not send the most anointed person. In fact, He had already sent the most anointed person and His name is Jesus, I will get to that in a minute. Many people laid hands on me, but there was no change. I spent almost five years in counseling rooms, but still there was no peace in my heart.

When I heard the stories of these so-called 'specialists', I found that their problems were the same as, or worse than, mine. I went to attend a special meeting of one of those 'specialists' and I wanted to sit as close as I could to the front. I thought, in case the anointing jumps off of him, I should be close enough for it to fall on me. But, these specialists have other specialists (people with money and pastors of large churches) that follow them or are their partners and only they get to sit in the front rows. I did not have that kind of money, and I was not a pastor of a large church. My place belonged all the way in the balcony where I had to use a binocular to see the person on the stage.

I had to use my 'Indian way' to get through the security line and I found a seat in the third row. I told them I was a minister from India. I said to myself, "This is the day. He is going to snap his finger and call me to the platform to lay hands on and prophesy over me. I am going to go down to the floor under the *power* and, when I get up, I will be anointed and my worldwide ministry will begin!"

So, I sat there looking so pious and holy and did not take my eyes off of the 'specialist' on the stage because, if he snapped his finger at me, I did not want to miss it. All of a sudden, I began to feel uneasy inside. I began to feel pain in my body like never before. I became so sick I did not hear a thing the preacher said. It felt like hundreds of needles were penetrating my skin and the pain all over my body was excruciating. I have never been sick like that before or since. I could not wait for the meeting to be over—since I had 'worked' my way so close to the front, I did not feel comfortable getting up and walking out.

After the meeting, I ran to my hotel room confused and disappointed. I confessed all my sins *once again* and cried out to the Lord for His mercy. The only benefit I had was that one of the followers of the specialist that was sitting in front of me realized that I was from India. He put his hand in his pocket and took out a hundred dollar bill and slipped it to me behind his chair. He might have thought, "This poor guy really needs some help, he looks like he is from a third- world country." From that point on, I stopped looking to the specialists. The reason I believe I got sick was because my focus was on the man and not on Jesus. The specialist is not the author and finisher of my faith; Jesus is. Later, I learned that all I needed was to look to Jesus and the Word to know what He did for me.

All this time I had been running around trying to receive something from men that I already had (the anointing). The Bible says in 2 Corinthians 1:21,

"Now He who establishes us with you in Christ and has **anointed us** *is* **God**, who also has sealed us and given us the Spirit in our hearts as a guarantee."

> 1 John 2:27 says, "But the **anointing which you have received from Him abides in you**, and you do not need that anyone teach you; but as the same anointing teaches you concerning all things, and is true, and is not a lie, and just as it has taught you, you will abide in Him."

Do you know that, according to the New Testament, every New Covenant believer is equally anointed? That might surprise you but that is the truth. I did not receive a small portion of the Holy Spirit and someone else received a bigger portion. The above scripture doesn't say, "Well, I am Paul, the anointing upon my life is more than what you have." John didn't say, "You know we are special apostles, you need to receive your anointing and blessings from us. When we come we will lay hands on each of you so be ready with a special offering." Have you heard such things in your life before?

Instead, they said, "It is God who anointed you. The anointing you have received from Him abides in you...the same anointing teaches you concerning all things." It's time for the body of Christ to believe God and His Word. We all are equally anointed but we are not all called to do the same thing. That is why we read in Acts 8 that Peter and John went to Samaria to lay hands on the believers to receive the Holy Spirit. They had a clear understanding of what each one was called to do. In Acts 6, we see apostles appointing anointed believers to serve at the table. They did not receive the anointing from the apostles; the apostles merely delegated them to their area of function.

The reason we are running after someone is we do not know that we are anointed and we do not know what we are supposed to do with our life. So, we feel that if we can get his or her anointing, we can do what he or she is doing. Before we can discover our *destiny* we need to first discover our *identity*. We are different members of the same body with different functions. We all received the same Holy Spirit and are equally anointed. The same blood and life that runs through my head also runs through my feet; the blood and life I have in my head is not any more valuable or different than in my feet. The same life, the same blood, but different body parts with different functions: that is the way it works in the body of Christ, so stop looking at someone as super anointed or more special. Find your place in the body and let the anointing that is on you flow to other members, and you will know that you are special too.

If the anointing and the life you have come from the Head (Jesus), then it is the same anointing in you that is working in the person you admire. Stop thinking someone is more anointed than you. They are anointed to do something different than what you are anointed to do, that's all. They might have started functioning in (exercising by faith) that anointing earlier than you because they realized the possibility sooner. Now it's time for you to start!

Another misconception that is keeping the body of Christ ineffective is this: They believe if someone is really anointed, they should be able to do miracles and signs and wonders. So, they tap into spiritual power that is not of God, and we have many false apostles who do signs and wonders by demonic powers. Everyone is not anointed to do the same thing. Joseph was anointed to be a prime minister but he did not perform any miracles. Abraham, the father of our faith, was anointed but he did not cast out any demons. Isaac and Jacob were anointed, but they did not heal any sick.

Bezalel was anointed by God with the spirit of wisdom, knowledge, and understanding to imagine and create things (Exodus 31:3). Esther was anointed to influence kings. Moses laid hands on seventy elders, and the anointing came upon them. Unlike Moses, they did not do any miracles, but they were anointed to govern and solve problems. Daniel was anointed to be a statesman. Not everyone worked miracles in the New Testament, either. John the Baptist came with the spirit of Elijah, but he did not do any miracles (John 10:41). In the early Church, there were anointed people at the table serving food for widows. Joseph of Arimathea was a rich man and a disciple of Jesus. He did not perform any signs, but he was anointed to make money.

You need to find what God anointed you to do and come to peace with it, instead of comparing it with someone else and desiring to have what they have. The Bible says God anointed me with the Holy Spirit and He abides in me. He did not come to visit; He came to stay. Can you imagine how many people run around to receive a word or anointing from other people? They are still in the Old Testament. They use the example of Elijah and Elisha. If so, he could have laid his hands on anyone he wanted (maybe after a special miracle service). It was God who told Elijah to meet Elisha and anoint him. Neither Elijah nor Elisha initiated the process (1 Kings 19:16-19).

If God tells someone to anoint you, they will come to you. God knows your address. You do not need to run after anyone. It is not God who drives you to do that; it is your ignorance and insecurity. By my works, I was trying my best not to lose something I did not earn (my salvation). I was trying to receive something that I already had (anointing). The devil had his time with me and kept me in ignorance for a long time, until the Holy Spirit began to open my eyes to what the Bible really says.

First of all, you need to know deep down in your heart that God loves you. You need to be rooted and grounded in His love (Ephesians 3:17). People who live by the law believe that God loves them because of their good behavior. That is contrary to the Bible. The Bible says God loved me when I was still a sinner. When I was living in sin, a blasphemer and a heathen who never even thought about God, He loved me. God reconciled me to Himself, not when I was saved but when I was a sinner. Why?

> Romans 5:8 & 10 says, "But God demonstrates His own love toward us, in that while we were still sinners, Christ died for us."

> "For if when we were enemies we were reconciled to God through the death of His Son, much more, having been reconciled, we shall be saved by His life."

Stop thinking that He will stop loving you because you did something wrong. He did not start loving you based on your goodness or because you were keeping all the law. The Bible says, "Nothing can separate us from the love of God..." (Romans 8:39). When it says nothing, that's full coverage. Believe it. It is the truth.

People who are saved but still living under the law (Old Testament) have difficulty understanding the grace of God. To them, grace means loose living, sin, and getting out of control. They do not like the message of grace because they fear sin and fear they will lose their salvation. But, to those who understand grace, sin is not a problem because they are already free from the bondage of sin and are dead to it. Sin has no more power over them. If someone is *living* in sin and says they are under grace, they are deceived and they may not be saved yet, they are still in the kingdom of darkness. They might say they are saved. Once you are saved, you are free from the dominion of sin. As long as you are living in grace, you will not have the notion to sin. We sin when we slip away from grace and move under the law. As the Bible says, those who are born of God cannot sin.

> 1 John 3:7-9 says, "Little children, let no one deceive you. He who practices righteousness is righteous, just as He is righteous. He who sins is of the devil, for the devil has sinned from the beginning. For this purpose the Son of God was manifested, that He might destroy the works of the devil. Whoever has been born of God does not sin, for His seed remains in him; and he cannot sin, because he has been born of God."

People living under the law are not free from sin, neither are they dead to it. Sin is alive and thriving in them, just waiting for the right opportunity to manifest its evil deeds. The reason they are not sinning is not because they are free from it, but because of fear; fear of judgment, fear of losing their salvation, and fear of getting caught. For these, making it to heaven is their biggest life goal!

To become free from this, the first thing one needs to have is a revelation of Jesus: Why He came and what He preached and did. These people will say they know the gospel and they speak in tongues but let me tell you, they have no clue at all. They think Jesus came to add the grace message to the already existing law and its teachings. They think He came to give salvation as a reward to those already keeping the law. That is not true.

Jesus did not come to add grace to the message of the law. He came to fulfill the old so He could establish a new covenant (Hebrews 8:7&13). That is why it is called the New Testament (covenant). Let me tell you something, when God judges you on the final day, He will not judge you based on the Old Covenant because He did not make that with you or for you. He will judge us based on the New Covenant. So, do not waste your life and time trying to observe the law, it will not do you any good. When I say Old Covenant, I mean the entire Old Testament—the law and the prophets.

Jesus said, "The law and the prophets were until John the Baptist" (Luke 16:16). Where God put a period, do not add a coma or a sentence. Paul says in Romans 10:4, "For Christ is the **end** of the law for righteousness to everyone who believes."

According to the above scripture, Christ is the end of the law, not a continuation of it. How then does one become righteous? It says everyone who believes becomes righteous, not by doing something or keeping the Ten Commandments. The next question is, by believing what? I will explain this more. Keep going.

Jesus became sin for us so that we might become the righteousness of God.

> 2 Corinthians 5:21 says, "For He made Him who knew no sin *to be* sin for us, that we might become the righteousness of God in Him."

In the New Testament, no one becomes righteous by good works. We do not earn it; we can only receive it as a free gift. The reason is this, we did not become a sinner by committing sin; we were born sinners. We inherited sin from Adam by birth, and that is why we sin. By the new birth, we inherit righteousness from Jesus Christ (Romans 5:12-18). That is why the Bible does not call the believer a sinner. It is against the birthright in Christ of a Kingdom citizen. Once we receive

146

the free gift of righteousness, we do good works because we are born (new birth) righteous, not the other way around. When we receive the righteousness of God, we are no longer poor sinners saved by grace. Instead, our confession should be, "I am a child of God and the righteousness of Christ Jesus by faith." Jesus did not become sin for us to continue to live in sin. He became sin for us to set us free from it so that we could become the righteousness of God.

First of all, the Law (Old Covenant) was given to the children of Israel, the Jews, not the Gentiles. A Gentile has nothing to do with the covenant God made with the Israelites. To the Jews and God, we were called, "Uncircumcised, without Christ, being aliens from the commonwealth of Israel and strangers from the covenants of promise, having no hope, and without God in the world" (Ephesians 2:11-12). This was our spiritual and social status before Christ came. So, putting a Jewish prayer shawl on your head will not make you any more spiritual, neither will it make you a Jew. Living in a barn won't make you a cow!

Many are trying to become Jews these days by putting on a prayer shawl or sticking something on the doorpost of their house (I hope they are not getting circumcised because that is the first requirement to be a Jew and keep the law). These are called Judaisers; they existed in the first century also. I know people who call themselves Christians but have officially converted to Judaism. Just because you keep a bunch of rules doesn't make you a Jew. Please don't misunderstand me. I am not anti-Semitic; I love the people of Israel and pray for their salvation.

> Romans 2:28-29 says, "For he is not a Jew who *is one* outwardly, nor *is* circumcision that which *is* outward in the flesh; but *he is* a Jew who *is one* inwardly; and circumcision *is that* of the heart, in the Spirit, not in the letter; whose praise *is* not from men but from God."

> Romans 9:4-6 says, "Who are Israelites, to whom *pertain* the adoption, the glory, the covenants, the giving of the law, the service *of God,* and the promises; of whom *are* the fathers and from whom, **according to the flesh, Christ *came*,** who is over all, *the* eternally blessed God. Amen. But it is not that the word of God has taken no effect. For they *are* not all Israel who *are* of Israel."

The above verse says that according to the flesh Christ came through the people of Israel. But, no longer do we know Christ after the flesh. Once He died and rose again, He is no longer a Jewish carpenter. He is the King of kings and Lord of lords.

2 Corinthians 5:15-16 says, "And He died for all, that those who live should live no longer for themselves, but for Him who died for them and rose again. Therefore, from now on, we regard **no one** according to the flesh. Even though we have known Christ according to the flesh, yet now we know *Him thus* no longer."

Some others say we have to discover our Jewish roots to receive our blessings. Let me tell you what we should be rooted in. We need to be rooted and grounded in love. That is the biggest problem in church today; very few are rooted in the love of God but they are rooted in some sect, culture, or ideology. Be free in Jesus' name. Please pray the prayer Paul prayed in Ephesians 3:14-21. He did not pray we should be rooted and grounded in our Jewish roots.

Jesus came to fulfill the law (Matthew 5:17). Why did He have to fulfill the law? Because no one else could do it. Except Jesus, no human being has ever kept the whole law without breaking one. Many people think that since He fulfilled it, now we have to fulfill it too. Well, if that is what you believe, then go ahead and try it and let me know what happens. He died on the cross for us; we do not need to die like He did. The secret behind it is this: the whole sin problem started because of one man's disobedience. God also decided to solve the sin problem by one Man's obedience, Jesus (Romans 5:17-19).

That is why the Bible says, "All have sinned." Jesus came and fulfilled the law for us so that the blessings God promised to those who keep the law might come upon us. That sounds like a good deal to me! Jesus fulfilled the righteous requirement of the law for me so that I can enjoy the blessings (Romans 8:3-4). Then He grafted us (the Gentiles) into the Olive Tree (Israel), so that every promise and blessing God gave to them is now ours for free. That is why the gospel is called good news. If He had put all the burden of keeping the law on our head, that would not sound like good news to me, my friend.

The Bible tells us to whom the law was given. 1 Timothy 1:8-9 says, "But we know that the law *is* good if one uses it lawfully, knowing this: that the law is not made for a righteous person, but for *the* lawless and insubordinate, for *the* ungodly and for sinners, for *the* unholy and profane, for murderers of fathers and murderers of mothers, for manslayers, for fornicators, for sodomites, for kidnappers, for liars, for perjurers, and if there is any other thing that is contrary to sound doctrine." If you belong to one of those groups mentioned above, please keep the law—you need it.

"So," you may ask, "What is the solution?" I want to share with you a little bit about how God saved us through Christ and what He did for us. It has nothing to do with what we did or what we do; it is all based on what Christ did on the cross.

For religious people, it is difficult to comprehend. Though we think we know it, we do not. It is a process. The good news is you are not alone in this. The majority of believers are in the same boat. They are under the influence of a religious spirit. That is why the world is in this shape. So, do not feel bad thinking it is only you that has to go through this. No.

The road to freedom for me began with thinking about the disciples of Jesus. These were fishermen, not ministers, before Jesus called them. They had never been to seminary, nor did they have the spiritual qualifications we would look for in a preacher. I believe the reason Jesus selected fishermen, and not the Pharisees from the temple (who were educated in the Word and looked holy and righteous), is because He wanted to show His grace to the world.

I grew up close to the ocean and have seen fishermen before. They do not speak the same 'language' as other people. When we were little, fishermen used to bring fresh fish to our home to sell. They did not have the same lifestyle as others. If someone were to choose leaders for their church or organization, they would never go to the seaside and pick a bunch of old fishermen. It is out of the question. You cannot change them or teach them anything new.

Well, that is our perception but not the perception of the grace of God. The moment Jesus called them He gave them power, and appointed them as apostles (Matthew 10:1; Mark 3:13-15), giving them power to heal sicknesses and diseases and to cast out demons. Apostles? When did they get the training to qualify them to be apostles? I was wondering how that could be. How could Jesus give power to these people? I know people who have been in church for thirty or forty years and still have never healed the sick (they carry medicine in their own purse) or cast out a demon. They think they are still not ready or holy enough to do it. We take people through healing school, prophetic school, and every other school you can imagine and still we do not see the results we would like to see.

How long did these men pray before He gave them the power? Did they speak in tongues for 8 hours the night before? Did He walk them through their generational tree to break all the curses? Did He do family counseling with them to heal their marital problems before they did this? If they cast out demons while they had family problems, could the demons or sicknesses that were on the people jump on them or their children because they were not spiritual enough? We do not see any such things in the New Testament and, if it is not mentioned, that means it is not our job to assume.

These disciples did not even say grace (they did not know how to or need to) or wash their hands before they ate. They were that primitive. After a couple of years, maybe at least one year, they had the guts to ask Jesus to teach them to pray. That means they had not prayed until then because they did not know how; no one had taught them. Even after three years of training with Jesus, they could not stay awake for an hour and pray. I believe every time they tried to pray they nodded off to sleep after a few minutes. Remember their experience in the Garden of Gethsemane?

They did not fast before they cast out demons. In fact, the Pharisees complained to Jesus that His disciples did not fast as they should. They were eating too much! Those poor Pharisees were praying, fasting, tithing, and doing all the right things, but they could not cast out a fly, let alone a demon! These fishermen did not grow up in church as some of us did, and that is our problem. We have too much *churchism* in us. The first thing that needs to be cast out is our *Churchianity*. Jesus gave them power and they were doing miracle-ministry from day one; the kind of ministry most of us have been dreaming about for fifty years. We think we are not ready yet. That is a religious spirit, my friend. God made us ready before the foundation of this world (please read Ephesians 1:3-4; 2 Timothy 1:9).

It is unfortunate that today we look at people who are operating in the gifts of the Spirit and think they are super heroes who attained some spiritual heights that we could not. In the Bible, that was the *first* practical lesson the disciples (when they were still carnal) did for their discipleship 101 class, not after their graduation. Today, we put that as the last and highest degree anyone could achieve and that is why most people do not operate in their spiritual gifts. That is why our Christianity remains only in word, but has no power to prove it.

The Corinthian church operated in more spiritual gifts, knowledge, and revelation than any other church mentioned in the New Testament (1 Corinthians 1:4-7). They were also the most carnal church. There were sins in that church that even the heathens were afraid to commit! There was division, immorality, dissension, abuse of communion, believers suing one another, partiality—the list goes on. Paul said he could not deal with them as saints, but as carnal people (1 Corinthians 3:1-3). He said he could only give them milk. That means there is no meat in the books of Corinthians, but they were operating in the spiritual gifts.

The religious church has set the bar so high that no one is able to reach it. We have been praying (some people attend at least one prayer meeting a day), fasting, spitting, and speaking all kinds of jibberish for so long but are not able to do anything. What is the solution? We need to be re-educated in the Holy Scriptures. We need to understand the grace of God. The first scripture I want to share with you is 2 Timothy 1:8-9. I want you to receive this in your heart (spirit).

> "Therefore do not be ashamed of the testimony of our Lord, nor of me His prisoner, but share with me in the sufferings for the

gospel according to the power of God, **who has saved us and called *us* with a holy calling, not according to our works, but according to His own purpose and grace which was given to us in Christ Jesus before time began.**"

Do you believe the above scripture? If you are saved, you have a calling. He does not need to call you again; it came with your salvation. Stop waiting for a burning bush or Damascus Road experience. The only thing we need to make sure of is what we are called for (2 Peter 1:10). We are saved and called not according to our works. Our calling is contingent on neither the works we did before our salvation nor those we do after to 'remain' saved.

How are we saved? Ephesians 2:4-9 says, "But God, who is rich in mercy, because of **His great love with which He loved us,** even when we were dead in trespasses, made us alive together with Christ (by grace you have been saved), and raised *us* up together, and made *us* sit together in the heavenly *places* in Christ Jesus, that in the ages to come He might show the exceeding riches of His grace in *His* kindness toward us in Christ Jesus. For by grace you have been saved through faith, and that not of yourselves; *it is* the **gift of God**, not of works, lest anyone should boast."

It is the pattern and style of all great kings to show off their wealth, glory, and military power to other kings and kingdoms. They hold demonstration parades to show off their wealth and might. Even today, nations do military exercises to show off their weapons, and firepower, to other countries. The above verse says God who is rich in mercy and grace shows off the exceeding riches of grace in that in His kindness He saved us. It has nothing to do with us. All that we need to do is believe and receive it.

Do you know why God loves us with such great love? There is only one reason; He *is* Love. Do you know how many believers are stuck in their life because they made some mistakes and do not feel worthy, or feel like they lost their calling? Let me tell you my friend, first of all, God didn't call you because you did not make any mistakes. God knew when He called you what He was getting into. God knew every mistake you would ever commit before you were born. It is not a surprise to Him. It's a surprise to us. When God bought us with a price, He knew the defects that came with the product! He was not cheated or misguided by the sales guy, as some seem to think.

Salvation and the forgiveness of sins are gifts of God to sinners, not rewards for good behavior to perfect people. Now, the question is, "How do I remain saved? Don't I have to do the right things to keep my salvation?" No, not if it was a gift. The gift was not given based on how good you were. It was free. It is hard to believe, but it is the truth. The Bible says that once we are saved we are kept by the power of God. Let's read 1 Peter 1:5, "…who are kept by the power of God through faith for salvation ready to be revealed in the last time."

What keeps us from stumbling or falling? Jude 24-25 says, "Now to **Him who is able to keep you from stumbling**, and to present you faultless before the presence of His glory with exceeding joy, **to God our Savior**, who alone is wise, be glory and majesty, dominion and power, both now and forever. Amen."

CHAPTER 10
THE LAW AND GRACE

CHAPTER 10: THE LAW AND GRACE

Since the fall, God's relationship with man and man's relationship with God has changed dramatically. God did not change nor did His love for us, but our capacity to understand has changed from age to age. We are living in a world that is deteriorating daily because of sin. Though outwardly it looks like we are making progress, in many ways, life is not any better now than it was a thousand years ago. We have more conveniences, luxuries, and technology, but there are more sicknesses, and it has become less safe than any previous time.

In each age, God began to deal with man differently. The ways (norms and terms by which) God dealt with man in one age is called a dispensation. A dispensation is a period of time in which God deals with man based on a particular covenant, promise, or principle. From the creation of Adam until now, there have been six dispensations or covenants, meaning six different ways God related to man. There is one more dispensation to be fulfilled. It will begin after the Second Coming of Christ.

This book is not about dispensations, but I want to cover them briefly so you can know what they are and what dispensation we are living in right now. When one dispensation is completed and a new one is introduced, the old one becomes invalid. God does not require us to keep the norms of the old when He begins to deal with humanity based on a new dispensation (covenant). Only the promises and benefits continue to the next, not the rules (terms and conditions). That is very important to understand; otherwise, it will create a lot of confusion in our walk with God.

To simplify it, God is not dealing with us now as He dealt with Noah or Moses. Thank God! We are in the best dispensation God has made with man since the fall. Everyone since the fall has desired to see and live in the day we are living in. It is unfortunate that many look to the Old Testament and wish they lived then.

The seven dispensations are these: 1) Dispensation of Innocence: This period began with the creation of Adam and ended when he sinned. 2) Dispensation

155

of Conscience: After the fall, man lived for a while based on his conscience and it lasted until the time of Noah. 3) Dispensation of Human Government: Man began to make his own rules and establish kingdoms on this earth. This lasted from Noah until the time of Abraham. 4) Dispensation of Promise: From the time of Abraham, God began to deal with man based on the promise He made with Abraham and it lasted until the law was introduced through Moses. 5) Dispensation of Law: God made a covenant with the people of Israel and gave them His Law, which is called the Old Testament or Old Covenant. It lasted until John the Baptist. 6) Dispensation of Grace: God began to deal with man based on His love and grace and not based on man's performance. It began with John the Baptist and will go on until His Second Coming. 7) Dispensation of the Millennial Reign: It will begin when Christ comes to set up His Kingdom on this earth and we will reign with Him for a thousand years.

We are now living in the Dispensation of Grace. This means God decided to show His favor, or grace (acceptance), to anyone who will respond to His love, and His love was demonstrated to us through giving us His only Son. Whoever believes in His Son Jesus, God will accept them, forgive their sins, and make them His children. No other condition is involved, nothing whatsoever. He does not deal with us based on the Old Testament law because we are not in that time period right now. We will see this in detail in the following pages.

> Ephesians 3:2 says, "If indeed you have heard of the **dispensation of the grace of God** which was given to me for you."

> Titus 2:11 says, "For the grace of God that brings salvation has appeared to all men."

> 2 Timothy 1:9 says, "Who has saved us and called *us* with a holy calling, not according to our works, but according to His own purpose and grace which was given to us in Christ Jesus before time began."

Jesus came to preach the acceptable year of the Lord. Though it says a year, it does not mean a literal year but represents an age.

> Luke 4:18-19 says, "The Spirit of the Lord *is* upon Me, because He has anointed Me to preach the gospel to *the* poor; He has sent Me to heal the brokenhearted, to proclaim liberty to *the* captives and recovery of sight to *the* blind, *to* set at liberty those who are oppressed; **to proclaim the acceptable year of the Lord.**"

Following Christ or seeking the Kingdom of God is not obeying a bunch of rules and regulations. It is a relationship with the King of kings and the Lord of lords. Many people have reduced Christianity to a bunch of rules. That is far from the truth. We are going to see how we fulfill every commandment in the Bible by having a relationship with Jesus Christ and with one another.

HOW DOES A BELIEVER IN CHRIST FULFILL THE REQUIREMENTS OF THE LAW OR THE TEN COMMANDMENTS?

The Ten Commandments were given as part of the Law. In fact, it was the introduction to the rest of the Law. When Moses started speaking what God wrote and gave to him, he started with the Ten Commandments.

There is a big fight going on in America for the Ten Commandments. The government wants to remove them from public places and some people in the Church think the country is going to go downward because they are removing them. Do you want to fulfill the Ten Commandments? Read the following verses and do what they say. No nation or person will go under if they practice the following two verses from the Bible. You will fulfill the whole law if you obey the following two verses.

Romans 13:8-10 says, "Owe no one anything except to love one another, for he who loves another has fulfilled the law. For the commandments, "You shall not commit adultery," "You shall not murder," "You shall not steal," "You shall not bear false witness," "You shall not covet," and if *there is* any other commandment, are *all* summed up in this saying, namely, "You shall love your neighbor as yourself. Love does no harm to a neighbor; **therefore love *is* the fulfillment of the law.**"

We do not fulfill the law by keeping rules, by observing certain rituals, following spiritual disciplines, by adopting a certain dress code or focusing on outward appearance. We fulfill the law by doing the following:

Galatians 5:13-15, "For you, brethren, have been called to liberty; only do not *use* liberty as an opportunity for the flesh, but through love serve one another. **For all the law is fulfilled in one word**, *even* in this: "You shall love your neighbor as yourself." But if you bite and devour one another, beware lest you be consumed by one another!"

Many believers are traveling in two boats, with one foot on the law and the other foot on grace. As a result, they are not going anywhere and they are not sure which one is which. This happens mainly because they fear losing their salvation. The second reason this happens is because most did not have a foundational teaching about the Christian faith. The third reason is we do not know what it means when the Bible uses the word *love*. Most of us were never loved unconditionally by any human, so we do not know how to receive the love of God or give it to others. The only love many of us know is the love between a man and a woman, which is mostly lust. The Bible says the love of God is beyond our comprehension (Ephesians 3:19).

We all received a little bit of this and that from somewhere but never gained a systematic teaching about the doctrines of the New Testament Church. People take scriptures from the law and mix them with the scriptures from the New Testament and the result we get is spiritual constipation. Paul said four times in the epistles that God will judge the hearts of men based on his gospel and not according to the Law or Ten commandments.

> Romans 2:16 says, "In the day when God will judge the secrets of men by Jesus Christ, according to **my gospel**."

> Romans 16:25 says, "Now to Him who is able to establish you according to **my gospel** and the preaching of Jesus Christ, according to the revelation of the mystery kept secret since the world began."

> 1 Timothy 1:11 says, "According to the glorious gospel of the blessed God which was committed to **my trust**."

> 2 Timothy 2:8 says, "Remember that Jesus Christ, of the seed of David, was raised from the dead according to **my gospel.**"

How can Paul make such bold statements? Even Jesus did not say such things. None of the authors of the four gospels made such a statement. Jesus came to reveal the mystery of the Kingdom of God. That is what we lost because of the fall. He came to restore to us the Kingdom. I am not saying here that Paul is greater than Jesus. No way. The reason he said it is this; the mystery of God, Christ, the Church, the gospel, and the grace of God was revealed to Paul and not to anyone else, including the other apostles. How do I know that? Please read the following verses.

Romans 16:25 says, "Now to him that is of power to establish you according to my gospel, and the preaching of Jesus Christ, according to the revelation of the **mystery**, which was kept secret since the world began."

Ephesians 3:2-5 says, "If indeed you have heard of the dispensation of the grace of God which was given to me for you, how that **by revelation He made known to me the mystery** (as I have briefly written already, by which, when you read, you may understand my knowledge in the **mystery of Christ**), which in other ages was not made known to the sons of men, as it has now been revealed by the Spirit to His holy apostles and prophets."

Ephesians 3:8-9 says, "Unto me, who am less than the least of all the saints, is this grace given, that I should preach among the Gentiles the **unsearchable riches of Christ**; and to make all men see what is the fellowship of the **mystery**, which from the beginning of the world hath been hid in God, who created all things by Jesus Christ."

Ephesians 6:18-19 says, "Praying always with all prayer and supplication in the Spirit, and watching thereunto with all perseverance and supplication for all saints; and for me, that utterance may be given unto me, that I may open my mouth boldly, to make known the **mystery of the gospel**."

Colossians 2:2 says, "That their hearts might be comforted, being knit together in love, and unto all riches of the full assurance of understanding, to the acknowledgement of the **mystery of God, and of the Father, and of Christ**."

Colossians 4:3 says, "Withal praying also for us, that God would open unto us a door of utterance, to speak the **mystery of Christ**, for which I am also in bonds."

There is coming a time when the mystery of God will be completed. That means we will know God the way we are supposed to know Him, not as a mystery.

Revelation 10:7 says, "But in the days of the voice of the seventh angel, when he shall begin to sound, the **mystery of God** should be finished, as he hath declared to his servants the prophets."

There is a time coming when the revelation of the grace of God will fill the whole earth. God will raise up many preachers to preach the grace of God more than anything else. They will be misunderstood and persecuted in the beginning just as it happened in the days of the Bible. We need to believe and preach the gospel Paul preached. Then the end will come.

A BELIEVER AND THE WORKS OF THE LAW

What is the relationship between a believer in Christ and the Old Testament law? How much of it do we need to observe? Will we be judged based on the law or grace?

Galatians 3:10-14 says, "For as many as are of the works of the law are under the curse; for it is written, "Cursed *is* everyone who does not continue in all things which are written in the book of the law, to do them." But that no one is justified by the law in the sight of God *is* evident, for "the just shall live by faith." Yet the law is not of faith, but "the man who does them shall live by them."'

'Christ has redeemed us from the curse of the law, having become a curse for us (for it is written, "Cursed *is* everyone who hangs on a tree"), that the blessing of Abraham might come upon the Gentiles in Christ Jesus, that we might receive the promise of the Spirit through faith."'

Nowhere in the New Testament does it say we need to keep the Old Testament law. Instead, it says we are free from it and its curses. If you want to remain under a curse, then just try to keep the law.

THE SIDE EFFECTS OF KEEPING THE LAW

When I say side effects, I mean unwanted troubles. I already mentioned one above, which is to have the curses that are mentioned in the Old Testament. That is one of the main side effects. No one wants to be cursed or live under a curse, but many do and they do not even know it. There are others mentioned in the New Testament and I want to share them with you.

IT BRINGS KNOWLEDGE OF SIN

Romans 3:20 says, "Therefore by the deeds of the law no flesh will be justified in His sight, for **by the law *is* the knowledge of sin.**"

Romans 7:7 says, "What shall we say then? *Is* the law sin? Certainly not! On the contrary, **I would not have known sin except through the law**. For I would not have known covetousness unless the law had said, "You shall not covet.""

Those who are living under the law cannot forget their sins, nor do they feel forgiven (Hebrews 10:3). The law that is in your heart keeps reminding you of every wrong thing you ever did from childhood until now. You will misunderstand, thinking it is the Holy Spirit who is reminding you. No, it's the law. The Holy Spirit will not bring to your remembrance the sins God forgave. He does not remember them at all (Hebrews 8:12; 10:17). Consequently, most believers never go beyond the basic doctrine of Christ, which is repentance (Hebrews 5:12-6:1-2). They, like the Old Testament believer, keep repenting every year. They never go beyond that. After Christ died, repentance does not mean confessing our sins; it means a change of mind, changing the way we think.

IT KEEPS EMPOWERING THE SIN CONSCIOUSNESS

A believer in Christ is supposed to live by the consciousness of righteousness. As long as a person remains under the law, they will not be able to exercise the consciousness of righteousness because the law keeps reminding and empowering their sin consciousness.

Hebrews 10:1-4 says, "For the law, having a shadow of the good things to come, *and* not the very image of the things, can never with these same sacrifices, which they offer continually year by year, make those who approach perfect. For then would they not have ceased to be offered? For the worshipers, once purified, would have had no more **consciousness of sins**. But in those *sacrifices there is* a reminder of sins every year. For *it is* not possible that the blood of bulls and goats could take away sins."

IT BRINGS WRATH

Romans 4:14-15 says, " For if those who are of the law *are* heirs, faith is made void and the promise made of no effect, because the **law brings about wrath**; for where there is no law *there is* no transgression."

If you are under the law, you will always be afraid of God's judgment and wrath. You will live in constant fear of punishment. You will have no assurance of salvation, nor comfort of the Holy Spirit. One of the reasons people do not experience the benefits of grace now is because they trust the law more than the grace of God. In the spirit and in the natural, whenever you break a law there is a consequence, and He is not responsible for that.

Also, the law makes you angry. If you are a person who follows the law, you will become angry when you see others breaking the law that you are keeping. If you are under grace, when you see someone making a mistake, you will feel compassion and mercy toward them. That is why Jesus was compassionate toward sinners while the Pharisees were angry and wanted to kill them. The law was given through Moses, but grace and truth came through Jesus Christ (John 1:17).

THE LAW MAKES SIN ALIVE

Do you wonder why you cannot overcome sin though you are saved? Though by new birth you are dead to sin, the commandments cause sin to come alive in us. If there is no law, sin remains dead.

Romans 7:8-11 says, "But sin, taking opportunity by the commandment, produced in me all *manner of evil* desire. For apart from the law sin *was* dead. I was alive once without the law, but when the commandment came, sin revived and I died. And the commandment, which *was* to *bring* life, I found to *bring* death. For sin, taking occasion by the commandment, deceived me, and by it killed *me*."

YOU WILL BE UNDER THE DOMINION OF SIN

Romans 6:14 says, "For sin shall not have dominion over you, for you are not under law but under grace."

As long as you keep and obey the law, you will be under the dominion of sin. This is against New Testament theology. After Christ died and paid for our sins, sin lost its dominion and no one needs to remain under its power.

THE LAW IS THE STRENGTH (EMPOWERMENT) OF SIN

Do you know why you feel the tendency to sin so strongly in your life? It is because of the laws you are keeping, consciously or subconsciously.

Romans 15:56 says, "The sting of death is sin, and the **strength of sin is the law**."

1 Corinthians 15:56-57 says, "It is sin which gives death its power, and **it is the law which gives sin its strength.** All thanks to God, then, who gives us the victory over these things through our Lord Jesus Christ!" (Philips)

IF YOU KEEP THE LAW, YOU ARE SEPARATED FROM CHRIST AND HAVE FALLEN FROM GRACE

If you keep one commandment from the law, you are obliged to keep the whole law.

Galatians 5:3-6 says, "And I testify again to every man who becomes circumcised that he is a debtor to keep the whole law. You have become estranged from Christ, you who *attempt to* be justified by law; **you have fallen from grace.** For we through the Spirit eagerly wait for the hope of righteousness by faith. For in Christ Jesus neither circumcision nor un-circumcision avails anything, but faith working through love."

Any time you think that you need to *do* something to receive anything from God, other than believing, you are going back to the law. When we do, we are saying that what Jesus did is not good enough or sufficient—that we have to complete the work or add to it. This happened to me several times. I would say to myself, "Maybe if I fast for a week, I will feel anointed." That is the law working in me, not my spirit living in grace. If I think according to the finished work of the cross, I will say, "Thank you Jesus for anointing me," whether I feel it or not. That does not mean you never need to fast. You fast when God tells you to, not do it as a ritual.

Do you want to know if you are living under the law or grace? If you feel guilt or condemnation in your heart, that means you are still under the law. When you live by grace, you feel freedom in your heart. If you do not feel confidence in your faith or in your prayers, it means you are living under the law. If you are not experiencing the love, joy, and peace God has promised, then you are under the law. When you are under the law, know that you also live under the dominion of sin. If you are afraid of God or the devil, you are living under the law.

Feeling the conviction of your sin is different from feeling guilty and condemned. The reason you feel guilty and condemned is you do not believe in your heart that God loves you unconditionally. You do not trust what His Son did for you. When you are convicted, you repent once and keep moving. Do not stay there for another second.

Recently, something happened to me. I sowed a financial seed into someone's life and it was one of the largest seeds I have ever sowed. After I gave the amount, I felt in my heart, "Now all the generational blessings will be released into my life." In my spirit, I did not feel right, as if something was wrong. Then, the next day, the Holy Spirit told me, "You gave that money because you are blessed; you are not blessed because you gave that money." Right then I knew I had returned to the law again. I repented and renounced that law and thanked God for the blessing I received through Jesus Christ. Do you see the difference, my friends?

Any time you attach a condition or perform a work to receive something that God already promised or gave you through Christ Jesus, you are depending either on the works of the law, or your own works and you have fallen from grace. To fall from grace does not mean you lose your salvation. It means you are not free anymore and have brought yourself back to the yoke of the law. If one thing is conditional, then everything else is conditional. God did not give some things for free and put a price tag on others. No. He freely gave us *all* things.

> Romans 8:32 says, "He who did not spare His own Son, but delivered Him up for us all, how shall He not with Him also **freely give us all things**?"

Why do we feel that God has not blessed us with some things? Why do we think certain things are conditional? It is because, in that area of our life, we are living under the law; maybe a law from the Bible or one we made ourselves. When you renounce that law and exercise your faith, you can have anything you believe.

YOU CAN RECEIVE THE GRACE OF GOD IN VAIN

Do you know why many do not walk in the power of God? They believe they have to obey the law and, as long as they believe that, the grace they received becomes void. If we could better our life ourselves in any way, then there was no need of Christ dying for us.

> 2 Corinthians 6:1 says, "We then, *as* workers together *with Him* also plead with *you* not to receive the grace of God in vain."

YOU CAN MAKE YOUR FAITH VOID AND THE PROMISES OF GOD INEFFECTIVE

Though you have received a measure of faith from God, you can make it void, meaning it will do you no good. You will be like a person in the world who lives and walks by what they think and feel (sight).

Romans 4:13-16 says, "For the promise that he would be the heir of the world *was* not to Abraham or to his seed through the law, but through the righteousness of faith. For if those who are of the law *are* heirs, **faith is made void** and the **promise made of no effect,** because the law brings about wrath; for where there is no law *there is* no transgression. Therefore *it is* of faith that *it might be* according to grace, so that the promise might be sure to all the seed, not only to those who are of the law, but also to those who are of the faith of Abraham, who is the father of us all."

YOU CAN FRUSTRATE THE GRACE OF GOD

When God made you a righteous person in Christ Jesus and you keep going back to the law to become righteous, you are frustrating the grace of God. You are trying to earn what God has given you for free. The Bible says He has freely given us all things. Do not frustrate the grace of God. Repent and accept His offer and let your soul find peace and rest in Jesus' name. If you could become a good person and be accepted by God by keeping the law, then Christ died in vain.

Galatians 2:21 says, "I do not frustrate the grace of God: for if righteousness come by the law, then Christ is dead in vain" (KJV).

THE PURPOSE OF GIVING THE LAW

THE LAW WAS GIVEN TO INCREASE THE OFFENSE

The more you try to keep the law, the more you mess up because it was given to increase the offense so that people will realize their need and cry out for a Savior. When you get tired of trying to keep the law, tired of trying to live right and still not meeting the standard, you give up. But, if you go to God, He will give you the revelation of His grace. He will say, "I never told you to try, I have done it for you, so you enter into My rest."

The whole Christian life is summed up in six words: "It is written," and, "It is finished." We need to know when to say which, that is the wisdom we need to receive from the Spirit of God.

Some people become like monks to utterly keep the law with the utmost intensity. They are not suited for living with other people, only in a cave somewhere. Jesus did not live in a cave even though He kept all the law and fulfilled it for us. He mostly hung out with sinners, drinking and eating (Matthew 11:19).

Romans 5:20-21 says, "Moreover the **law entered that the offense might abound.** But where sin abounded, grace abounded much more, so that as sin reigned in death, even so grace might reign through righteousness to eternal life through Jesus Christ our Lord."

THE LAW WAS GIVEN TO BRING US TO CHRIST

Galatians 3:23-25 says, "But before faith came, we were kept under the law, shut up unto the faith which should afterwards be revealed. Wherefore the law was our schoolmaster to bring us unto Christ, that we might be justified by faith. But after that faith is come, we are no longer under a schoolmaster" (KJV).

We all may begin with the law, the schoolmaster, when we start our walk with the Lord. But, once we are in Christ and receive freedom through His Spirit, we should not remain under the schoolmaster (law) even for a day, choosing instead to live under grace and be led by His Spirit. Who needs rules and regulations? Children and spiritual children need the law, not matured and adult children. Paul calls those who teach the law instructors of babes.

Please read the following verses.

Romans 2:20 says, "…an instructor of the foolish, a teacher of babes, having the form of knowledge and truth in the law."

Galatians 4:1-7 says, "Now I say, That the heir, as long as he is a child, differeth nothing from a servant, though he be lord of all; but is under tutors and governors until the time appointed of the father. Even so we, when we were children, were in bondage under the elements of the world: But when the fullness of the time was come, God sent forth his Son, made of a woman, made under the law, **to redeem them that were under the law,** that we might receive the adoption of sons. And because ye are sons, God hath sent forth the Spirit of his Son into your hearts, crying, Abba, Father. Wherefore thou art no more a servant, but a son; and if a son, then an heir of God through Christ" (KJV).

Every child needs rules and regulations because their conscience is not developed or trained to know the difference between right and wrong. But, there comes a time when each child needs to make his or her own decisions. The sooner it happens, the better it is for the child and the parents. We all start with the same rules, "Do not touch, do not taste, do not handle." The Bible calls them the elementary things (rudiments) of this world (Galatians 4:9-11; Colossians 2:20-23).

When you become an adult, you do the right thing not because someone forces you but because the law is in your heart. You do not keep a set of rules in your pocket that was given by someone so that you can take it out and read it to know good from evil. That is what God said in the scriptures, "I will put my law and Spirit within them and cause them to walk in my ways" (Hebrews 9:8-13; 10:15-17).

Hebrews 6:13-14 says, "For everyone who partakes *only* of milk *is* unskilled in the word of righteousness, for he is a babe. But solid food belongs to those who are of full age, *that is,* those who by reason of use have their senses exercised to discern both good and evil."

Unfortunately, today there are many believers who have not made that transition in their life. They are still under the tutor (rules and regulations) though they have been children of God for many years. They are spiritual babes. It's time to make that transition and walk in the freedom Christ has given us. Many people, when they hear of their freedom in Christ, only think about freedom from the Old Testament animal sacrifices or lawless living. That is not all it is talking about. It is freedom from the spirit of bondage and freedom to walk in the Spirit. As I said earlier, we all need the law until we receive the revelation of the love and the grace of God in our heart, which is supposed to happen when we come to Christ. For many, it takes a long time to figure it out. Once we receive it, we are no longer under the law. Otherwise, no one would be able to safely live on this earth.

THE LAW WAS GIVEN TO SHOW US OUR HOPELESSNESS

The Israelites couldn't keep the law, but not because they did not want to. They tried to and realized there was no way they were able to fulfill all that was required. No one in the Old Testament was made righteous because they obeyed the law. Otherwise, God did not have to send Jesus to die for us. The Psalmist says, "There is none who does good, No, not one" (Psalm 14:3; 53:4).

What the law could not do because of sin, God sent His Son to fulfill so that the righteousness of God could come upon us who believe in Christ.

Romans 8:3-4 says, "For what the law could not do in that it was weak through the flesh, God *did* by sending His own Son in the likeness of sinful flesh, on account of sin: He condemned sin in the flesh, that the righteous requirement of the law might be fulfilled in us who do not walk according to the flesh but according to the Spirit."

THE LAW WAS GIVEN AS A SHADOW OF GOOD THINGS TO COME

Hebrews 10:1 says, "For the law, having a shadow of the good things to come, *and* not the very image of the things, can never with these same sacrifices, which they offer continually year by year, make those who approach perfect."

JESUS FULFILLED THE LAW FOR US

Matthew 5:17 says, "Do not think that I came to destroy the Law or the Prophets. I did not come to destroy but to **fulfill**."

Besides Jesus, no human being ever fulfilled all the requirements of the law, so stop deceiving yourself by thinking that you are some spiritual superhero who can keep the law. No one did and no one can. God knew that when He gave the law, but He gave it to let man see what was in him. Jesus fulfilled everything that was required by the law for us, so we do not need to try keeping it anymore.

According to the Old Testament, when you fulfill the requirements of the law, all of the blessings that were promised by God will come to your life. So, because of what Jesus did, you and I are freely blessed by every blessing promised by God. Do not let the enemy, who will tell you to keep the law, cheat you out of your blessing. Cast him out and say, "Devil, Jesus fulfilled the law for me and all the blessings God mentioned in the Old Testament are mine. Amen."

GOD INTRODUCED A NEW LAW

The world we live in, and the universe, are governed by laws. There are natural and spiritual laws. Gravity is a natural law, and the law of aerodynamics is a superior law to gravity. When you apply the law of thermodynamics, cold water turns into steam. The problem with humanity was that we were held in bondage under the law of sin and death. God gave the law (commandments) to make man know his depravity and inability to do anything good without Him. He knew that humans do not admit defeat or weakness that easily. They will always find a good deed to hang onto; thinking that will make them righteous and save them from hell. There is a tendency in us to think that we are (our sin is) not as bad as someone else out there in the world. We try to justify ourselves through such comparisons. God wants man to admit his sin and ask Him for help. In truth, the law accomplished that.

> Galatians 3:23-26 says, "But before faith came, we were kept under guard by the law, kept for the faith which would afterward be revealed. Therefore the law was our tutor *to bring us* to Christ, that we might be justified by faith. But after faith has come, we are no longer under a tutor. For you are all sons of God through faith in Christ Jesus."

If the law of sin and death (Romans 7:23,25; 8:2) is to be broken, there has to be a superior law. That law is called the law of the Spirit of life in Christ Jesus. We remained under the law of sin and death until the new law was introduced.

> Romans 8:2-4 says, "For the law of the Spirit of life in Christ Jesus has made me free from the law of sin and death. For what the law could not do in that it was weak through the flesh, God *did* by sending His own Son in the likeness of sinful flesh, on account of sin: He condemned sin in the flesh, that the righteous requirement of the law might be fulfilled in us who do not walk according to the flesh but according to the Spirit."

GOD GAVE US NEW COMMANDMENTS

You might ask if a Christian needs to obey any commandment at all. Yes, we do. In fact, we need to obey two commandments. Jesus gave us two new commandments.

> John 13:34 says, "**A new commandment I give to you**, that you love one another; as I have loved you, that you also love one another."

John 3:18 says, "He who believes in Him is not condemned; but he who does not believe is condemned already, because he has not believed in the name of the only begotten Son of God."

John 8:24 says, "Therefore I said to you that you will die in your sins; for if you do not **believe** that I am He, you will die in your sins."

1 John 3:22-23 says, "And whatever we ask we receive from Him, because we keep His commandments and do those things that are pleasing in His sight. **And this is His commandment:** that we should believe on the name of His Son Jesus Christ and love one another, as He gave us commandment."

1 John 5:2-3 says, "By this we know that we love the children of God, when we love God and keep His commandments. For this is the love of God, that we keep His commandments. And His commandments are not burdensome."

According to the above verses, a believer in Christ is required to keep two commandments. They are to believe in Jesus Christ and to love one another.

GOD'S ONLY REQUIREMENT

There is only one way to obey the new commandment; that is to walk in the Spirit. The one and only thing God requires from us now to obey Him is to walk in the Spirit. When you walk in the Spirit, you will automatically fulfill all the righteous requirement of the law. You will not fulfill the lust of the flesh. Do not follow any rules and regulations, but follow your re-generated spirit and the Holy Spirit. Those who are led by the Spirit of God are the children of God, not those who keep rules and regulations. Be free in Jesus' name.

When you walk in the Spirit, neither the flesh, sin, the law, the devil, nor the world, will have any effect on you. Romans 8:13-15 says, "For if you live according to the flesh you will die; but if by the Spirit you put to death the deeds of the body, you will live. For as many as are led by the Spirit of God, these are sons of God. For you did not receive the spirit of bondage again to fear, but you received the Spirit of adoption by whom we cry out, 'Abba, Father.'"

WE CAN MAKE OUR OWN LAW

A law in someone's life did not necessarily come from the Bible. People make their own laws all the time, and bring themselves under bondage. Whatever rules or regulations you apply to your life thinking, "If I do this, God will be pleased with me and if I do not do that, God will be mad at me," becomes a law in your life. Or, when you say you will never do or say something again, you have put yourself under a law. Sooner or later, you will break that law and feel condemned.

For example, if someone says, "I will NEVER drink coffee in my life," they just put themselves under the law. After a couple of weeks, they go out to breakfast with their friends and are tempted by the smell of the coffee that was coming from their friend's cup. They give in to the temptation and take a sip. Bang! The law that was in them suddenly brought the sin nature alive and brought guilt and condemnation into their heart.

The devil, taking the occasion, begins tormenting them. "Look at you, you just broke a law; you cannot even keep one, single rule. You are worthless and you are going to be punished." As a result, we feel bad about ourselves. That whole day might be ruined until we make a new law. Life keeps going like this. That is not the kind of life Christ came to give to us. Drinking coffee is just an example; it could be anything that pertains to life.

Our parents put so many laws into our lives. When we were growing we heard, "You can't do that," "Don't touch that," "Never say that again," etc., etc. The Bible calls them the elementary principles (rules) of the world. They are all laws by which our mind has been programmed. Once you come to Christ, you are free from them but, because we have been programmed from childhood, it is difficult for us to think differently.

> Colossians 2:20-23 says, "Therefore, if you died with Christ from the basic principles of the world, why, as *though* living in the world, do you subject yourselves to regulations— "Do not touch, do not taste, do not handle," which all concern things which perish with the using—according to the commandments and doctrines of men? These things indeed have an appearance of wisdom in self-imposed religion, *false* humility, and neglect of the body, *but are* of no value against the indulgence of the flesh."

> Galatians 4:9-11 says, "But now after you have known God, or rather are known by God, how *is it that* you turn again to the weak and beggarly elements, to which you desire again to be in bondage? You observe days and months and seasons and years. I am afraid for you, lest I have labored for you in vain."

People have made all sorts of laws that have nothing to do with the Bible or the law of the Spirit of life. Make sure you unearth all the laws you are keeping or have brought upon yourself and throw them at the foot of the cross, never to pick them up again. We are not to be led by the law but by the Spirit. One reason the blessings of the New Covenant are not manifesting in our life is not because of the devil, but because we are living under laws we ourselves have made.

That is why Paul said there is nothing unclean in itself, unless to someone who thinks it is unclean. Romans 14:14 says, "I know and am convinced by the Lord Jesus that *there is* nothing unclean of itself; but to him who considers anything to be unclean, to him *it is* unclean."

Romans 2:14-15 says, "For when Gentiles, who do not have the law, by nature do the things in the law, these, **although not having the law, are a law to themselves,** who show the work of the law written in their hearts, their conscience also bearing witness, and between themselves *their* thoughts accusing or else excusing *them*."

Paul said in 1 Corinthians 6:12, "All things are lawful for me, but all things are not helpful. All things are lawful for me, but I will not be brought under the power of any."

Any time we keep a law we kick-start the curse of the law. Whether it is one from the Bible or one we make, those who follow the law are under a curse.

Galatians 3:10 says, "For as many as are of the works of the law are under the curse; for it is written, "Cursed *is* everyone who does not continue in all things which are written in the book of the law, to do them.""

You cannot take one law and avoid the next; either you do it all, or do not do any at all. James 2:10 says, "For whoever shall keep the whole law, and yet stumble in one *point,* he is guilty of all."

BENEFITS OF GRACE

Now that we have learned about the law and its purpose, let's learn about the grace of God and the benefits of living in grace.

THERE WILL BE NO TRANSGRESSION

Romans 4:15 says, "Because the law brings about wrath; for where there is no law *there is* no transgression."

172

Do you want to know the secret of living free from sin? Be free from the law. When there is no law, there is no transgression. When you are free from the law, you lose the desire to sin. Without the law, sin is dead. It has no power because the law empowers our sin nature. The law was not given to cure sin but to bring the knowledge of sin.

Many people are afraid that if they do not keep the law, their life will get out of control and they will commit some horrible sin. The opposite is true. When you are free from the law and come under the dominion of grace, you will be free from the grip of sin and, for the first time, you will be free to live the life God wants you to live without fear.

> Romans 7:8 says, "But sin, taking opportunity by the commandment, produced in me all *manner of evil* desire. For apart from the law sin *was* dead."

Sin is no longer a problem. The devil uses fear to keep us from knowing the truth. He does not want us to be free. If you are still bound by sin and the law, you are his illegal prisoner. He has no right to keep us under his dominion because his right of ownership was broken (taken away) by the blood of Jesus. The whole world is free and can be free, but they do not know that yet. We must tell them this truth. Amen.

NO MORE GUILT AND CONDEMNATION

> Romans 8:1 says, "*There is* therefore now no condemnation to those who are in Christ Jesus, who do not walk according to the flesh, but according to the Spirit."

The reason we feel guilty and condemned when we do something wrong is because of the law. When you are in Christ and under grace, condemnation has no place in your heart because you know in your heart you were accepted as the beloved of God in spite of what you did or did not do.

SIN WILL NOT HAVE ANY DOMINION OVER YOU

> Romans 6:14 says, "For sin shall not have dominion over you, for you are not under law but under grace."

One of the main concerns legalistic people have against the grace of God is, if we preach grace and not enough law, people will become lawless and commit sin or receive a license to sin. This is a total misconception. As the above verse says, when you come under grace, sin loses its dominion over you and gradually you stop sinning altogether. On the other hand, people who are living under the law commit sin like every other person in the world. They cannot stop sin by keeping the law; instead, the law empowers sin.

YOU HAVE THE FREEDOM TO COME TO GOD'S PRESENCE ANYTIME, ANYWHERE

> Hebrews 4:16 says, "Let us therefore come boldly to the throne of grace, that we may obtain mercy and find grace to help in time of need."

As a child of God, you have the freedom to come to the presence of God (your Father) at any time and in any location. Because of what Jesus accomplished for you, God will not and cannot reject you.

WE ARE JUSTIFIED BY FAITH

> Romans 3:21-24 says, "But now the righteousness of God apart from the law is revealed, being witnessed by the Law and the Prophets, even the righteousness of God, through faith in Jesus Christ, to all and on all who believe. For there is no difference; for all have sinned and fall short of the glory of God, **being justified freely by His grace** through the redemption that is in Christ Jesus."

> Romans 3:28 says, "Therefore we conclude that a man is justified by faith apart from the deeds of the law."

> Acts 13:38-39 says, "Therefore let it be known to you, brethren, that through this Man is preached to you the forgiveness of sins; and by Him everyone who believes is justified from all things from which you could not be justified by the law of Moses."

If observing the law could have justified and made a person righteous before God, then God did not have to send His Son to die and endure all that pain.

WE ARE DEAD TO THE LAW AND FREE FROM IT THROUGH JESUS CHRIST

> Romans 7:4 says, "Therefore, my brethren, you also have become dead to the law through the body of Christ, that you may be

married to another—to Him who was raised from the dead, that we should bear fruit to God."

Romans 7:6 says, "But **now we have been delivered from the law**, having died to what we were held by, so that we should serve in the newness of the Spirit and not *in* the oldness of the letter."

WE HAVE BEEN REDEEMED FROM THE LAW

Galatians 4:4-5 says, "But when the fullness of the time had come, God sent forth His Son, born of a woman, born under the law, to redeem those who were under the law, that we might receive the adoption as sons."

Most of us are waiting for Jesus to appear in a vision, or to send an angel, or even for that special anointed one to come and lay hands on us to set us free. My friend, there is nothing left for Jesus to set you free from. You are free from those things you believe you are free from. It's up to you now; the choice is yours.

Jesus said, "And you shall know the truth, and the truth shall make you free (John 8:32). The reason we feel we are not free in some areas is because we do not yet know the truth. When you know the truth, you will experience it in your life. Please read the chart below to understand the difference between the Old and the New Covenant and see which covenant you are living under.

Old Testament (covenant)	New Testament (covenant)
If you obey, I will bless you	You are already blessed (Ephesians 1:3; 2 Peter 1:3)
The land I will give to you	All things are yours (1 Corinthians 3:21-22)
If you do not obey My voice, I will leave you to your enemies	I will never leave you nor forsake you (Hebrews 13:5)
If you sanctify yourself…	You have been made holy and blameless (Ephesians 1:4)
If you walk in My ways…	I will cause you to walk in My ways (Hebrews 8:9-11)
If you obey, I will not put any sickness on you	You are healed (1 Peter 2:24)

I will go before you and defeat your enemies	Our enemy is already defeated (Colossians 2:14-15)
If you bring the right sacrifice, I will forgive you	All sins are forgiven because of one perfect sacrifice (Hebrews 10:11-12)
If you are holy, I will dwell among you	We are the temple of His Spirit. He dwells in us (1 Corinthians 3:16; 6:19)
Some special people are anointed	Everyone is anointed (2 Corinthians 1:21)
Servants	Sons (John 1:12)
A select few are priests and kings	Each believer is a king and a priest at the same time (Royal priesthood) (1 Peter 2:9; Revelation 1:6; 5:10)
Priests need to offer the sacrifices every year	Christ offered Himself once and for all (Hebrews 9:12)
No permission to come to His presence	Come to His presence anytime boldly (Hebrews 4:16)
If you do this, based on works and keeping rules…	Based on faith and belief only (Hebrews 11:6)

RIGHTEOUSNESS IS A FREE GIFT

Again, you did not become a sinner by sinning. We all became sinners because of Adam's transgression. So, it is unfit for God's justice system to punish us. Also, it is unreal for God to demand that we do everything right when He knows it is impossible for fallen humans. So, He decided to forgive our sins and make us righteous in spite of who we are and what we did.

Romans 5:17-19 says, "For if by the one man's offense death reigned through the one, much more those who receive abundance of grace and of the gift of righteousness will reign in life through the One, Jesus Christ. Therefore, as through one man's offense *judgment came* to all men, resulting in condemnation, even so through one Man's righteous act *the free gift came* to all men, resulting in justification of life. For as by one man's disobedience many were made sinners, so also by one Man's obedience many will be made righteous."

176

You do not need to look or act pious in order to receive the free gift because it does not depend on your behavior. It depends solely on what Jesus did on the cross.

SALVATION IS A GIFT

Just like righteousness is a free gift, salvation is a free gift. You do not need to crawl on the floor or climb any hill to be saved; just believe.

> Ephesians 2:8-9 says, "For by grace you have been saved through faith, and that not of yourselves; *it is* the gift of God, not of works, lest anyone should boast."

We are not saved by prayer or baptism but by simple faith in Christ Jesus and what He did for us. That's it.

EVERYTHING ELSE GOD GIVES US IS FREE

God gave everything to Adam for free. Genesis 2:16 says, "And the Lord God commanded the man, saying, 'Of every tree of the garden you may **freely** eat.'"

> Romans 8:32 says, "He who did not spare His own Son, but delivered Him up for us all, how shall He not with Him also **freely give us all things?**"

> 1 Corinthians 2:12 says, "Now we have received, not the spirit of the world, but the Spirit who is from God, that we might know the things that have been **freely given to us by God.**"

> 2 Peter 1:3 says, "As His divine power has given to us all things that *pertain* to life and godliness, through the knowledge of Him who called us by glory and virtue."

There is nothing we could earn from God by our good works or through keeping any law. He has already blessed us with everything we need. It was given to us as a free gift. The only thing we can do is receive it with thanksgiving.

WHEN THERE IS NO LAW, SIN IS NOT IMPUTED

> Romans 5:13 says, "For until the law sin was in the world, but **sin is not imputed when there is no law.**"

If Christ is the end of the law and by grace we are freed from the bondage of sin and the law, then sin is no longer imputed. What does that mean? To impute means to credit something to your account. When God says sin is not imputed, it means that when you commit a sin now, it is not credited to your life; God imputes that to the cross and to the blood of Jesus. God is not walking behind you taking note of every little thing you do wrong so that He can write it down in His book. There was a time like that, but that was during the Old Covenant. Jesus nailed the writing that was against us to the cross and removed it forever (Colossians 2:14).

Grace is not a license to sin, but the power to walk in victory. You will not sin if you walk and live in grace; believe me. But, if you try to keep the law, you will stumble, you will sin, and you will never enjoy the Christian life God has purchased for you on this earth.

I used to be afraid of sin when I was not free from the dominion of sin. I believed that if I sinned, God was going to be mad at me and take away my anointing and that I would lose my calling or salvation. Now I know why most believers are miserable, defeated, and waiting to get out of this earth. They are being tormented by the devil for the sins and mistakes they commit because they are still living under the law. Every time you transgress a law, there is punishment. But, if you are in Christ, you are not under the law and are free from the dominion of sin. There is no transgression or condemnation. The devil has no right to make you feel condemned. You need to rebuke and renounce it any time you feel condemned. You have passed from judgment to life.

If you look at the life of Abraham, the father of our faith, you will learn how to live the Christian life. He was the first person to whom the gospel was preached (Galatians 3:8). He was the first individual who lived under grace. Abraham was not a perfect man. He committed many sins in his life, but we do not see God punishing him for them. Is God partial? Was Abraham God's favorite? No, but he understood something about God that very few people discover in their lifetime.

Abraham saw the day of Jesus on this earth and lived in it, by faith, thousands of years before Jesus' coming (John 8:56). He saw the day when God forgives people's sin not based on their goodness but on His love. He believed it and God accounted that to him for righteousness.

When God told Abraham to leave his country and his father's house, he took his nephew Lot, and his father. That was his first mistake. He lied twice about his wife, but God rescued him (and his wife) anyway. He slept with Hagar, trying to produce the seed of the promise. God did not punish him for it. Why? First of all, he was not under the law. The law was not yet given. Remember, when you are not under the law, sin is not imputed. Secondly, He was living under the grace of

God. God was showing us through Abraham what it means to live in the age of grace. Man has the freedom to live under the law or grace. It is our choice.

What would you do if you did not feel condemned? How different would you feel if you knew that God had forgiven all your sins and that He does not keep a record of wrongs? What would you do if you knew that God loves you unconditionally, not based on your works? Would you have more confidence toward God? Would you share that love with more people? Yes, of course. Or, would you feel like sinning more? I don't think so. You are loved, you are forgiven, and you have victory over sin and the devil. If you truly know you are forgiven, you will love God all the more (Luke 7:46-48). Get up and dance now!

It is not easy to live in the grace of God. Though it is a free gift, we have a natural tendency to go back to the law. As fallen humans we like rules and regulations, we like the feeling of being in control. Remember, man chose the way of good and evil in the beginning, which was a foreshadowing of the law. Adam tried to be like God based on his own merits. Knowingly or unknowingly, we try to make the free gift of God conditional. Though the Israelites were freed from Egyptian slavery, when things did not seem to go the way they thought they should, their first tendency was to go back to Egypt. Though they knew it was slavery, they found out that it was harder to live free trusting in God than living in bondage. As long as we live on this earth, there will be a tendency in us to go back to the law (bondage). We need to examine ourselves to see if we are in faith.

> 2 Corinthians 13:5 says, "Examine yourselves *as to* whether you are in the faith. Test yourselves. Do you not know yourselves, that Jesus Christ is in you?—unless indeed you are disqualified."

We need to grow in the grace of God. "You therefore, beloved, since you know *this* beforehand, beware lest you also fall from your own steadfastness, being led away with the error of the wicked; but **grow in the grace and knowledge of our Lord and Savior Jesus Christ**" (2 Peter 3:17-18). May the Lord help us all.

CHAPTER 11
THE SECOND MOST IMPORTANT DECISION OF YOUR LIFE

CHAPTER 11: THE SECOND MOST IMPORTANT DECISION OF YOUR LIFE

DISCOVERING YOUR PURPOSE - DECIDING WHAT YOU WANT TO DO WITH YOUR LIFE

After you are saved and your relationship with God is in the right place, **the second most important decision is deciding what you want to do with your life: Discovering your purpose.** Everything on this earth was created for a purpose. Next to salvation, discovering your purpose is the greatest discovery of your life. In order to reach full potential, it is best for a person to discover his or her purpose between the ages of 16 and 25. I believe God will communicate His purpose to a person between those ages. Sometimes, God will communicate it earlier than that and, other times, one may discover it later in life.

You can choose God's purpose for your life or you can follow the system of this world, which is to go to school, get a degree, find a job, and retire when you are sixty-five. Wherever I look, I see people who are dissatisfied, frustrated, and wounded. Right Management, a subsidiary of the giant staffing firm Manpower Group, released a survey that says about 81% of people who are working are not happy with their job. They are enduring it because they need a job to survive. Imagine doing something that you do not enjoy for forty hours or more a week. Is there a solution to this dilemma? I believe there is.

When I watch Christian Television and see the faces of believers in some churches, there is no life in their expression. Many look lost, empty, and sad. They look like they are just waiting to die. I asked the Lord, "Why is it? Your people are supposed to be the most joyful, fulfilled, and productive people on this earth. Instead, they look dejected and disappointed."

They got caught up in the rat race of the American Dream to get a piece of the pie, but many did not get the pie. Instead, they missed their purpose and time and now have no motivation for living. No one taught them about their purpose.

183

They believed the lie of the "Dream Big" philosophy and went after riches and fame, but most did not make it.

The "Dream Big" philosophy is a virus (actually, it is a spirit) and, when it attacks your system, you will never be happy again. You will not be content with anything. Instead, anxiety, dissatisfaction, worry, stress, and all sorts of things will manifest in your life. The end result of all these will be physical illness. Not everyone is called to run a business or to be an entrepreneur or to pastor a mega church. You might be called (your purpose) to be a receptionist in a doctor's office or to be a hair stylist. Your goal should be to do that job like no one else did before and be the best receptionist or the best hair stylist in the world. You might be called to work at a Day Care center. Be the best you can be and do an extraordinary job.

Let me tell you my friend, fulfilling your purpose is the most satisfying thing on this earth. It does not need to be something BIG all the time. When you live your purpose that is the "BIGGEST" thing, whatever that may be. It could be being a mother and a wife or a driver of a taxi. Being in God's will is the safest place in the world. We have all heard the slogans, "The American Dream," "Dream big," "Take the limits off," "If you can think it, you can achieve it," "Don't limit yourself." Have you been to one of those seminars? They are nothing but humanism at its best controlled by the spirit that is working in this world. If you follow after that vanity, pain and regret will be the end result. That is the thrust of western civilization.

Let me tell you what God says, "Before you were formed in your mother's womb, I knew you." Our response should be, "To do your will, O God, I come." You are His workmanship, created in Christ Jesus to do a specific task. God never appeared to anyone, in the Bible or in history, and told them to dream big or to take the limits off. If you heard a voice like that, it is not God; it's the devil.

Whenever God called someone to do something, He gave them a specific job that needed to be done a specific way, within a specific boundary. Everything God created has boundaries. When He called Noah, He did not say, "Noah, I want you to dream big, take all the limits off, and make the biggest ark you can think of." No. He gave him the exact measurements, the type of wood to use, the number of windows, and every other detail he needed.

When God called Moses to make the Tabernacle, it was made exactly as God showed him. There are more than sixty chapters of details regarding the Tabernacle and its tools and service. When God sent Jesus, He sent Him to the lost sheep of Israel. He could not just go anywhere He wanted and preach any message just because He was the Son of God. Jesus Himself said, "...The Son can do nothing of Himself, but whatever He sees the Father do, the Son also does in like manner" (John 5:19).

When Jesus called Paul He told him the exact purpose for which He was calling him, to bring the light of salvation to the ends of the earth. The good news is whenever God calls you to do something, it will be different from what others do, or did in the past, and it will always be better than anything that happened before.

When I came to the West and heard the philosophy of the 'unlimited' and the 'supersize', I was really attracted to it at first. America is known as the land of "unlimited opportunities," "unlimited refills," "all you can eat buffets," "you can have it the way you want it," "you can become a millionaire," "mega churches," "supersize." When I first came here, I was enticed by these. I said to myself, "I am going to be the greatest, nothing can stop me, I will have the biggest ministry in the world, there are no boundaries." I quickly found that none of my pants fit me anymore. The 'boundaries' of my body were enlarging in every direction because of the unlimited buffets!

As I said before, everything God created has a specific boundary and a specific purpose. The land and the oceans have their boundaries. The sun was created to rule the day and the moon was created to rule the night. They cannot take their limits off and be whatever they want to be. It does not matter how much you confess or what you do; you cannot have sunlight at night.

Then, I heard the sermons in the church like, "You can have whatever you say." The Bible says, "Whatever you ask the Father in My name will be done." "I can do all things through Jesus Christ who strengthens me." "God will do exceedingly, abundantly more than you can ask or think." I thought this philosophy was in the Bible too, so I began to ask God for big things. I confessed them until I broke my throat.

Later, I found the truth. It says in 1 John 5:14, "Now this is the confidence that we have in Him, that if **we ask anything according to His will**, He hears us." Wow, that opened my eyes! It says, whatever we ask according to His will. Before I ask, I need to discover what His will is for me. Then, within the 'limit' of His will (purpose) for my life, there is no 'limit' for what I can ask Him. He will answer me. Do you understand the difference?

This is what He is saying: Once you discover your purpose, within that purpose you can ask God for anything you want and He will grant your desire. For example, if you are called to run a restaurant, you do it well and people like the food. If you do the groundwork and know what you are doing, you can open another restaurant in a different part of town. That is God's will for you. Then, if you are really good with your business and know how the system works, you can start a franchising deal that will open restaurants all over the country or world. Whatever you do, God wants it to grow and expand.

If you are called to be an Evangelist, and remain faithful to your calling, God will expand your ministry. He said that when we are faithful with a little, He will entrust us with more. It's not doing anything you want when you want.

What is purpose? Purpose is the original intent of something. It is the reason for your creation and existence on this earth. God can communicate your purpose to you at any time. Ideally, He does it between the ages of 16 and 25. The reason He reveals it then is because that is the time people decide which direction they want to go in life. Once you discover your purpose, you need to find the right kind of education to help you fulfill that purpose.

God's method of training to fulfill His purpose is done more outside of a classroom than inside. His Kingdom education works differently than the world's way of education. In the world, if you graduate and receive a certificate, you can apply for a job. In the Kingdom, it does not work that way. I want to share with you in the lines below a little bit about how the Kingdom operates.

THE GOOD NEWS

Before God decided to create you, He first saw a need on this earth and then decided your purpose, which is to meet that need. He designed your physical body and form and prepared everything (resources) it will take for you to fulfill that purpose. Finally, He released your birthplace and time and you were born. That includes every resource you will ever need to do anything He called you to do. There is no instance in the Bible where God called someone to do something but they could not do it because they did not have access to any money. It does not exist. Be encouraged. However big your purpose is; there is provision. Your provision is in your purpose.

I have heard that in third-world countries the two major problems are population and poverty. There is no such thing as a population problem, only a purpose problem. There are millions of people in the third world countries who do not yet know their purpose. There is no such problem as a poverty problem, but there is a productivity problem. People do not produce anything, so they remain poor.

WHY IS PURPOSE IMPORTANT?

Discovering your purpose is important for the following reasons.

1) Your provision is connected to your purpose

Your financial blessing is attached to your purpose. The reason for poverty on this earth is because people do not know their purpose. Many nations think population is their problem, and the reason for poverty. Population is not a problem. People not knowing their purpose is the real problem. Many developed nations do not have enough people to do the work, so they allow people from other nations to migrate to their countries.

2) Your provision is in the place of your purpose

Your purpose is also connected to a place. Once you discover your purpose, you need to know where you are supposed to fulfill that purpose. Each person has a specific place and nation where they are supposed to fulfill their purpose.

3) Purpose gives you freedom

We all like freedom to do what is really important to us. We like to see places and help other people. When you are doing what you were created to do, it frees you up from being a slave to a system or being tied to a mundane schedule.

4) Purpose gives you fulfillment

Nothing else gives you more satisfaction and fulfillment than when you do what you were created to do. Many are not satisfied and feel unfulfilled so they try to find those things in wrong places. Or, they need a hobby to make them happy.

5) Purpose gives you direction and focus

So many people do so many things, but they do not do anything well because they do not have any focus. Every journey has a destination. Your life has a destiny, which is your destination. When you know what you are supposed to do, you can really focus on it. Also, it gives you direction about where to go with your life.

6) Purpose gives you boundaries

Everything God created has a boundary. Jesus said the path to life is narrow and difficult (Matthew 7:14). It means that living dedicated to your purpose, single-heartedly, is not easy. Purpose keeps you undistracted and on a narrow path.

PURPOSE OF MAN

Before you discover your individual purpose, you need to discover the corporate purpose of human beings. Why did God create man? What was in His mind when He thought about creating the human race? Traditionally, I was taught that man was created to worship God. Then, I found that everywhere I went people all over the world are taught the same thing. If I was created to worship God and if worship means singing some songs, then how many hours a day do we worship? Why do only a few people on this earth have the real ability to sing? Did God make a mistake by not giving most people the ability to sing? Or, were we misled?

I began to read the Bible to find out where it says man was created to worship God. To tell you the truth, I could not find it. I found the place where it says everything that has breath praise the Lord. And, everything God created praises Him (Psalm 148). But, that is not their purpose. An apple tree was created to produce apples. The sun was created to rule the day. Birds were created to fly. A cow was created to give milk and meat. This is how they praise him.

BOTH THE OLD AND NEW TESTAMENTS SAY THE SAME ABOUT THE PURPOSE OF MAN

In Genesis 1, God said that we are created to rule on the earth and in Revelation 22:5, we read that we will be reigning on this earth forever and ever. He did not change His mind in between either. In Romans 5:17, we read that we are supposed to reign in life. 2 Timothy 2:12 says that if we endure with Him, we shall reign with Him. The questions to ask are, "How should each of us reign, and "Why, then, should we worship God?"

There has been much teaching about praise and worship, but I never heard anyone teaching about how to reign in this life. There are some who teach that we are created to reign, but I never heard the "how" part until the Holy Spirit revealed it to me from the first chapter of Genesis. I will share that with you in this book. But, before I do that, let me share with you why we worship God.

WHY DO WE WORSHIP?

The greatest commandment in the Bible is to love God. Worship is an expression of our love to God but not the purpose of our creation. Worship is not always singing either. In many places where the word 'worship' is mentioned in the Bible, it has nothing to do with singing. Worship deals with the posture and attitude of our heart. God created millions of angels to worship (sing to) Him and they are doing it in heaven non-stop.

Jesus never asked anyone to sing to Him. He did not come to teach us how to sing. The disciples did not sit around Jesus every morning singing to Him. Neither did Jesus sing songs to the Father while He was on this earth. There is no record of it in the gospels other than after the Passover when they sang a hymn (Matthew 26:30). He was teaching and showing them how to live in His Kingdom. Jesus said at the end of His ministry, "I have glorified You on the earth. I have finished the work which You have given Me to do" (John 17:4). I believe the greatest form of worship is discovering and fulfilling our God-given purpose on this earth.

Another thing I was taught by church tradition was that when we get to heaven we will be worshiping God day and night. We will be flying around like angels and singing Hallelujah for all eternity. So, I thought I'd look for proof of that in the Bible. I began to read the book of Revelation and it says the same thing about man that the book of Genesis says. The first chapter of Genesis says man was created to have dominion (reign) on the earth and the last chapter of Revelation says we will be reigning with Christ forever and ever on the earth.

> "There shall be no night there: They need no lamp nor light of the sun, for the Lord God gives them light. And they shall reign forever and ever" (Revelation 22:5).

Another interesting thing I found in the book of Revelation is the song the living creatures and the twenty-four elders in heaven sing is about us reigning on this earth.

> Revelation 5:8-10 says, "Now when He had taken the scroll, the four living creatures and the twenty-four elders fell down before the Lamb, each having a harp, and golden bowls full of incense, which are the prayers of the saints. And they sang a new song, saying: "You are worthy to take the scroll, and to open its seals; for You were slain, and have redeemed us to God by Your blood out of every tribe and tongue and people and nation, and have made us kings and priests to our God; and **we shall reign on the earth**."

The person from the Bible most people use as an example for worship is David. He wrote songs and danced before the Ark of God. But, have you ever wondered what David's purpose was? What did he do with his life? His purpose was to be a king of Israel. In fact, he was the greatest king of Israel and God said his throne shall endure forever. I do not mind if you worship or dance like David danced, but I also want you to fulfill your purpose like David did. Reign in life!

There are a few verses and incidents in the Bible that people use as an example for worship and to defend the reason for all the lengthy 'so-called' worship that goes on in some churches. Again, I am not against worship, I am all for it, but we need something to praise and shout about before we start singing.

One experience is the story of Jehoshaphat in 2 Chronicles, where he appointed singers to go in front of the army to the battle. But if we study that incident in detail, we see that when the enemy came against him he declared a fast and decided to seek the Lord with all his heart. He prayed a powerful prayer before God and all the people of Israel.

> 2 Chronicles 20:3-4 says, "And Jehoshaphat feared, and set himself to seek the Lord, and proclaimed a fast throughout all Judah. So Judah gathered together to ask *help* from the Lord; and from all the cities of Judah they came to seek the Lord."

As a result of prayer and fasting the Lord told him to send Judah first in the battle against his enemies. How absurd is it that we copy his experience without following the principles he applied before he started singing, and expect the same result? Both the Old and New Testament give more importance to prayer than singing.

Another major incident people use for worship is in the New Testament when Paul and Silas were put in prison. Usually, preachers use that incident and say they sang praises and God sent an earthquake. But, again, if we read the Bible carefully we see that they prayed before they praised God. I believe they prayed so earnestly that when they received the assurance that God was going to answer their prayers they began to sing praises to Him for answering their prayers.

First of all, Paul and Silas were put in prison because they cast a demon out of a girl who had the spirit of divination. The Bible says in Acts 16:16, "Now it happened, as we went to **prayer,** that a certain slave girl possessed with a spirit…" Paul and Silas were going to pray when they met this girl.

> Acts 16:25 says, "But at midnight Paul and Silas **were praying** and singing hymns to God, and the prisoners were listening to them."

We see in the above scriptures that they prayed before they sang. As you know, if two of us agree on earth and ask anything in Jesus' name, He will do it. Paul and Silas prayed in agreement and God answered their prayer. There are three other scriptures people mainly use to support their worship theology. The first is when Jesus said, "If I be lifted up I will draw all men unto me." They use that verse to support worship. This is one of the best examples of using a verse out of context. If you read the verse after, you will see this particular verse has nothing to do with worship. Instead, He was talking about His death.

> John 12:31-33 says, "Now is the judgment of this world; now the ruler of this world will be cast out. And I, if I am lifted up from the earth, will draw all *peoples* to Myself." This He said, signifying by what death He would die.'"

Do we need to lift Jesus up in our songs and worship? Of course we do, but we should not use scriptures out of context to support our limping theology. I pray that churches would remove songs from their praise and worship list that do not lift or praise Jesus or do not mention the name of Jesus, Christ, God, or any of His names.

The second verse people use to support their worship services is when Jesus told the Samaritan woman the Father seeks true worshipers who will worship Him in spirit and in truth.

> John 4:23-24 says, "But the hour is coming, and now is, when the true worshipers will worship the Father in spirit and truth; for the Father is seeking such to worship Him. God *is* Spirit, and those who worship Him must worship in spirit and truth."

We cannot use the above verse and declare the whole human race is created to worship God. I have seen very few people who understand the meaning of the above verse. Here Jesus was explaining to a woman who believed God must be worshiped only on a particular mountain, or a certain place, in a certain way. Jesus was saying the hour is coming, where people would worship the Father from every known place, not just on a mountain or in a particular building.

Worship in the spirit means two things. Old Testament worship did not include the spirit of man, it was an outward (body) worship, dance, shouts, etc. In the New Testament, since our spirit is born again, God wants us to worship Him with our spirit (Romans 1:9; Philippians 3:3). Notice the small "s" used for the word spirit in these verses, which represents our spirit. 1 Corinthians 14:15b says, "I will sing with the spirit, and I will also sing with the understanding."

> Ephesians 5:19-20 says, "Speaking to one another in psalms and hymns and spiritual songs, singing and making melody in your heart to the Lord, giving thanks always for all things to God the Father in the name of our Lord Jesus Christ."

191

The second meaning of that verse is to worship without limit. Now, people can worship God anytime, anywhere. It was not the case in the Old Testament; they were allowed to worship only in the place chosen by God and only at the times appointed by God.

The third is the most popular, where it says our God dwells in the praises of His people. "But thou art holy, O thou that inhabitest the praises of Israel" (KJV). This is an Old Testament concept because He could not dwell in people then, though it has always been His desire. So, there had to be praises all the time to sustain the presence of God among the people. In the New Testament we are the temple of God and He dwells in us permanently (if you are born again) (1 Corinthians 3:16; 6:19; Ephesians 2:21-22; 1 Peter 2:5). Wherever we go God goes with us. Whether we praise or sing, He is always with us. That is why Jesus did not ask anyone to sing to Him. Instead, He wanted them to stop singing and not limit Him to only dwell in their praises but allow Him to live in, and with, them.

WHY DID THE OLD TESTAMENT PUT MORE EMPHASIS ON WORSHIP?

We do not see as many references to praise and worship in the New Testament as we see in the Old Testament. That was not the primary focus of Paul when he wrote letters to the churches. There is a reason for it. The reason we see more references to worship in the Old Testament is because, in that dispensation, God could not dwell in people. They were not redeemed, or born again as we are, by the blood of Jesus. He dwelt (His presence) in a tent (tabernacle), in a temple, or in the praises of His people (Psalm 22:3).

David was a man who loved God and His presence very much. He did not like the idea of the Spirit of God coming and leaving. He wanted something that remained or was constant. He had a revelation, or an idea, to keep the presence of God continually around him. The idea was to implement non-stop praise and worship. So, constant praises and singing were arranged to sustain His presence. Sometimes, when they went to fight a war, they ordained a praise and worship team to precede them in battle. In the New Testament, we are the temple of God, the dwelling place of God. We are the household of God. Because He lives in us, wherever we go He goes with us. We do not need to sing to sustain God in our lives. He lives in us. That is why Paul said to make melody in our hearts, singing to the Lord with our spirit (Ephesians 5:19).

The New Testament gives more importance to prayer than praise. If we spent as much time praying as we spend singing, this world would not be in the shape it is in. It would be different. God's house (us) is supposed to be a house of prayer for all nations (Mark 11:17). Paul exhorted believers to pray (not praise) without ceasing. When the Church discovers her original mission on this earth, then the change and transformation we want to see will begin to happen.

Everyone God used in the Bible was a worshiper, but that was not their purpose. Moses was a deliverer, Joseph was a prime minister, Job was a businessman, Daniel was a statesman, Paul was an apostle, Esther was a queen, Luke was a doctor, etc. What about you?

We are created in the image and likeness of God. The DNA of our spirit is of God. God likes to create and rule. That is His nature. Whatever comes of God bears His nature and attributes. Everything that God created rules over something. He created the sun to rule the day. He created the moon and stars to rule the night (Psalm 136:8-9). Birds rule the sky, animals rule over the forest, and fish rule in the oceans. You and I, created in His image and likeness, are supposed to do the same thing God does.

The Bible says God surrounds us with songs of deliverance (Psalm 32:7). Just because He sings does not mean that is His purpose. He is a King and His Kingdom rules heaven and earth. A kingdom has music, songs, worship, and dance, but that is not the primary function of a kingdom. We are His children. Let's find out our purpose.

The whole creation is waiting for the manifestation of the sons of God to be set free from bondage (Romans 8:19-21). Unfortunately, most sons and daughters of God are busy singing inside a four-walled building that we call church.

CHAPTER 12
6 REASONS GOD CREATED MAN

CHAPTER 12: 6 REASONS GOD CREATED MAN

When I say 'purpose of man,' I mean the human race, which includes both men and women. From the first three chapters of the book of Genesis we understand that God created man for a six-fold purpose. Let us see what the Creator says concerning our purpose.

1) MAN WAS CREATED TO HAVE DOMINION OVER THE EARTH

Genesis 1:26-28 says, "Then God said, "Let Us make man in Our image, according to Our likeness; let them have **dominion** over the fish of the sea, over the birds of the air, and over the cattle, over all the earth and over every creeping thing that creeps on the earth." So God created man in His own image; in the image of God He created him; male and female He created them. Then God **blessed** them, and God said to them, "Be **fruitful** and **multiply**; **fill the earth** and **subdue it**; have **dominion** over the fish of the sea, over the birds of the air, and over every living thing that moves on the earth.""

In the above verses, God the Creator mentions the purpose for creating man. Only the manufacturer knows the purpose of a product. It is very important that we understand this. We all have preconceived notions in our heart and mind that were taught by the religious spirit. So, when we read the above scripture, we assume we know it but, in truth, very few people on this earth fully understand its meaning.

In order to understand our individual purpose, we need to understand why God created the human race. The above verses tell us how and why God created us. We are created in the image and likeness of God to have dominion over the earth. Each of us is created to have dominion over a particular area of life and God has equipped each human being with the capacity and ability to do it. This could be a purpose, vision, product, or calling. He deposited our purpose in us in seed form. When we discover that seed and follow the principles, or the steps he laid out in verse 28, we will prosper.

There is no one born on this earth without that seed. The problem is many have not discovered it yet. We also call the seed "potential," or "talent." Each seed needs a particular environment in order to grow and be fruitful.

Man's eternal purpose is to be a king on this earth. Kings have kingdoms and kingdoms have dominion. But, because of the fall, God added two other dimensions to man's life, which is to be a priest and a prophet. Those two dimensions are temporary until we are redeemed from this present life. Once we are redeemed, we will reign on the new earth once again, forever and ever (Revelation 5:10; 22:5). Adam was a king, and at the end there will only be kings like it was in the beginning.

There is a teaching among the body of Christ that says you are either a king or a priest. People who are in ministry are called priests and people who work in the secular world or run a business are called kings. The New Testament does not advocate this teaching. Christ is a King, Priest, and Prophet at the same time. Each believer is also supposed to function in all of these capacities. Abraham, David, and other Old Testament saints, who lived in the revelation of life in Jesus, functioned in all of these three roles. The Hebrew word for dominion is *Radah* (Strong's Hebrew Lexicon), which means to rule, have dominion, dominate, tread down.

From Genesis to Revelation, it is God's plan to establish His Kingdom on this earth as it is in heaven, and for man to have dominion over the works of His hands. God is a king and we are His children. Whatever He does from Genesis to Revelation has a kingdom flavor. Kings rule over a territory and that territory is called a kingdom. That is why whenever God mentions the position of man, He always put the kingship first and not the priesthood. Please read the following verses and you will see what I am talking about.

Right now everyone in the body of Christ is a king and priest at the same time. When God brought the people of Israel out of Egypt, He said He wanted them to be a kingdom of priests. Exodus 19:6 says, "And you shall be to Me a **kingdom of priests** and a holy nation.' These are the words which you shall speak to the children of Israel."

We see the same thing in the New Testament. 1 Peter 2:9 says, "But you *are* a chosen generation, a **royal priesthood**, a holy nation, His own special people, that you may proclaim the praises of Him who called you out of darkness into His marvelous light."

Revelation 1:5-6 says, "And from Jesus Christ, the faithful witness, the firstborn from the dead, and the ruler over the kings of the earth. To Him who loved us and washed us from our sins in His own blood, and has **made us kings and priests** to His God and Father, to Him *be* glory and dominion forever and ever. Amen."

Revelation 5:10 says, "And have **made us kings and priests** to our God; and we shall reign on the earth."

Revelation 22:5 says, "There will never be night again. They will not need the light of a lamp or the light of the sun, because the Lord God will give them light. And they will rule as **kings** forever and ever" (NCV).

None of the above scriptures say that God made some kings and others priests. Instead, it says He made us kings *and* priests." That includes everyone. Revelation 22 mentions only kings. That is the finale. Amen.

God wants each of us to exercise our royalty first before we move into any other capacity He created us for. Royalty is your identity and when you exercise your kingship (dominion) over an area of life you will have provision for your living.

Jesus is a King, Prophet, and Priest. When He was on this earth He functioned as a Prophet and a Priest and not as a King. But when He comes back the second time, He is coming as a King, not just a King, but as the King of kings.

The enemy knows that if he can keep us busy singing songs inside a building, we will not bother him with the dominion of the earth. We will stay inside our homes and church buildings, singing songs. God did not ask Adam to sing to Him. He did not give Adam a guitar or a violin and tell him to sit in the Garden and sing to him on the seventh day!

Throughout the Bible, God says we are created to reign on this earth. What if a cow stays in its stall and sings all day long? Will it fulfill its purpose? No. A fig tree is created to produce figs. When Jesus saw a fig tree and it did not have any fruit, He cursed it. He did not say, "Well, at least it is praising me, so let it remain fruitless." He said that no one would eat fruit from it ever again (Mark 11:14).

David had a passion for worship, but his primary purpose was to be a king. It is a common song we sing, "When the Spirit of the Lord comes upon my heart I will dance like David danced." Well, let us not only dance like David danced, but reign like he reigned. It is easy to dance, but not so easy to reign. To reign, you need to discover your purpose and master at least one area of life.

Another big deception the enemy has used is to make people believe that God created us to live in heaven. I do not see that anywhere in the book of Genesis or in the book of Revelation. The devil knows if he can keep us ignorant of the fact that the earth belongs to us, then he can freely misuse the whole earth and its resources for his purpose, and man will not bother him. God created man to live on this earth and gave him the earth to manage. We are going to reign with Christ on the new earth, not in heaven. But, only if we learn how to reign in this life will we know how to reign with Him in the next.

2) MAN WAS CREATED TO HAVE A RELATIONSHIP WITH GOD AND WITH EACH OTHER

We are created as sons of God. Our sense of worth and identity come from our relationship with our Heavenly Father. Unfortunately, we try to find our identity from what we do or based on where our body (color) came from. We received our body from our parents, but they did not create our spirit. God did! So our identity comes from Him. Unless our relationship with God is in the right place, nothing else will flourish in our life. We will always feel empty inside, or like something is amiss in our heart.

We were also created to have intimate relationships with each other. Family life is the best example for that. We are always longing for a close and intimate relationship with another person. That is part of our nature. When any of our relationships are not in order, nothing else will work out for our good. The number one commandment in both the Old and New Testaments is to love God with all our heart, soul, and mind, and to love others as we love ourselves (Matthew 22:37-40). Everything in the Kingdom of God flows through relationship.

God looked at everything He created and said, "It is good," except man. When He looked at man (human being) He said, "It is not good that man should be alone..." (Genesis 2:18). He was not referring to a manufacturing defect, but to the social and emotional aspects of man. Man was not created to be alone or "all in one" like some equipment we buy from a store. Both men and women need healthy and close relationships for their well-being and for the fulfillment of their purpose on this earth.

The first task God gave to man, other than tending the garden, was to name the creatures God had created. Every creature had a mate except Adam. He created a help-meet for Adam. Worship was not on God's priority list for man. He wanted man to know that He cares more about his relational need than singing to Him.

He wanted him to know that He cares more about His family life than to hear him sing.

Our greatest blessings and challenges may come through relationships. When God decides to bless you or promote you, He will connect you with a person you never knew before. The enemy also knows that in order to fulfill your purpose God always uses relationships, so he will try to mess up godly relationships through misunderstandings, miscommunication, jealousy, and pride or bring wrong relationships to your life. We need to take seriously the relationships God brings to us.

3) MAN WAS CREATED TO WORK OR ACHIEVE

God recreated the Garden of Eden and put man in it to till it and to keep, or guard, it.

> Genesis 2:15 says, "And Jehovah Elohim took Man, and put him into the garden of Eden, to till it and to guard it" (Darby Bible).

It is interesting to see what God asked Adam to do in the Garden. He was not only to till the Garden but also to guard it. Guard it from what? God knew the devil would try to get back into the Garden and He warned and prepared Adam for it. As it says in Ezekiel, Lucifer was in that Garden once before (Ezekiel 28:13). The Hebrew word used for keep, or guard, is shamar.

> shamar (shaw-mar'); a primitive root; properly, to hedge about (as with thorns), i.e. guard; generally, to protect, attend to, etc.: From which we get our English word *watchman* (Strong's OT 8104).

It was Adam's responsibility to protect the Garden from evil forces entering it. Adam did not pay attention and Satan disguised himself by entering the serpent to come into the Garden under cover. Satan knew he could not directly enter the Garden because Adam was guarding it. He had to find a way to enter the Garden and he found it through the serpent, because the serpent was more cunning than any other creature God had made.

God did warn man by telling him to guard the Garden, take dominion over the earth, and subdue it. Then, God gave him absolute authority over all the creatures on the earth. He gave him dominion, power, glory, and finally, He gave man His Word. Man's only responsibility was to keep and obey that Word. The only Word God gave him to keep was not to eat the fruit of one tree. As long as he obeyed the Word of God, no power on this earth could defeat the man.

What Adam and Eve might not have known was the history of the earth. They stepped into a realm where Lucifer had once ruled, and he was not happy that now man was occupying and ruling his former territory. He became jealous once again and wanted to take over the earth by any means. His desire was to rebuild his kingdom and, for that purpose, he needed to use man as his culprit.

As believers, we need to guard our minds. Our mind is the garden of the Lord and is where He plants the seeds of great ideas, creativity, and invention (2 Corinthians 11:3). Just like Adam, most of us do not guard our mind against the assault of the enemy. Instead of creativity and motivation, negative thoughts dominate. We remain discouraged and as hopeless as the rest of the world. You and I were created to do a specific work. I call it purpose. Adam's purpose was to work in and expand the Garden. The Bible says that we are His workmanship created in Christ Jesus for good works (Ephesians 2:10). Jesus came to do the work His Father gave Him to do. Do you know the work your heavenly Father has given you?

4) MAN WAS CREATED TO EXPAND AND GROW

Whatever we do, we are created to expand and grow. There is a seed of greatness in each of us. As I said earlier, a seed is something that has unlimited potential. God expects you to grow and increase. If He has given you one talent, He is expecting two in return. If He gave you five, He wants ten back. Many live and die without making any significant difference with their life because they do not understand the purpose and principles God established for us.

It is in the heart and spirit of every man to achieve and accomplish something. Though our identity comes from our relationship with our Heavenly Father, there is a part of us that feels good when we do something worthwhile. Man is constantly looking for a new mountain to climb, an ocean to cross, a new horizon to reach, constantly pushing the limits. We do this because we are created in the image and likeness of God, and because His Kingdom has no end (Daniel 4:34b). Whatever He created is constantly expanding and growing. It's been discovered by scientists that our universe is constantly expanding. I was reading on BBC online that there are 17 billion earth-sized planets out there. This is just a recent scientific discovery; it could change tomorrow to a hundred billion.

The Garden of Eden was a comparatively small place on this earth. As man multiplied and increased, they were to expand and make the whole earth like the Garden. God showed them an initial plan, man had to duplicate it and fill the earth. In order to show that we are created for expansion and growth, God made a river from the Garden that flowed to the four corners of the earth. He did not make a lake, a stagnant body of water, but rivers that were full of life and vigor.

We are going to look at the rivers that started from Eden and spread across the land. A river in the Bible always pictures the anointing of God, or life. Jesus said that from our belly rivers of living water would flow (John 7:38). In Psalm 46:4 we read, "There is a river whose streams shall make glad the city of God." Rivers show growth and expansion because most of them flow into an ocean, or into a larger body of water. Keep in mind that before the fall the whole earth was like one continent. The dry land was in one place and the sea in one place. These rivers sprang from Eden and spread across the whole earth.

The name of the first river was Pishon, which in Hebrew means 'increase.' Can you believe God named the first river increase? He wanted them to know what He was expecting of them, which was to increase. God did not start a lake in the Garden to water it; a lake is a stagnant body of water, it does not flow or increase. But a river flows unstoppably over every obstacle that is in its path. It is in the DNA of a river to expand and spread forth. God put that river in you. He did not put a lake or a tank in you; it has to flow, it needs outlets.

The river Pishon encompassed the whole land of Havilah, which means 'circle,' meaning it flows to one region and then it spreads and goes to the next. The Bible says there was gold in Havilah, which is very precious, along with bdellium and onyx stones. There was no mention of any gold in Eden. If they had remained in Eden, they would not have found these precious metals and stones. They had to move and expand to find the new treasures that God had hidden on this earth. As long as you remain in one place, you will not discover the treasures God has deposited for you and in you. It is God's idea for you to expand and grow.

The second river was called Gihon, which means in Hebrew 'bursting forth.' You cannot stop this river; it bursts forth from you. This same meaning was used when Jesus said that out of your belly shall flow rivers of living water. The more you give out; the more God will put into you and you will reach a place of bursting forth. If you keep it for yourself, you will lose it or God will take it and give it to someone who will use it (Matthew 25:14-30).

The third river was called Hiddekel, which in Hebrew means 'rapid.' Whatever God does He does rapidly, because it is not by might nor by power but by the Spirit of the Lord. What we try to make happen in twenty years of effort God can do in one minute. This river goes toward the land of Assyria, which means a 'step.' Sometimes all you need to take is one step in order to step into the destiny God has for you. God is waiting for you to take a step by believing in Him.

The fourth river was called Euphrates, which in Hebrew means 'fruitfulness.' That is what God wants from all of us, fruitfulness. Jesus told us to go and bear fruit. There are different kinds of fruit that we can bear as a Christian. There is the fruit of our body, the fruit of righteousness, the fruit of the spirit; even every invention is a fruit of our imagination.

The breath of God that was in man had all of these qualities. After the fall, man lost that creative ability and succumbed to his own circumstances. He lost the anointing to expand and spread out. They remained in one place and increased in number, but failed to expand the Kingdom of God on this earth.

5) MAN WAS CREATED TO MANIFEST THE GLORY OF GOD

Man is the only visible form of God on this earth. God wanted to work through man so that all who saw him would see God. So, He gave us His glory. When we hear the word 'glory,' it is possible to have a pre-conceived idea. We usually use and hear the word glory in relation to worship or a shining light around our head or smoke appearing on the ceiling of a church building. That is not the only type of glory mentioned in the Bible, it is just one kind. When the Bible says the earth shall be filled with the glory of the Lord, that does not mean the whole earth will be filled with smoke!

> Numbers 14:21 says, "But truly, as I live, all the earth shall be filled with the glory of the LORD."

When Adam sinned, he lost the glory of God. That is why the Bible says *all* have sinned and come short of the glory of God (Romans 3:23). Jesus restored our lost glory. Once again, we are able, by His grace, to manifest God on this earth.

Each of us carries a deposit of God's glory that is waiting to be revealed. In truth, the whole creation is waiting for the manifestation of that glory through you. As children of God, you and I are created to set free a particular aspect of creation from its bondage. Creation was brought under bondage because of Adam's sin (Romans 8:18-22). Now that we are redeemed, it is waiting for us to act like the sons of God on this earth.

> Ephesians 1:18 says, "The eyes of your understanding being enlightened; that you may know what is the hope of his calling, and what are the **riches of the glory of his inheritance in the saints.**"

204

The Bible talks about the seven dimensions of the glory of the Lord we are created to reveal on this earth.

1) MAN'S GLORY - GLORY RELATED TO THE SONS OF GOD

Man was filled and covered with the glory of God in the Garden. That is our inherent glory. It did not come through worship or doing anything, but just being the children of God. When we sinned, we lost the glory of God. Because we lost the glory through sin, we also lost both the capacity to know God and the ability to represent Him.

Jesus came to restore that glory. Those who believe in Him become the children of God and receive His glory. He said in John 17:22, "And the glory which you gave me I have given them..." Through redemption man is restored back to his original glory. The ability to know and represent Him on this earth is given to you and me.

Every son of God must bear the glory of his Father. John 1:14 says, "And the Word became flesh and dwelt among us, and we beheld His glory, the glory as of the only begotten of the Father, full of grace and truth." What was Jesus' glory? He was not walking around with a glow around His head all the time or saying, "Glory," to the Father. The Father sealed Jesus as His Son and He is the express image of His glory. You and I are sealed by God until the day of redemption (John 6:27; 2 Corinthians 1:22; Ephesians 1:13; 4:30).

2) SOLOMON'S GLORY - GLORY RELATED TO OUR WISDOM AND PROSPERITY

> Luke 12:27 says, "Consider the lilies, how they grow: they neither toil nor spin; and yet I say to you, even Solomon in all his **glory** was not arrayed like one of these."

What was Solomon's glory? It was the glory of God manifested through his wisdom and prosperity. He was the wisest and the richest man that has ever lived. God chose him to reveal His wisdom and riches to this world. People (both wealthy and famous) from all over the world came to Jerusalem to see the wisdom and the wealth God gave to Solomon, and his fame reached to the ends of the earth.

Your prosperity is in direct proportion to your wisdom. The wisdom and riches of our God are unsearchable. We are created to manifest these on this earth. Wisdom, riches, and honor go hand in hand. The Bible says that in the right hand of wisdom is long life and in her left hand riches and honor (Proverbs 3:16; 8:21).

205

When we manifest God's wisdom and prosperity, we are manifesting His glory to the world and the rest of creation.

3) MIRACLES – GLORY RELATED TO THE SUPERNATURAL

In the Gospels we read that Jesus manifested His glory through the miracles He did. His first miracle was to turn water into wine. The Bible says, "This beginning of signs Jesus did in Cana of Galilee, and **manifested His glory**; and His disciples believed in Him" (John 2:11).

When Jesus was informed that Lazarus was sick, He told His disciples that the sickness was not unto death but for the glory of God. When He came to raise Lazarus from the tomb, He told Martha that if she believed, she would see the glory of God (John 11:40). When we move in the supernatural power of God, we manifest His glory.

4) CREATION – GLORY RELATED TO OUR WORK

All of creation reveals the glory of God. Psalm 19:1 says, "The heavens declare the glory of God; and the firmament shows His handiwork." Everything God created carries the DNA of God. From the minutest atom to the largest mountain, they all declare the glory, or the revelation, of God. We are supposed to manifest the glory of God through the works we do. Whatever we do should represent our God. Jesus revealed the glory of His Father through the works He did.

God is the most creative Person in the universe. When we look at what He made, we do not see any duplicates. God wants to release the same creativity through His children. It is revealed through the products we make and the things we do. It is often a new thing that no one has ever done before.

The Bible says He has done all things well (Mark 7:37). When Jesus did something, He did it with excellence and people marveled at it. At the end of His life He said, "I have glorified you on the earth. I have finished the work which You have given Me to do" (John 17:4). That should be our testimony, too. We do not glorify God when we walk around saying, "Glory to God," all day long.

When you do something, do it in a way that no one else did it before, even if it is a small task like cleaning your own room. Keep your room clean and in order like no other room and watch what God will do through your life.

Psalm 90:16 says, "Let **Your work** appear to Your servants, and **Your glory** to their children."

There are works that God has prepared just for you to do on this earth. We are His workmanship created in Christ Jesus unto good works (Ephesians 2:10). We are created to manifest God's glory through what we do.

5) WORSHIP - GLORY RELATED TO WORSHIP

We are familiar with this kind of glory. This is the glory we experience when the presence of God manifests while we worship. Many times, the reason we do not experience the glory of God in times of worship is because most of the songs we sing have nothing to do with praising or worshiping God. They are statements we make about what happened to us or what will happen in the future. Praise and worship is what we give to God. It is not the time for asking Him for something or for prayer requests.

I have a humble request to worship leaders. There are many kinds of songs: prayer songs, request songs, statement songs, declaration songs, and nonsense songs. When you come to praise and worship, select songs that give God all the glory, honor, power, and everything that belongs to Him. Make sure the song you are singing is going to Him. These days, the songs are mostly to entertain people and make them happy but have little to do with God.

> 1 Kings 8:10-11 says, "And it came to pass, when the priests came out of the holy *place,* that the cloud filled the house of the LORD, so that the priests could not continue ministering because of the cloud; **for the glory of the LORD filled the house of the LORD.**"

The reason the glory of the Lord filled the temple Solomon built was because of the preparation. They took years to practice, build the temple, and set everything in order. Finally, when the moment came, the glory of the Lord showed up! May the glory of the Lord show up in every true worship service!

6) ETERNAL GLORY – (RESURRECTION GLORY) -WE SHALL BECOME LIKE JESUS

> 1 Corinthians 15:42-43 says, "So also *is* the resurrection of the dead. *The body* is sown in corruption, it is raised in incorruption. It is sown in dishonor, it is raised in glory. It is sown in weakness, it is raised in power."

Paul says the present affliction is nothing compared to the exceeding and eternal weight of glory (2 Corinthians 4:17).

207

Romans 8:18 says, "For I consider that the sufferings of this present time are not worthy *to be compared* with the glory which shall be revealed in us."

1 John 3:2 says, "Beloved, now we are children of God; and it has not yet been revealed what we shall be, but we know that when He is revealed, we shall be like Him, for we shall see Him as He is."

7) MARRIAGE – THE FEMININE AND MASCULINE GLORY OF GOD

1 Corinthians 11:7 says, "For a man indeed ought not to cover his head, since he is the image and glory of God; but woman is the glory of man."

Man reveals the glory of God and, in turn, woman is the glory of man. When a man and woman come together in marriage, they reveal the nature and character of God. Man or woman alone cannot reveal His glory. God is revealed in the Bible as a father as well as a mother.

Trios appear in everything God made. There is heaven, earth, and hell; water can turn to vapor, ice (solid), or liquid. An atom has three particles: protons, neutrons, and electrons. Man has three parts: spirit, soul, and body. Family life is made of father, mother, and children. No wonder the institution of marriage is being attacked on every side; the devil knows that if the man and woman do it right, they will reveal the glory of God on this earth and he hates that!

6) MAN WAS CREATED TO REPRESENT GOD AND HIS KINGDOM ON THE EARTH

We are supposed to manifest God on this earth. We are the ambassadors of His Kingdom, representing Him and His Kingdom on the earth (2 Corinthians 5:20). An ambassador is a person who represents a government in a foreign country. Whatever we do is to represent our God. He wants to work through us and we are the only legal outlet He has on this earth. He created us to demonstrate His nature, purpose, and plans. We are the household and the temple of God (Ephesians 2:19-22).

God does not dwell in a temple or a building (including church buildings) made with hands (Acts 17:24). Unfortunately, many still believe that He does. We need to live with the constant awareness that God wants to reveal His character, power, creativity, love, wisdom, and glory through us to this world.

THE LAST ADAM

The first Adam messed up the plan of God for the rest of humanity, so God decided to send a second Adam. The Bible calls Him the last Adam (1 Cor. 15:45), who is Jesus the Son of God. Adam was a son of God just like Jesus is the Son of God. Jesus did not operate in His divinity while He was on this earth. He is the only example of the perfect man. He came to show us how to live on this earth. He did not come to sing songs to His Father. He exemplified all of the above six purposes for which mankind (except marriage; that is yet to be done) was created. He is our example. He came with a definite purpose.

Sometimes, when we look at Jesus, we see Him only as God. But, in the Gospels, He was living as a human being and called Himself the Son of man. There are many references in the Gospels of Him comparing Himself to us. The best example is in John 21:17, 'Jesus said to her, "Do not cling to Me, for I have not yet ascended to My Father; but go to My brethren and say to them, 'I am ascending to My Father and your Father, and *to* My God and your God.'"'

Jesus also said that if we believe in Him we shall do greater things than He did (John 14:12). No one can do greater things than God, but Jesus was referring to Himself as a human being.

CHAPTER 13
THE PROCESS OF HAVING
DOMINION

CHAPTER 13: THE PROCESS OF HAVING DOMINION

Since we have learned that man was created to have dominion on this earth, we are going to learn how each one of us needs to exercise that dominion. Before I explain the process of dominion, I would like to share with you the methods, or ways, God uses to exercise dominion. We see in the Bible that God uses six major ways to help man exercise his dominion on this earth. Each of us is created to exercise dominion through one or more of those ways.

The six major ways are: 1) Through demonstrating the power of God 2) Through prayer 3) Through a business or product 4) Through wisdom and skill 5) Through government 6) Through demonstrating God's love.

Since this book is not about dominion, I am not going to spend much time explaining each one but I will explain the foundational principles mentioned in the book of Genesis that need to be used regardless of what area you are called to reach. The reason we are not able to reach this world is because we do not know how to exercise our dominion. No one taught us how to reign. The only way most Christians know anything about having dominion is through power and prayer. These are not the only ways God wants us to exercise dominion.

Prayer and love are a necessity for everyone, just like water and air for life. But, there are people that God calls to specialize in them. For instance, Jeremiah, Epaphras, Anna, and Simeon specialized in prayer and in praying for other people and nations. Everyone is commanded to love, but people like the Apostle John specialized in it—he is known as the apostle of love.

If you look at people like Bill Gates or Steve Jobs, or companies like Coca-Cola, Disney World, Toyota, or Sony, they are more influential in the world than the whole Church combined. They came up with products that the world needs or wants. That is one of the ways God wants His children to exercise dominion on this earth.

When we look at people like Mother Theresa, she did not do any miracles or cast out any demons (at least that is not what she is known for). But we read in her story that many people died in her arms. Through her service of love, many experienced love and forgiveness for the first time in their lives. She exercised her dominion through demonstrating God's love to the poor and the hurting. She might have touched more lives around the world than most miracle-working evangelists that we know of. Almost everyone in the world knows who Mother Theresa is. She also won a Noble Peace Prize. Though she passed away, her ministry has branches in 133 countries on the earth and is still growing. We need more people like her in the body of Christ.

People like Joseph, Mordecai, Nehemiah, Daniel, and Esther influenced the governments of their time through prayer and the wisdom of God. Through prayer, Moses, Elisha, and Jeremiah shook up more kings and kingdoms than any army did in the Bible.

People like Solomon and Bezalel demonstrated God's wisdom and wealth through their lives. The Bible says people from all over the known world came to Jerusalem to hear and see Solomon's wisdom. "And men of all nations, from all the kings of the earth who had heard of his wisdom, came to hear the wisdom of Solomon (1 Kings 4:34). That is called exercising dominion. One of the main purposes of the Church is to make known the manifold *wisdom* of God to the principalities and powers (Ephesians 3:10). Instead, we have been trying for a long time to make known the *power* of God to them by pulling them down or by binding them and it is not happening! In the New Testament, women like Tabitha and Lydia, and men like Joseph of Arimathea, were business owners who had products and sold them. They were influencers of culture.

Unfortunately, the body of Christ has been divided into groups based on these six methods while it is God who is working through all people as He wills. At present, people whom God uses to demonstrate His power do not like, or agree with, the people He uses to demonstrate His love or wisdom. They think everyone needs to walk in power as they are. Through power alone we will never reach this world, just as we will not reach the world without it. When we understand the difference and work hand in hand, we will be able to reach this world for Christ. It takes tremendous maturity and the love of Christ to appreciate the difference.

In the Old Testament, God mostly demonstrated His power. What was the result? The majority of the people did not know Him. The People of Israel saw massive demonstrations of His power in Egypt and in the wilderness, but the majority of them died in the wilderness because of unbelief, without fulfilling their destiny. In the New Testament, He chose to demonstrate His love by sending Jesus. This world has never been the same. When we embrace each other instead of dividing, God's Church will impact the world the way He intended.

The table below shows you how God used His people in the six different methods/ways to influence this world with His Kingdom.

	Power	Prayer	Business/ Product	Wisdom/ Skill	Government	Love
Moses	*	*	*	*	*	
Elijah	*	*			*	
David		*	*	*	*	
Samuel		*	*		*	
Solomon			*	*	*	
Elisha	*	*			*	
Bezalel			*	*		
Esther		*.			*	
Mordecai		*			*	
Nehemiah					*	
Daniel		*		*	*	
Joshua		*		*		
Jeremiah		*			*	
Abraham		*	*		*	
Jonah		*			*	
Stephen	*					*
Jesus	*	*	*	*	*	*
John						*
Paul	*	*	*	*	*	*
Joseph of Arimathea			*		*	
Job			*	*		
Tabitha			*			
Mother Theresa						*
Ethiopian Eunuch					*	
Lydia			*			

215

In this chapter, you will learn what to do once you discover your purpose. Unfortunately, among Christians, the religious spirit has created an escapist mentality. We have been taught that we do not belong here and are going to fly away soon. Most churches have secluded themselves and are not making any real difference on this earth. We became one of the most consuming communities; we are supposed to be the most productive people on earth. That is what we see in the Bible. God's children were the best in everything. God wants His children to be productive and He put that in the first chapter of Genesis itself.

> Matthew 13:24-25 says, "Another parable He put forth to them, saying: "The kingdom of heaven is like a man who sowed good seed in his field; but while men slept, his enemy came and sowed tares among the wheat and went his way.""

One of the mysteries of the Kingdom of God is seed. The whole earth functions according to the principle of seed. When God gives you something, He gives it to you in seed form. The reason many people think God did not give them anything is because they do not recognize the seed God has given them. Seeds are usually tiny in nature but, most of the time, we are looking for something big from God.

The problem with most of us is that we have both seeds and weeds in us. Many of us are more aware of our weeds (weaknesses and flesh) than the seeds God has planted in us. Let me tell you the good news, God is more aware of the seed He planted in you than the weeds you are worried about. He did not plant any weeds in you, it is the devil that planted those weeds and Jesus said that everything His Father did not plant will be uprooted. In fact, God created you, your body, and your life in which to deposit that seed. That is the whole purpose.

> Matthew 15:13 says, "But He answered and said, "Every plant which My heavenly Father has not planted will be uprooted."

Throughout history, God used people in spite of their weaknesses or failures (weeds) because of the seed He planted in them. This is so important that I want you to grab this truth with both of your hands, hold onto it, and never lose it! Everything you need in life is in that seed. When you look at someone you might see only the weeds but do not throw that person out; everyone has received a seed from God. Our job is to help them find that seed. The reason the weeds have overgrown the seed is because they failed to recognize the seed and give it the needed attention. I can guarantee you that God will never take back the seed He planted in you.

Your miracle is not with someone else or going to come from somewhere else. **Your miracle is in your seed**. The seed to the miracle you are believing God for is with you right now. That is why whenever God did a material miracle in the Bible, He always used something the people already had.

When Moses cried out to God because of the Red Sea in front of him, God told Him to stretch forth his rod over the sea. He already had the key to the miracle in his hand. When the people of Israel were enslaved in Egypt and cried out to God for deliverance, God sent a fellow Israelite, Moses. When a widow complained to Elisha about her debt, the man of God asked her what she had in her house. She had a jar of oil. That was the seed to her miracle.

The first miracle Jesus did was turning the water into wine. He told the people to fill the jars with water and it became wine. The same principle goes with the five loaves and two fishes. These were all seeds that had unlimited potential when given to God.

Your purpose is hidden in you as a seed. God deposited that in you when He created you. You need to recognize it and develop it as early as possible. Everyone has a purpose. Whether it is small or great, God has put something in you or in your hand that has the ability to multiply and reproduce. When you do that; you will prosper.

Your food is in your seed: When God gave man the seed He said it was for food. The reason many people are hungry and in poverty is because they do not recognize the seed God gave them. Every nation and person has received seeds. There is not a country on this earth that does not have seeds. They do not value the seed God gave to them, so they starve while they are waiting for someone to come and feed them.

> Genesis 1:29 says, "And God said, "See, I have given you every herb *that* yields seed which *is* on the face of all the earth, and every tree whose fruit yields seed; to you it shall be for food.""

The good news is that God gave the seed to every single human on this earth. When I say seed, it does not always mean something that grows on a tree or in a fruit. A seed is anything that has unlimited potential to reproduce its own kind.

Your words are seeds, which determine your future. You will reap the harvest of the seeds that you sow today. The harvest you have today is the result of the seeds you have sown in the past.

Your purpose is a seed: God has hidden the purpose of your life in you in seed form. It needs to be recognized, planted, nurtured, and cultivated. Most of the time, when we eat or cut a fruit or vegetable, we throw out the seeds. Because we do not value them, we think they are unnecessary but, to God, those seeds are the important factor.

Your future is in your seed: The Bible mentions different kinds of seeds. Your children are your seed. Your children are your future. The Bible calls us the seed of Abraham. If you nurture, train, and cultivate your children in the ways of the Lord, you will have a great future and a blessed generation after you.

Your financial miracle is in your seed: The Bible calls money a seed. When you are believing God for a financial miracle, He may not give you the full amount you are believing for. In fact, most of the time He won't. Many people get mad at Him because they think He did not provide for their need. He promised to supply the seed, but we are looking for a harvest. When we sow the seed, He is faithful to produce a harvest.

> 2 Corinthians 9:6-10 says, "But this *I say:* He who sows sparingly will also reap sparingly, and he who sows bountifully will also reap bountifully. *So let* each one *give* as he purposes in his heart, not grudgingly or of necessity; for God loves a cheerful giver. And God *is* able to make all grace abound toward you, that you, always having all sufficiency in all *things,* may have an abundance for every good work. As it is written, "He has dispersed abroad, He has given to the poor; His righteousness endures forever." Now may **He who supplies seed to the sower**, and bread for food, supply and multiply the seed you have *sown* and increase the fruits of your righteousness."

When you sow a financial seed, it is a harvest for someone. In turn, when they sow a seed, it will become a harvest for others. The cycle goes on. You are created to be an answer to someone else's problem. You are not your own. The Bible says you were bought at a price (1 Corinthians 6:20).

Remember the parable of the talents that Jesus shared. A talent was like a seed. If you keep it as it is, it remains the same but, if you plant it or invest it, it will produce a harvest. God has given to each of us seeds according to our ability.

After you recognize the "seed" in you, you need to create the right environment or acquire the necessary education to grow that seed. Not all types of seed grow everywhere. Most of the trees, plants, and fruits that grow in India are not in the United States. Many of the animals and creatures that I see in India are not here either. Each seed requires particular weather and environment. That is why God takes people away from their birthplace to train and develop them. The way God develops us is not the same as the way the world does. His system of education works differently than our regular schools and colleges.

In Genesis 1:26 we read that God said, "Let Us make man in Our image, and according to Our likeness..." Then He said, "Let them have dominion over the fish of the sea..." In creation God said, "Let *us* create." But, in having dominion over the earth, He did not include Himself. He said, "Let *them* have dominion." That means man had total freedom in what he could do on the earth. God was not going to intrude into man's business or freedom of choice.

God created us to have dominion over this earth. There are two applications to this truth. The first is natural and the second is spiritual. The natural application is this: In verse 28, God is explaining how to exercise that dominion over the earth. First of all, He blessed them. Then, He explained the process of obtaining dominion. He said to be **fruitful, multiply, replenish, subdue,** and then have **dominion.** This five-fold process is the key to understanding and fulfilling our purpose. Being fruitful means not only to have children but also to be productive. God wants us to be productive.

That means God deposited at least one seed in each of us (1 John 3:9). That seed needs to grow (be cultivated) and produce fruit. This also means there is a product in each of us that is waiting to be released. That is the key to your prosperity. When you discover your product (purpose), you become an essential part of life on this earth. Thousands, maybe millions, die without ever discovering their product. The reason for the poverty on this earth is because people do not know their purpose.

God put a desire in your heart to do something on this earth. That is a clue to the product that is hidden in you. It could be ministry, an idea, business, invention, ability, song or book writing, music, serving, giving, a talent, etc. There are a variety of ways God wants us to manifest that product to the world.

Once you discover your product (fruit), you need to multiply it. You need to manufacture or to mass-produce it. After you manufacture it, you need to fill (replenish) the earth. That means you need to market that product so others can benefit from it. The next step is to subdue, which means take control or implement a system of operation to manage your business. As a result, you will have dominion over a particular area of life on this earth.

When we think of computers, two names come to our mind: Bill Gates and Steve Jobs. Why? It is because they implemented the above principle and took dominion over the computer business. What if Bill Gates and Steve Jobs sat in their living room and sang, "Amazing Grace, how sweet the sound," all day? Or, "This earth is not my home, I am just passing by...?" They may not be tongue-talking, holy-rolling believers, but they fulfilled their purpose based on the principles that are written in the Bible by taking dominion over a particular area of life. What about you and me?

You are created to take dominion over a particular area or sphere of life. The seed of God in you is waiting to be released. Do not go to the grave with that seed. My prayer to God is to help me die empty. Before I die, I want to release everything to this earth that God put in me. One part of my purpose is to help others identify that seed in them. You need to discover and reproduce that seed to bless humanity. Do not leave the earth before you make your mark in the pages of history, because the whole earth is waiting for the manifestation of the sons of God.

In verse 28 of Genesis 1, God blessed them and explained to them how to have dominion. Once you discover your purpose, you need to fulfill that purpose by applying the following steps. There are five steps to having dominion.

THE PROCESS OF HAVING DOMINION

1) BE FRUITFUL

The first command God gave man was to be fruitful. To have a fruit, you first need a seed. Fruit does not grow on its own: it needs a tree. The tree needs ground and the seed must be planted in that ground. In turn, the tree produces the fruit to disperse the seed. The tree also bears fruit, not for it to enjoy, but for someone else. You are created to be a blessing to someone. God does not explain the whole process when He says something. He will tell you the end-result, but we have to go through the process. There are multiple meanings to the word fruitful. The Hebrew word used for fruitful is *Parah* (Strong's Hebrew Lexicon), which means to bear fruit, be fruitful, branch off, to make fruitful, to show fruitfulness.

The general idea of being fruitful is to have children, which is the fruit of our body. Even for that, there is a process involved. A baby does not just appear out of man. He needs to deposit his seed into a womb and then it takes 9 months for a baby to develop and grow.

Man is a three-part being: spirit, soul, and body. Each of these parts has the ability to produce fruit. When God said to be fruitful, He was not just talking about the fruit of our body (children). He also meant for us to produce fruit in the other two parts. Unfortunately, most people only produce the fruit of their body while the other two areas remain barren; that is why they do not prosper in life. If you keep producing only children and do not produce any other fruit, then you will not have anything to feed your children. That is the reason for poverty in many parts of the world. They produce children but their souls and spirits are barren.

The key to prosperity lies in the fruit of the other two parts of our life, the soul and spirit. At the same time, our soul and spirit cannot function without our body. The fruit of our mind and spirit have to manifest through our body. This fruit is a product. Children are our natural product, the product of our bodies. You also need to bring forth some products from your mind and spirit. Just like God has put seeds in your body that produce children, He also put seeds in your mind and spirit. We need to discover and develop these if we are going to prosper and fulfill our purpose. The Bible talks about different kinds of fruit. I am not talking about fruit we eat here.

A fruit is something that benefits others. When you go to a store you pay money to buy a product (fruit) someone else made. A tree does not eat its fruit. The fruit is there to attract others to the tree. When you bear fruit, it is for someone else. They want to eat or use that fruit and, if it is good, they will compensate you for it. If your fruit (product) feeds or meets the needs of others, they will pay you for meeting that need. Every product you buy from stores is the fruit of someone. It meets your need and you spend your money to have it. That is the secret to prosperity. No fruit; no money.

Just having fruit will not necessarily bring you money. There are other steps involved before you can make any money with your fruit. I will explain this more. Just say, "Father, thank You for making me fruitful in my spirit, soul, and body." The Bible talks about the fruit of each of these areas. Please read the following verses.

FRUIT OF OUR BODY

The children we give birth to are the fruit of our body. We also labor, or work, with our body to produce fruit. This is called the fruit of the land, or fruit of our hands. If we do not work, there will not be any fruit.

> Deuteronomy 7:13 says, "…He will also bless the **fruit** of your womb and the **fruit** of your land…"

> Exodus 23:16 says, "…when you have gathered in the **fruit** of your labors from the field…"

> Proverbs 31:31 says, "Give her of the **fruit** of her hands, and let her own works praise her in the gates."

221

Deuteronomy 28:4 says, "...Blessed shall be the **fruit** of your body..."

FRUIT OF OUR LIPS - WORDS

The words we speak are seeds. Sooner or later, they will bring a harvest into our lives. Our prosperity and health depend on the words of our mouth. The Bible says both life and death are in the power of the tongue.

Proverbs 12:14 says, "A man will be satisfied with good by the **fruit** of his mouth..."

Proverbs 18:20 says, "A man's stomach shall be satisfied from the **fruit** of his mouth; from the produce of his lips he shall be filled."

Isaiah 57:19 says, "...I create the **fruit** of the lips..."

FRUIT OF OUR MIND - SOUL

The first and foremost commandment in the Bible is to love God with all our heart, soul, and mind (Matthew 22:37). How do we love God with our mind? It is not done by just thinking about God all day long, but by using our mind to produce something on this earth. The creativity and innovative nature of God has to manifest through our mind and through what we do. Your prosperity depends on the fruit of your mind and spirit, not necessarily the fruit of your body.

Our soul is made of emotions, imagination, intellect, creativity, will, and memory. The fruit of our mind is our imagination. Every product and invention on this earth is the fruit of someone's imagination (mind). Some minds do not produce anything good because their imagination is constantly evil.

Do you know that you can choose to think what you want? Otherwise, the Bible would not tell us to think, or meditate on, good things. The soil (thoughts) of our mind is the garden of God where He plants the seeds of ideas and innovation for the next generation. We need to train our mind to think good thoughts because every thought has the potential to produce fruit, whether good or evil. Consider every imagination as a seed, which has the potential to grow and reproduce.

Every good and evil deed we ever did began as an imagination, or a thought, in our mind. It is easy to train your mind; all you have to do is speak to yourself. When you recognize a thought that you do not want to think, just speak and say, "I do not want to think that right now, I want to think about this (say something you want to think about)." All of a sudden, you have made a choice for your mind on what to think. Do not become a slave to your thoughts; make your mind your best servant, which will do your bidding. Live from the inside out, not the outside in.

God put the picture of our future in our mind. The mind is not bad and all imaginations are not evil. Our mind is a blessing from God if we use it for the right cause. Fruit of the mind can be ideas, books, songs, drawings, specific knowledge, creativity, inventions, products, speech, etc. Anything that we use our imagination to think, do, build, or work is a fruit of our mind. The Bible says we have the mind of Christ (1 Corinthians 2:16). We should be the most productive people on earth.

The mind of Christ is the most fruitful mind. Everything that was created originated in the mind and the Spirit of Christ. He is the Master Architect of this universe. He put together the stars, planets, and galaxies. He made the oceans and the sandy beaches. He made the mountains and the northern lights. Unfortunately, most Christians do not use their minds to produce anything good. They are always looking for the next demon to bind without knowing the greatest bondage (ignorance) exists between their ears. If unbelievers can come up with the most useful products and transform cultures on this earth, how much more should the children of God? If we become more God-conscious than demon-conscious, we will see more transformation in our lives. If we become more righteousness-conscious than sin-conscious, we will experience the freedom Christ has promised.

> Colossians 1:16 says, "For by Him [Christ] all things were created that are in heaven and that are on earth, visible and invisible, whether thrones or dominions or principalities or powers. All things were created through Him and for Him."

What are we doing with it, Church?

> Proverbs 16:3 says, "Commit your works to the LORD, and your **thoughts** will be established."

> Proverbs 21:5 says, "The **plans** of the diligent lead surely to plenty..."

> Jeremiah 6:19 says, "...The **fruit** of their thoughts..."

People who prosper on this earth are those who put their mind to work. It's been said that most people will not utilize even ten percent of the capacity of their mind in their lifetime. God set a limit and boundary to everything He created; everything, that is, except our mind. He put no limit on our imagination. Through your imagination, you can travel and be at any place for no cost and in no time. Even our spirit is limited and will be until we are resurrected. Whatever man can imagine in his mind, he can accomplish.

> Genesis 11:6 says, "And the Lord said, Behold, the people are one, and they have all one language; and this they begin to do: and now nothing will be restrained from them, which they have **imagined to do**" (KJV).

Most inventions and achievements have come from people that were not born again. That was not the case in the Old Testament. I believe the reason for that is whenever God plans to reveal something new on this earth He puts it in the mind of His children first. He usually does that for more than one person simultaneously and worldwide. Most of His children do not know how to turn an idea into a product. They are busy in church practicing new songs! Then, God takes that idea and gives it to a heathen who knows how to turn an idea into a product. They make it happen and earn billions of dollars with it.

Do you know that you do not need to be a Christian nor speak in tongues to run the largest corporation in the world? Do you know that you do not need to speak in tongues to invent a new product? Do you know that you do not need to go to church to build a spacecraft and go to the moon? Do you know that you do not need to be born again to design and build the tallest building on this earth? Do you know that you do not need to confess the Word or give a tithe to live healthy and long on this earth? Do you know that you can climb Mount Everest and do not have to pray even once? Wow! These are the questions God asked me personally. You do not need to be a Christian to be a successful businessperson, artist, or musician. Just like He asked Job, I was asking God why Christians are not productive and influential. Why doesn't the Church have any voice on any issue that is happening in this country though we say we are the majority?

Many Christians shut off their mind and do not use it to do anything creative. They are always busy with spiritual activities that do not produce any fruit. Monday night prayer, Tuesday morning men's breakfast, Wednesday night mid-week service, Thursday afternoon women's fellowship, Friday cell group, Saturday football practice, and then worship on Sunday again. That is our general routine. God have mercy.

Heathens do not use their spirit to do things; they use their mind. Everything God created works according to a law. Everything we see (and do not see) in the universe and our spirit, soul, and body all work according to laws. The law by which our spirit works is called the law of the Spirit of life (Romans 8:2). The law by which our body works is called the law of sin (Romans 7:23, 25). That is why the Bible says those who follow their body (flesh) will die. The wages of sin is death. The law by which our mind works is called the "law of the mind" or the "law of imagination."

> Romans 7:23 says, "But I see another law in my members, warring against the **law of my mind**, and bringing me into captivity to the law of sin which is in my members."

One difference between rich and poor people is that, generally, the rich are those who put their mind to work and the poor are those who only work with their body. The part of our life we use the least for good is our mind, but it contains the most potential. Those who learn to tap into the capacity of their mind will accomplish extraordinary things in this life.

THE DIFFERENCE BETWEEN RICH AND POOR PEOPLE

The poor use physical strength to make money

The rich use mental strength to make money

The poor work for a salary or wage

The rich work to meet a particular need

The poor do not have specialized knowledge

The rich make money based on specialized knowledge

The poor work for money

The rich make their money work for them

The poor make money to meet needs

The rich make money to meet needs and create wealth

The poor spend everything they earn

The rich budget their spending and save some

The poor ask for money

The rich look for opportunity

The motto of the poor is survival

The motto of the rich is to make a difference

FRUIT OF THE SPIRIT

Our spirit can produce fruit. We are familiar with the fruit of the spirit (love, joy, peace, etc.). We also need to bear a different kind of spiritual fruit: souls. When you bring a person to Christ, they become fruit of your spirit—your spiritual children. The more spiritual children you have, the more blessed you will be.

Galatians 5:22 says, "But the **fruit** of the Spirit is love, joy..."

Proverbs 11:30, "The **fruit** of the righteous is a tree of life, and he who wins souls is wise."

Fruit of the spirit can also be an idea, speech, book, song, or message, etc. when they are received from God instead of our own imagination. But, they all have to come through our mind and body to benefit other people.

FINANCIAL FRUIT

When we sow a financial seed, it produces a harvest. This is also fruit.

Philippians 4:17 says, "Not that I seek the gift, but I seek the **fruit** that abounds to your account."

GOD WANTS US TO BE FRUITFUL IN EVERYTHING

Both the Old and New Testaments tell us to do the same, which is to be fruitful. Jesus explains the method of bearing fruit, which is to dwell in Him.

John 15:5 & 16 says, "I am the vine, you *are* the branches. He who abides in Me, and I in him, bears much fruit; for without Me you can do nothing." "You did not choose Me, but I chose you and appointed you that you should go and bear **fruit**, and that your **fruit** should remain, that whatever you ask the Father in My name He may give you."

Colossians 1:10 says, "That you may walk worthy of the Lord, fully pleasing Him, being **fruitful** in every good work and increasing in the knowledge of God."

Even if you do not sing a song to God for the rest of your life, He will not punish you for it because He knows that is not the reason He created you. But, if you do not bear any fruit, do not fulfill His purpose for your life, and do not multiply the talent

He has given you, beware, you will have nothing but regret at the end. Remember the story of the fig tree that Jesus cursed, and also the parable of the talents.

After we recognize the seeds God planted in our spirit, soul, and body and begin to produce fruit, we need to move on to the next step, which is to multiply.

2) MULTIPLY

The next thing God told man to do was multiply. After we produce fruit, we need to multiply that fruit. That means we need to find a way to mass-produce it. I am not talking about children here. I am talking about the fruit of your mind and spirit. When a person invents a product, he or she goes to a manufacturing company and asks them to reproduce it. The Hebrew word used for multiply is *Rabah* (Strong's Hebrew Lexicon) which means, be or become great, be or become many, be or become much, be or become numerous (of people, animals, or things), to make large, make many, enlarge.

You might be a secretary or a teacher, and might be wondering how you can use this principle at your workplace. You can use this principle in any field, and any place, regardless of your geography and arena. For example, if you are a secretary, be the best secretary and learn everything that is out there about that job. Once you master that field, you write it down and make your own training manual or write a book about it. Then, you find other people whose desire is to be a secretary and offer your training to them. Slowly, you start doing small seminars and become an expert in that field. I want to tell you, it is not easy but, if you put some effort and time into it, you can do it. A lack of knowledge is our first problem. We have to awaken our frozen brain cells and put them to work.

I also want to tell you that this is not for everyone. This is for people who feel they are born to do something more than what they are doing right now, or those who want to take it to the next level. This is for those who believe that there is more to life than what they are experiencing.

When you have an idea, song, book, or anything God puts in your spirit or mind, you need to design it. Make it a product and find a way to multiply it. If they are souls, disciple them and have them reproduce others into the kingdom. After multiplication, we move to the next stage.

3) FILL THE EARTH

To fill the earth means to distribute or market whatever you have produced. Many of us fail to prosper not because we do not have an idea or a product, but because we do not know how to turn an idea into a product. Others have a product but do not know how to distribute it. The more you distribute; the more you prosper.

The Hebrew word for fill the earth is *Male* (Strong's Hebrew Lexicon), which means to fill, be full, fullness, abundance, be accomplished.

The people in the world are smarter in these things than believers in the Church. You need to fill the earth with your product. Companies spend billions of dollars to advertise their products. It does not matter how valuable or beneficial a product is, if you do not advertise it no one will know about it and, as a result, you will not prosper.

Most of the companies out there started very small. They applied the wisdom and principles that are mentioned in the Bible (whether they realized it or not) and became large. Companies like Coca-Cola, Pepsi, McDonald's, and Microsoft filled the earth with their product and they are some of the richest in the world. Once you fill the earth, then you move on to the next stage.

4) SUBDUE

Once you distribute your product, then you take control of that one area you are focusing on with your product. For a long time, Bill Gates subdued the area of computer technology and software all over the world. Subdue means to take authority over something. Do it like no one ever did it before. The Hebrew word for subdue is *Kabash* (Strong's Hebrew Lexicon), which means to subject, subdue, force, keep under, bring into bondage, make subservient.

To subdue something you need power and authority. Your product gives you the power and authority to subdue that area of life. When you subdue, you can take dominion over that area; which is the next step.

5) HAVE DOMINION

When you apply the above four principles to an area of life, the end result will be dominion over that arena of life. You will become a 'king' over it. That is why some people are known to be king of that or king of this, while we talk about their lives. Dominion is the ultimate purpose of God for man. Most people know in their heart that they are created to rule and have dominion but, since the fall when man lost his dominion over the earth, people do not understand the *process* of dominion. Instead, they began to dominate each other.

People who do not have dominion over an area of life through their purpose and product will always try to dominate or control fellow human beings with force because they feel insecure. Others may use their money and power to dominate. We are not created to dominate people but to serve them in love.

THE SPIRITUAL APPLICATION OF DOMINION

There is a second (spiritual) application of Genesis 1:26-28. The Word of God is a two-edged sword. That means everything mentioned in the Bible has a natural application and a spiritual application. If a natural thing is mentioned, it also has a spiritual application; if a spiritual thing is mentioned, it also has a natural application. For example, when the word 'wicked' is mentioned, it represents evil men as well as the devil. When it says a sower went to sow seed, the seed also represents the Word of God. The parables Jesus taught were based on natural stories, but they contain deep spiritual truths.

We see that when God created Adam, He told him to subdue and have dominion over the earth (Genesis 1:26). It is very important to notice that He said to subdue and take dominion over the earth; not people. What was there to subdue and to take dominion over before the fall? You need to subdue something only if there is a rebellion. God repeated the same thing in verses 26 & 28, telling man to have dominion and subdue the earth and all the living creatures that were on it, starting with the fish of the sea, birds of the air, cattle, and every creeping or living thing.

Wow! How could those creatures be any danger to Adam and his existence on this earth? How can birds and fish rebel against man without the help of external spiritual forces? This was before the fall, but there should have been a reason for God to tell Adam to take dominion over those creatures when there had not yet been any rebellion in the animal kingdom.

Before the fall, man and the animal kingdom lived in peace. But, demon spirits were allowed to enter the animal kingdom: fish of the sea, fowl of the air, and the creeping things of the earth. They were never intended to be in any human and that is why we cast demons out of human beings. Man was supposed to keep the animal kingdom subdued, not listen to them.

As a loving Father, He was preparing Adam for a possible assault from the enemy, who would most likely use one of those four mediums. Since Satan and demons are spirit beings, they need a physical body to operate on this earth. There were not allowed to enter Adam and Eve, so they had to use either the fish of the sea, birds of the air, cattle of the earth, or the creeping things. Satan chose the serpent because it was more cunning than any other creature God had made on this earth. Even in our world today, in any culture, creatures from those four categories God told man to subdue are worshiped or considered gods.

229

God wanted Adam to subdue (make submit by force) any rebellion or attempt to usurp his authority. He was to put it out immediately. It was man's duty to keep them where they belonged. Unfortunately, Adam did not do it, but listened to the serpent and willfully disobeyed God.

There is another incident in the New Testament that supports this teaching. When Jesus was casting the demons out of the man of Gadarenes (Mark 5:1-13), there were many demons in this one man. The demons asked Jesus' permission to enter the herd of swine that was feeding nearby. Jesus gave them permission and those demons left the man and entered the pigs, which ran violently over the cliff and into the water, killing them. Why did Jesus give them permission to enter the herd? It was because He knew they had the right to be in animals, but do not have the right to be in human beings.

We also see that when Jesus was fasting for forty days, the Bible says He was with wild beasts (Mark 1:13). Why? What would wild beasts have to do with Jesus' fast? Keep in mind that He is the last Adam who came to take back the dominion of this earth. He had to start from where the first Adam left off, and it was through a beast of the field that Satan first tempted Eve. Jesus gave us authority over serpents and scorpions and over all the power of the enemy.

In any heathen culture (either one that is mentioned in the Bible or in the modern world) where idol worship is active, you will see they always worship animals as gods. In India, people worship all kinds of animals; from rats to snakes, everything is a god. They are not worshiping those animals, but the demons that are in those animals.

KINGDOM EDUCATION

Once you decide what you want to do with your life, you need to get the education that helps you fulfill that purpose. I have seen many precious people go to colleges and universities to earn degrees but, later, they found that they are called to do something entirely different than what they learned in school. They wasted money and their precious time doing that.

Kingdom education is different from worldly education. Kingdom education is focused on developing your God-given seed, talent, and abilities to influence the world. It is focused on your spirit. Another important thing about Kingdom education is that it is all about gaining wisdom. Without wisdom there is no foundation.

In the world today, we see so many "educated people" who have degrees from prestigious universities but lack basic wisdom. They do not even understand the basic difference between humans and animals, male and female. They regard both in the same category. This is because their spirit has not received any education. Their mind has knowledge but they did not acknowledge God, so He gave them up to become reprobate in their minds (Romans 1:28).

When we read the Bible, we see that God founded the earth by wisdom and established the heavens by understanding (Proverbs 3:19). A house also needs to be founded on wisdom and understanding (Proverbs 24:3). When we read about Jesus, we see that He grew in wisdom and stature (Luke 2:52). We do not read that He was enrolled in the Roman school system and was the best student. No. His life was founded on wisdom; even the Pharisees were amazed at His teaching.

The majority of Christians are following the world system but do not even have as much wisdom and understanding as the world about how it operates. When a person is educated, he is a master of that area of study. When you master a talent, ability, skill, profession, subject, or a trade, you become educated in that area. You subdue and take dominion over it. Then, you are ready to rule over that area and have a following.

You do not need to go to a college or university all the time to be educated. Many times those who do are not truly educated because they know a little bit about many things but master nothing. Being educated does not mean you graduate from a university with a certificate! I have seen people who have never been to school but they have mastered an art, or ability, and make a much better living than so-called educated people. Some of the inventors and great entrepreneurs of our time dropped out of school or college, but they became famous because they mastered an area of life like no one else before.

That is Kingdom education. I have seen auto mechanics in India who have never been to school to learn, but they mastered their trade by practicing it and watching others. They joined the workshop as an apprentice and learned the job by doing it. Some of the best hairdressers that I know in India never went to school, not even grade school.

If you study the most famous people on this earth you will find one thing in common, they were all educated but they all did not necessarily graduate from a university. In the spirit and in the natural, they became famous because they mastered one area of knowledge, trade, technology, a talent, an idea, etc. That is what made them famous. Anyone can do it; it's not a secret. People like Moses, Joseph, Martin Luther King Jr., Mahatma Gandhi, Bill Gates, Steve Jobs, and the list goes on.

When we look at the people in the Bible that God used, we see the same pattern in their lives. The anointing gives you the ability to master an area of life. They learned the ways of God, not in a school setting but through life experience. The

Bible says John the Baptist was in the wilderness until he revealed himself to Israel. What was he doing in the wilderness? The Bible says He grew strong in spirit (Luke 1:80). He may not have known arithmetic, but he focused on what he needed to fulfill his purpose and mastered it, which was to become strong in spirit.

The Bible says that John the Baptist was the Elijah that was to come. He came in the spirit of Elijah, but he did not do any miracles or signs like Elijah did (John 10:41). Why not? Usually, we associate Elijah with his miracles (like bringing fire from heaven) and make songs like, "These are the days of Elijah." People who made that song and those who sing it do not understand what they are singing.

The spirit of Elijah manifests differently in each generation. In John, it manifested as a bridge between two dispensations (law and grace). It turned the spiritual tide (atmosphere) of this earth into a new era of grace. He was the forerunner of Jesus Christ. He gave birth to a new season in the Spirit. I believe if his spirit were to manifest today, it would be different than anything we saw in the Bible. May the Lord open our eyes to see what His Spirit is doing today!

HOW TO CREATE MONEY

Do you know you can create money? Money is a medium of exchange, an exchange for something of value. If you can make something that has a value of ten dollars, you created ten dollars. When you exchange that product, idea, information, skill, entertainment, etc. to someone who needs it, they will pay you ten dollars. It can be a product, idea, specialized knowledge, an art, a skill, ability; it could be anything.

You are created to do one or more of the below principles, which will generate financial income to your life. Your purpose will encompass one of those areas.

HAVE A PRODUCT

At any given time we might be using at least ten (the number might vary between men and women) kinds of products made by different companies on our body. We paid money to buy them. In our homes, we use hundreds of products and know that someone made those products, and they made money when we bought it!

You might be a person in whom God has deposited a product. The product does not have to be something like an airplane; it could be as small as a paper clip or a rubber band. Not everyone is created to produce a product so, if you do not have a product, there is no need to worry about it. You may be called to help someone who manufactures products.

There are other roles you can play in the process of making a product, and you might be called to play one of those roles. The first one is a designer. Every product needs a designer to design it. The next role is to be a manufacturer. You could start a company that manufactures products for others. Another is packaging. There are companies that specialize in making packaging materials. The next role is marketing. As I mentioned earlier, a product will do you no good if it is not marketed. Some more are distribution, transportation, and advertising. Or, you could provide raw materials, or any form of services or tools, to any of the above areas. All of the above services generate money and people who do those become blessed financially.

MEET A NEED

The second way money will come to you is when you meet a need. There are needs all around us. In our nation, church, and community there are needs waiting to be met. When you meet a particular need, you will be blessed financially. Food meets the need of hunger. Watches solve a time-telling problem.

SERVE A CAUSE

There are causes that are worth committing your life to. There are so many social and charitable organizations around the world and they all serve a cause. Our ministry has a Vision Center in India where we train orphans and destitute children to discover and fulfill their purpose. It's been one of the best programs we ever did as a ministry, to see children who never had any opportunity going to school, becoming entrepreneurs, learning skills, and becoming everything God created them to be. Everyone who has come to visit has said they have never seen a program like ours anywhere else before.

SOLVE A PROBLEM

You are created to solve a problem. Bill Gates solved a computer problem. Jesus solved the sin problem. Ford solved the automobile problem. Clothes solve the nakedness problem. Whatever grieves your heart and makes you cry; you might be created to solve that problem. Every business out there solves a problem, and people pay money when that problem is solved for them.

ADD VALUE TO OTHERS

When you add value to others through your wisdom, service, teaching, etc. you will in turn, be blessed financially.

EXERCISING YOUR DOMINION

Now that you know your purpose is to have dominion, and know the process of dominion, you need to know where you should execute that dominion. If you do not know what area you are to have dominion over, you will try to dominate other people. If you study the lives of the people in the Bible that God used, or in the present day, they were all used to influence the world with Kingdom power and principles.

The Bible mentions two different worlds. One is the world that God loves and the other we should not love. The Bible says, "God so loved the world..." (John 3:16). The Bible also says, "Do not love the world and the things in the world" (1 John 2:15). The first word 'world' is talking about the people on this earth; the second is the world system through which the kingdom of darkness operates on the earth. The world that we live in is influenced by the spirit world.

The Bible says we are in this world but we are not of this world. There is a world system by which the nations are operating in this present age. Just like different technology needs different operating systems, the earth that we live in is operated by a system called the "world." This present world system that we are living in is made of seven components. They are:

1) Culture

2) Religion

3) Government

4) Economy

5) Education

6) Media & Entertainment

7) Science and Technology

If you take the town, city, or nation that you are living in, it can be divided into these seven components. The kingdom of darkness operates through these seven segments to execute their purpose on this earth and God wants to influence it through His children. They are the seven mountains mentioned in chapter 17 of the book of Revelation.

When God chooses a person, He chooses him or her out of the world and trains them in His Kingdom. Then, He sends them back into the world to influence it (John 15:19; 17:18). He puts something in them that can be used to influence one or more of these segments. One of the main purposes of the Church is to train believers to influence this world with the Kingdom of God.

Below is the chart that shows some of the people who were used by God and in what area they were used.

	Culture	Religion	Government	Economy	Education	Media	Sc. & Tech
Noah	*	*	*	*	*	*	*
Abraham	*	*	*	*			
Joseph			*	*			
Moses		*	*				
Elijah		*	*				
Elisha		*	*				
David			*	*		*	
Abigail				*			
Ruth	*	*		*			
Bezalel							*
Esther	*		*				
Daniel		*	*				*
Paul	*	*	*				
Peter		*	*				
Jesus	*	*	*	*	*	*	*
Jonah	*	*	*				
Solomon			*	*		*	*

ALL OF CREATION IS WAITING FOR THE REVEALING OF THE SONS OF GOD

Romans 8:19 says, "For the earnest expectation of the creation eagerly waits for the revealing of the sons of God."

All of creation was brought under corruption and futility because of the fall of man. It is not directly responsible for the state it is in right now. Everything God created has a purpose: Everything. When man discovers his purpose and begins to exercise his rightful dominion on the earth it will affect the state of the creation around also.

For example, a piece of steel is *redeemed* when it is collected from ore and made into a beam and then used to construct a building, or a plate to make a piece of equipment, or other part to make a tool. Now, that steel has a redeemed purpose and value. Water seems to have no value when you see it in a river, but when you package it in a bottle or make a product with it, like a soft drink, you add value to it and, in turn, you prosper.

In the same way, the whole creation is waiting for the sons of God to declare their redemption and apply the principles of dominion. When each human being discovers their purpose and exercises their dominion, it will affect the entire creation. Thus, the ultimate purpose and plan of God will be fulfilled on this earth and it will be covered with the glory of God.

May the Lord help the Church worldwide to train believers to influence this world for Christ. Just having more Christians in a country does not necessarily change a culture, nor can they influence its future. Starting more churches will not in itself solve the problems in our society. It is when Christians understand how a kingdom operates and administer that to its community based on the principles mentioned above. Then you will see transformation.

Instead, we are waiting for revival. Revival is not the answer. God never asked us to pray for revival. He told us to pray for His Kingdom to come and for His will to be done on earth as it is in heaven. Shall we take at least one minute each day and pray that prayer? America had more revivals than any other country in the world and has more Christians and churches per capita than any other country in the world, but the situation here is going from bad to worse. May the Lord open our eyes to see what is really happening.

CHAPTER 14
10 KEYS TO DISCOVERING YOUR PURPOSE

CHAPTER 14: 10 KEYS TO DISCOVERING YOUR PURPOSE

If God has a purpose *for* us, how does He communicate it *to* us? Since no one can see God, how will we know and hear His voice? God communicates His purpose to us in ways that may not be the same for everyone. He knows what to use for each person because each person is unique. There are ten major methods God uses to communicate His purpose to us. Let's check them out!

1) THE HOLY SPIRIT

Have you ever wished God would send someone to let you know exactly what He wants you to do: maybe an angel, or a stranger, or your pastor, or...anybody? That is exactly what He did. He sent a Person who knows everything to this earth to be our helper and counselor: He is the super-genius Person in all of heaven and earth and His name is Holy Spirit. There is only one Person on this earth that knows the purpose of your existence and that is the Holy Spirit. He is the one who made you. The Bible says in 1 Corinthians 2:11 that no one knows what is in the mind of God except His Spirit. God sent His Spirit to this earth to be with us and in us, in order to guide us into all truth.

1 Corinthians 2:9-12 says, "But as it is written:

> Eye has not seen, nor ear heard, nor have entered into the heart of man the things which God has prepared for those who love Him." But God has revealed *them* to us through His Spirit. For the Spirit searches all things, yes, the deep things of God. For what man knows the things of a man except the spirit of the man which is in him? Even so no one knows the things of God except the Spirit of God. Now we have received, not the spirit of the world, but the Spirit who is from God, that we might know the things that have been freely given to us by God."

The Holy Spirit knows everything about you. Jesus called Him the Helper (John 16:7). Whenever you need help with anything, just ask, "Holy Spirit, please help me," and He will help you. The reason we do not get help is because we do not ask. He will not impose Himself on you to help. He will simply stand beside you until you say something to Him. He will use any of the following to communicate what He finds in the heart of God concerning you.

2) DESIRE

The second key to discovering your purpose is the desire in your heart. God often communicates His purpose through placing a desire in your heart. He usually does that between the ages of sixteen and twenty-five. Ideally, you should discover your purpose during that time and focus the rest of your life on accomplishing that purpose.

Desire is the seed of your destiny. God imprints an indelible desire in your heart that sticks with you for the rest of your life. You need to make sure it is the desire of your heart (spirit) and not just your head or a feeling. There is a difference between these. The desire of your heart will not go away but the desire of your head will change with every new circumstance, or diminish over time. The Bible says to delight in the Lord and He shall fulfill the desire of your heart (Psalm 37:4).

3) GIFTING

What are you good at? Your gifting can be a clue to your purpose. Many people are born with natural talent to do various things and it could be a clue to your destiny. I did not grow up speaking English. I knew only three words in English until I was 18 years old. Then, I went to a Bible college in India. Within three months, God opened my understanding and gave me the English language as a gift. I began to speak and preach in English. God said, "You need this for your future." I did not know at that time what my future would be.

Years went by. I became more fluent preaching in English than in my own native language. God gave me books to write and when He gives me a message, He gives it in English. The reason is that the message God gives is primarily for English-speaking people. I even dream in English. That is a clue to my purpose, though it took me a while to figure that out.

The gifting God gave you naturally by birth, or spiritually when He called you, is a clue to your purpose. Sometimes, God will use your natural gifting to fulfill your spiritual purpose. For example, God might help you start a business to provide for your call. Whatever your purpose is, God will equip you with the right gifts. You just need to trust Him and thank Him for it.

4) PASSION

You may not have an obvious outward gifting, or any special ability, but you have a passion to do or learn something. You need passion if you are serious about fulfilling your purpose. When I was a teenager, I had this passion to learn European languages, like French and German. Every time I saw an ad in the newspaper for learning those languages, I told myself I should go and join that school. But, I never did. I now wish that I had.

Also, make sure your passion is not a "strange passion." I have seen people with a passion for all sorts of things. It may not be the right kind of passion. You can be passionate about crazy things. Passion needs to be based on knowledge and God's purpose for your life.

You may be a woman and think you do not have a passion to do anything big. You may not have a big dream to achieve anything, but your desire and dream is to be a wonderful wife and mother. I want you to know you are perfectly fine. That is God's perfect will for your life so you can be happy about it. Not everyone is created to do the extraordinary, but we are all created to do what we do extraordinarily.

5) WHAT MAKES YOU ANGRY OR SAD?

You were born to solve a problem on this earth. What are the things that you feel need to be changed? What makes you angry? What makes you cry? What bothers you about life on this earth? They are clues to your purpose. After you decide what you want to do, get the right education to help you fulfill your purpose.

Several years ago, I watched a movie about Mahatma Gandhi. He was from India but was working as a lawyer in South Africa. One day, while he was traveling by train, he happened to sit on a seat that was reserved for white people. When the next station came, the people threw him out of the train. He was embarrassed and angry. That experience created in him a passion for his people. During that time, his country was under British rule. He left South Africa and went to India to begin the fight for freedom. Eventually, his non-violent tactics worked and he helped bring freedom to the people of India.

6) THE VOICE OF GOD

God speaks to you directly through His Word or through someone else concerning your purpose. We see that in the Bible. Sometimes, God tells parents about the purpose of their children. Their purpose is so unique that they need an entirely different upbringing than other children. Some examples of this are Samson and John the Baptist (Judges 13:3-5; Luke 1:13-17).

7) CIRCUMSTANCES

Where you were born and your family background can play an important role in discovering and fulfilling your purpose. Sometimes, children take over their parents' business or ministry after their passing. It does not have to be like that all the time. I have also seen children take over ministries and businesses they were not anointed for. God may have someone else in mind but, because of family ties, parents tend to put their children in those positions.

8) YOUR RELATIONSHIPS

Another clue to your purpose is the people you are connected to, and those with whom you get along the best. People with whom you connect easily may not necessarily be the people from your own culture. You get along well with the people of your purpose. God will give you supernatural favor with the people to whom you are assigned. Paul was called to the Gentiles, but his passion was for the people from his culture. He kept going back to them and, each time he did, was rejected and kicked out. When he went to the Gentiles, in most places they welcomed him or had a supernatural breakthrough.

9) PROVISION

Another clue to your purpose is from where your provision is coming. Who or what is God using to provide for you? Your provision is in the place of your purpose. Your purpose is in the place of your provision. God is committed to providing for your purpose. He will always send someone to help you no matter where you are. If there is no human available, He will send a bird or any other means necessary to get you what you need.

10) DREAMS

God may communicate your purpose to you through your dreams. There are multiple examples in the Bible where God did that. We need to be open to however God chooses to communicate His purpose. We cannot dictate to God what to do or how to do it. He is God.

THE ULTIMATE PURPOSE

Here is the ultimate purpose for all of our lives on this earth. You might be a doctor, housewife, mailman, businessman, minister, etc. Whatever your purpose, your ultimate purpose is to reveal Jesus Christ to this world. All of creation is eagerly waiting for the manifestation of the sons of God (Romans 8:19). Each of us is called to be transformed into the image and likeness of the Son of God.

When you read the Bible and study the people God used, whether they were kings, shepherds, statesmen, deliverers, leaders, or men and women of faith, they were all pictures and types of Jesus Christ. Everything that was made that is mentioned in the Bible was made to reveal Christ, the Son of God. All of creation was made to reveal the glory of God.

While on this earth, Jesus said, "I am in the Father and the Father in Me" (John 14:11). In the previous verse He said, "He who has seen Me has seen the Father…" When I read that I said, "Wow!" Jesus came to reveal the Father to us. Jesus was in the Father and the Father was in Jesus, and those who saw Jesus saw the Father. Read the following lines carefully.

Then He said, "And that day [the day the Holy Spirit comes] you will know that I am in My Father, and **you in Me, and I in you**" (John 14:20). A few verses later He said, "If anyone loves Me, he will keep my word; and My Father will love him, and **We will come to him and make Our home with him**" (John 14:23).

If the Father is in Jesus and Jesus is in the Father and, if those who see Jesus have seen the Father; then, if Jesus is in us and we are in Jesus, those who see us should see Jesus - not us. I hope you understand what I am saying.

If the world is to believe the Father sent Jesus to this earth, this needs to happen. It already happened, but the Church needs to receive and walk in that revelation.

> John 17:21 says, "That they all may be one, as **You**, Father, are in Me, and I in **You**; that they also may be one in Us, that the world may believe that **You sent** Me."

> John 20:21, "So Jesus said to them again, "Peace to you! As the Father has **sent** Me, I also send you."

He said this to His disciples, but for what purpose? I believe it was to reveal Jesus. Jesus was sent to reveal the Father and we are sent to reveal Jesus.

The Apostle Paul wrote, "If anyone is in Christ…" In another place he said, "Christ in us the hope of glory" (Colossians 1:27). If we are in Christ, and Christ is in us, those who see us should only see Jesus. We need to think like that, only then will our actions change. Most are more conscious of their old man (old self before they were saved) than their born-again spirit man and the new nature they have received. Put off the old man with all its traits, and put on the new man created in Christ Jesus. Say this out loud, "I put off the old man I received through natural birth, and I put on the new man created in Christ Jesus."

As we learned earlier in this book, when we are born again the scriptures say we are one spirit, one mind (soul), and one flesh (body), with Jesus. Do you see how we have been cheated by the devil and by the religious spirit in the Church? We have to shake off our pathetic look and poverty spirit and believe and act what the Word says about us. We were not saved just to make it to heaven. We have been saved to the uttermost; that means everything is saved. The Father is in us, Jesus is in us and we are in Jesus, and the Holy Spirit is in us and upon us. What else does God have to do for us? My God, please open our eyes to see the truth.

You might have heard the saying, "The only Jesus some people will see is us." That is a true statement; it is the essence of all Christianity and all of the other 'Christian' things we do. Whatever your purpose is and whatever you are called to do, the ultimate purpose is to reveal Jesus to those around you. If they do not see Jesus, we failed in our mission.

If you are called to be a businessman, athlete, entertainer, hairdresser, pastor, housewife, mother, or a construction worker, you need to reveal Jesus in that arena. There is an aspect of Jesus that can be revealed through every profession on this earth. When I say, 'reveal Jesus,' I do not mean saying "Hallelujah" and "Praise the Lord" to everyone you see or to all your customers. No. I mention a quote by Francis of Assisi in my books. He said, "Preach the Gospel at all times and when necessary use words."

Neither is it preaching 'hell and brimstone' to everyone you see and to all your friends. No. It is being the light and salt of the earth. The reason God created you is to manifest His glory. All of creation manifests His glory, but each is different in their glory, as Paul says in 1 Corinthians 15.

At the end of His earthly ministry, Jesus said, "I have glorified You on the earth. I have finished the work which you have given me to do" (John 17:4). That is the way we manifest His glory, when we do with excellence the work God gave us to do on this earth.

Once you discover your purpose, the next thing to do in order to fulfill your purpose is to recognize God's timing for that purpose. This is vital and will save you from a lot of headaches and unnecessary loss. I do not have enough room to explain all that in this book. Please get a copy of my book, "*Recognizing God's Timing For Your Life.*"

YOUR PURPOSE IS SEASONAL

As you begin to discover and walk in your purpose, you need to understand that your purpose is seasonal. That means you may not be doing the same thing all your life. What does that mean? When you study the people God used, you will see that God had a different purpose for each season of their lives. Each of those seasons worked its way to the next and what they did or learned in their previous season opened the door for what was to come.

Moses fed his father-in-law's sheep for forty years before he went to Egypt as a deliverer. Mahatma Gandhi was a lawyer in South Africa before he went back to India to protest the British. Jesus was a carpenter before He started His public ministry. The apostles were fishermen before being called by Jesus. Each of those seasons was a part of their purpose and played a major role in fulfilling their ultimate purpose.

One day I was talking to one of my spiritual sons from the Vision Center in India and he told me that he had a 'big' problem and wanted to talk to me about it. He sounded worried and sad and I asked him what was the matter. He said he did not know what to do with his life. We emphasize discovering their purpose to our children at the Vision Center from a very young age, and developing various skills. The reason he was confused and worried was because he did not know the ultimate purpose of his life. He is only 14 years old.

I asked him what are the opportunities he has right now for learning. So, he began to list them one by one. He said he has the opportunity to learn different musical instruments; he is learning violin and guitar, and he is one of our worship leaders. He goes to school. He speaks the English language, which he did not know before and the list went on. I said, "Wow!" You do not need to worry about your ultimate purpose now. What you do need to focus on right now is maximizing the opportunities God has given you and when the right time comes, He will use what you have learned to open the right door or to show you what your ultimate purpose is.

I feel that is the story of many in the body of Christ. Everyone is waiting for the 'big bang' or the 'big door' to open, while opportunities are passing them by daily. If they had recognized and taken advantage of them, God would have used what they knew to open the big door they had been waiting for all their life.

David was a shepherd boy, but while he was feeding the sheep he was not sleeping under a tree all day long. He focused on mastering two other skills that God used later in his life to open doors that no man could open, to fulfill his destiny. He developed the ability to shoot a stone with a sling and hit any target.

Secondly, he learned how to play the harp and compose music. I believe there were other older shepherds that he came in contact with from whom he learned those skills. He was not sitting in a cave and asking God to open a window in heaven and pour out some blessings. When he heard that a Philistine giant was challenging the army of God, he used what he knew to kill that giant. This opened a door for him to meet the king and eventually work for him. You might have heard the saying, "Success is preparation meeting opportunity."

Ephesians 5:15-16 says, "So be careful how you live. Don't live like fools, but like those who are wise. Make the most of every opportunity in these evil days" (NLT).

CHAPTER 15
THE THIRD MOST
IMPORTANT DECISION OF
YOUR LIFE

CHAPTER 15: THE THIRD MOST IMPORTANT DECISION OF YOUR LIFE

CHOOSING YOUR LIFE PARTNER - YOUR MARRIAGE

After you discover your purpose and get established, **the third most important decision is choosing your life partner.** How do you know if you are ready for marriage? You should have already made the two previous decisions in your life. Marriage may not be for everyone. There are some people God calls to lead a single life for His Kingdom, but the majority of the people on this earth get married. If you are someone who does not want to be married, or has received a special gift from God to remain single, you can still read this and teach others about it. Marriage is an honorable thing for all.

In my personal opinion about 98% of people get married for the wrong reason. Nearly 60% of marriages in the United States end in divorce. Another 25% have spouses living together but leading separate lives; there is no 'family life.' Another 10% are hanging in there enduring each other instead of enjoying each other. Only 5% have any kind of normal married life. Something has gone terribly wrong. It is an epidemic that is destroying the very foundation of our society and culture.

Because of the pain and the turmoil involved with most marriages, we are living in a society where people are losing respect for marriage, and they are looking for alternative lifestyles or want to redefine marriage. Marriage is not working not because it is not a God idea, but because we do not know how God instituted it. Most people think about love, sex, money, and prestige when it comes to marriage, but only a few have any idea about God's original design for marriage. When we do it in God's way and follow the manual He made for it, there is no greater blessing than being married.

Many of our children are growing up with a single parent or no parent at all. Starting a care group for single moms or opening a food pantry (though necessary) is not going to solve the epidemic that is going on around us. We have to deal with the root. Seven out of ten male and female teens are sexually active. Ladies and gentlemen, we have an issue that needs a solution. We need to tell the truth. We cannot keep ignoring these problems and expect them to solve themselves. Things are going from bad to worse. Everyone knows there is a problem, but only a very few know what to do about it.

It is not funny that people prepare and train for years to run in a race that lasts less than five minutes. They change their whole lifestyle to be fit enough to run in that race. Marriage is a lifelong race, but most people get into it with very little or no preparation at all. For some unknown reason, people keep making the same mistakes though they see heart-broken people all around.

There is a direct assignment from hell against family life and marriage on this earth. If you are married, you know what I am talking about.

If the body of Christ is going to make a difference on this earth, we need to start where God started. God began human life on this earth with a family, not a nation. When the family life is fixed and brought to God's order and original design, I believe 98% of the problems we have in the world and in our society will disappear automatically. If we trace the root of most problems, we will find them connected to a dysfunction in the family.

Instead of taking care of the root of the problem, many are waiting for a revival. God did not start life on this earth with a revival. The reason we are looking for a revival is because we are still not ready to accept responsibility and make a course correction. We want someone else to fix our problem. We keep doing the same thing thinking someday a different result will appear from the blue sky. If anything is messed up that is ordained by God, then it is family life.

We have a generation of men and women who do not know who they are or their specific role in life. That is why a man is looking to marry another man and a woman does not want to be a wife and a mother anymore. Everyone is fighting for equality, independence, and dominance. We do not have a drug, gun, rape, gay, morning-after pill, teen-age pregnancy, human trafficking, prostitution, crime, or a gang problem. These all stem from a family life that is out of order. Family is the basic and foundational unit of life on this earth. If the foundation is not in order, then nothing else will be in order.

We say the problem began when prayer was taken out of our schools. Let me tell you the truth, prayer was taken out of our family life way before it was taken out of our schools. If it were important in the family, it would have stayed important in our schools.

Our prisons will be empty if our family life is in order. It is not the responsibility of a government agency, non-profit organization, or the educational system to fix our family or change it. There is only one agency that God put on this earth to fix the problem, that is the CHURCH, the CHURCH, the CHURCH! But, the Church lost her "voice" and relevancy on any issue that is in society because many thought we were put on this earth to sing or to fly away.

The body of Christ has been employing an ostrich mentality for too long; burying our head in the sand pretending no one sees us. People do not come to church because they do not like the Church. Believe it or not, that is a fact. It does not matter how nicely we sing or how much money we put into our latest Easter or Christmas production. When most people think of 'church', what comes to mind is not a good picture. Who is to blame? The devil? No, we have to take responsibility for what we did with the Church. We are the Church that people see and interact with. When the people in the world look at us, we have the same problems that they do, so why should they be interested in coming to church?

I remember hearing a story about the dodo birds, which are now extinct. These birds could not fly but flocked together in large numbers and marched like an army. They believed they were superior to other creatures; thinking their way of life was better than other animals of their time. The reason for their extinction is also said to be the lack of basic intelligence to notice their surroundings when they marched. If one fell off a cliff, then others also did the same thing—falling to their death. Let's not be like dodo birds with our lives.

The Bible calls us sheep. There are good and bad things we can learn from sheep. I would like to quote something I found online. "Sheep have a strong instinct to follow the sheep in front of them. When one sheep decides to go somewhere, the rest of the flock usually follows, even if it is not a good "decision." For example, sheep will follow each other to slaughter. If one sheep jumps off a cliff, the others are likely to follow. Even from birth, lambs are conditioned to follow the older members of the flock. This instinct is "hard-wired" into sheep. It's not something they "think" about.

There is a certain strain of sheep in Iceland known as leader sheep. Leader sheep are highly intelligent animals that have the ability and instinct to lead a flock home during difficult conditions. They have an exceptional ability to sense danger. There are many stories in Iceland of leader sheep saving many lives during the fall roundups when blizzards threatened shepherds and flocks alike" (source: Sheep 101.info). Let us be the leader sheep for our future generations.

If marriage is a blessing from the Lord and is ordained by Him, what are the things we should take into consideration before we say, "I do"? If marriage is a life-long race then how should we prepare for it? Following are some guidelines that would help someone who is planning to get married.

WHAT YOU NEED TO LOOK FOR WHEN YOU CHOOSE YOUR LIFE PARTNER

1) HE OR SHE SHOULD COMPLEMENT YOUR PURPOSE

When you are considering marrying someone, you need to look for someone who will complement your purpose. This is where most people make a mistake and why many marriages fail. First of all, most do not know their purpose. Some others, though they know their purpose, make mistakes by marrying someone based on mere physical attraction but who does not want anything to do with their spouse's purpose; so war begins at home. Again, you need to follow God's order as I mentioned earlier in this book. I cannot emphasize that enough. First, focus on your relationship with God. Next, discover your purpose. Then, choose your mate who will support and complement that purpose. What usually happens with people is they see a 'body,' then jump on each other like a lion on its prey.

We are living in an upside-down world. I did not know this truth either when I made all these major decisions. But, because of His grace, from a very young age my desire has been to do His will and obey Him to the best of my ability. By His grace, God did these things in my life in this order. When I was sixteen years old, I gave my life to Jesus. When I was eighteen, I left my home to go to a seminary where I discovered my purpose, which was to be in the ministry. Again, you do not need to go to a seminary to discover your purpose. As I mentioned earlier in Keys to Discovering your Purpose, that was a desire in my heart to go to a seminary. Jesus did not appear in the sky, no angel came to me in a dream, and I did not hear any audible voice of God speaking to me.

Looking back at it now, I know God began speaking to my heart about it when I was twelve years old. That time I did not know it was God speaking to me. Based on that godly desire in my heart, I took a step and the rest is history. Then, when I was twenty-five years old, God brought my wife into my life. Though things happened in God's order, the process was not smooth and easy.

If you have made mistakes in your life and you did not even know Jesus when you made all these decisions, do not worry; there is hope. Once you give your life to Jesus and everything that happened in your life, He is the Master Craftsman and knows how to carve a beautiful piece of art or a picture from a shamble or from the broken pieces of your life. He gives beauty for ashes and works all things together for our good. But I also want to tell you this; unless you do two things, it will not happen. First, He wants you to cooperate with Him and, second, do not let the belief system that was formed in you based on your past experiences stop you.

I have seen married couples that seem as if one is from the South Pole and the other is from the North Pole. I wonder how they got together. What happened to them? Then, I see people who have a call on their life, married to a person that is not even saved yet. I see some others who are called to travel overseas (missions) married to a person who has never wanted to venture out of their hometown and cannot live without the coffee and chocolate they are used to for even a day. When I see that I say, "Lord, have mercy!" This world needs help.

Don't stop reading this book now if you are in that situation, there is a solution. Please keep reading. Divorce is not the answer, I can tell you that right now.

2) THE WOMAN YOU CHOOSE SHOULD BE WILLING TO HELP YOU FULFILL YOUR PURPOSE

Let me tell you ladies, with all respect and love, this might be revolutionary and may be against the cultural norm, but I can tell you it's not against the Word. God took you out of the man; you have something he needs. It does not matter how independent you are, which modern utopian culture you are living in, or what the current trend is about women and marriage. The Manufacturer did not change His manual because our cultures and times have changed. Unless we follow God's plan, life will not work.

One of the reasons for the epidemic rate of divorce in the Western culture is that there are two heads in the house. It can't work. Anything with two heads is a monster. Most people use the verse from Galatians 3:28 to support their argument saying, "In Christ, there is no male or female, we are all equal." That verse is talking about salvation, not about marriage. When it comes to receiving salvation through Christ, there is no difference between a Jew, Gentile, male, or female. We are all equal and we are in the same boat (Romans 10:12; Galatians 3:28). Imagine a country, a company, or an organization with two heads having equal position and power in everything they do. It will not exist for long.

We are created differently for different purposes and tasks. Because of the abuse, neglect, and domination by men, women rebelled and came up with the idea that they are the same as men. We all have the same spirit (the human spirit). Even in the Trinity there are different roles. They are "equal," but they do not do the same thing.

There is definitely a difference between a Jew and Gentile. Paul talks about that in the book of Romans 9:4-5. The covenant, promises, scriptures, and even Jesus were all given to the Jews first and came through the Jews. God decided to share that with the Gentiles and brought them together as one in Christ Jesus. Even in eternity there will be differences between a Jew and a Gentile; we read that in the book of Revelation. Now, if either is to be saved, there is only one way to the Father—Jesus. None of the Gentiles get to sit on twelve thrones in heaven, only the Jews (the original apostles) (Matthew 19:28).

Woman is designed to help man fulfill his purpose. Man was made to love, provide for, and protect the woman. Man, you need the woman God put in your life. There is something in her that you need. Maybe the reason for the challenges you are facing is because you are not listening to the woman God has put in your life. You need to love and honor her. That does not mean a woman cannot work, or do things on her own. She can be the governor of a state, or even the president of a country. That does not change the role God has designed for you.

When Jesus was questioned about marriage and divorce, He referred back to how it was in the beginning (Matthew 19:8). That means how it originated in the Garden is the protocol for marriage. If marriage is to work on this earth, we need to find out how it began and how God intended it. God never intended for any marriage to end in divorce. That is not His will. If He started it, He knows how it needs to be handled and what the solution is if a problem arises.

God did not create Eve to live an independent life. He did not form her from the dust, neither did He breathe into her. He didn't tell her a word about anything, like He did to Adam. If He did, we could say that man and woman were created equally, with equal strength, purpose, and roles. He said, "I will make him a helper comparable to him" (Genesis 2:18) then took her out of Adam and brought her to him. He did not create woman to shop as some may think or believe. If it was so, He would have made a shopping mall just for her like the Garden He made for Adam, and would have taken her there and told Adam to go and pay for what she bought!! Instead, He brought her to the Garden to be with her husband.

The Garden is a place of work; it takes a lot of effort and work to take care of a garden. Trees and plants need to be cultivated and nurtured for them to produce the intended fruit. Adam was given the dominion over the earth and Eve was brought to help him do that.

Spiritually, men and women are equal. There is no male spirit or female spirit; the same spirit that was in Adam went into the woman. Even today, men and women are spiritually equal. The same Holy Spirit that is upon the man is upon

254

the woman. I am talking about God's order here. The life that was in Adam gave life to Eve. Now, it was his responsibility to tell her everything God told him. Her life was connected to his purpose.

Whatever he told her became her life and reality. He showed her around the Garden, told her about the fruit and the tree. It was to Adam that God gave dominion. When Eve ate the fruit, her eyes did not open. If they had, Adam would not have eaten it. It was when *he* ate the fruit that both of their eyes simultaneously opened, because they were one. I am sharing what is mentioned in the manual, this is not just my personal opinion.

When Paul wrote about the relationship between husbands and wives, he compared it to the relationship Christ has with the Church. He wrote:

> "Wives, submit to your own husbands, as to the Lord. For the husband is head of the wife, as also Christ is head of the church; and He is the Savior of the body. Therefore, just as the church is subject to Christ, so *let* the wives *be* to their own husbands in everything.
>
> Husbands, love your wives, just as Christ also loved the church and gave Himself for her, that He might sanctify and cleanse her with the washing of water by the word, that He might present her to Himself a glorious church, not having spot or wrinkle or any such thing, but that she should be holy and without blemish. So husbands ought to love their own wives as their own bodies; he who loves his wife loves himself. For no one ever hated his own flesh, but nourishes and cherishes it, just as the Lord *does* the church. For we are members of His body, of His flesh and of His bones.
>
> For this reason a man shall leave his father and mother and be joined to his wife, and the two shall become one flesh." This is a great mystery, but I speak concerning Christ and the church. Nevertheless let each one of you in particular so love his own wife as himself, and let the wife *see* that she respects *her* husband" (Ephesians 5:22-33).

In some things, Christ and the Church are equal. We are seated with Him, we have received the same Spirit, we have authority through Him, and we are of His flesh and of His bones. Concerning other things, we are not equal with Christ. We are adopted as sons and Jesus is the only begotten of the Father. He is the creator and sustainer of all things. He is the head of the Church, and we are the body. He died on the cross for us. He is the second Person of the Godhead. He is the Alpha and Omega, the beginning and the end. He is the King of kings and the Lord of lords. Though we have the same Spirit as He does, our roles are different. This is the same with man and woman. Though we have received the same spirit, our roles are different in life. God made it that way, and no one can change it.

3) THE MAN YOU CHOOSE SHOULD BE WILLING TO CULTIVATE YOU

The reason God did not tell Eve about anything when he made her is because it was man's responsibility to cultivate her and help her become everything God created her to be. Let me tell you men, if you are looking for a perfect woman who has all the qualities you need, you will remain single for your lifetime. The woman God brings to you has everything you need. Some qualities might be in her as a seed, which you need to cultivate. Let me tell you ladies as well, if you think you have got it all together, you are in error. Everyone is looking for the Proverbs 31 woman.

Proverbs 31:10 says, "Who can find a virtuous wife [not woman]? For her worth *is* far above rubies."

It is not easy to find a virtuous wife. They are very rare and are more costly than rubies. Only a few have discovered the secret behind the virtuous wife in Proverbs 31: It was her husband. If you study that chapter, you will see that her husband is mentioned three times. There are three qualities of the husband that has a virtuous wife. I want to share them with you.

Proverbs 31:11 says, "The heart of her husband safely trusts her; so **he will have no lack of gain**."

The heart of her husband safely trusts her. This means a wise husband will trust his wife and will give some room for her to make mistakes, because he knows she is not perfect as he is not perfect. And, if he is smart with her in the beginning, then at the end he will have no lack of gain. Many husbands are like the man who owned the golden goose. They do not want to invest anything in the life of their wife, but they expect her to lay golden eggs every day. Sometimes, they want it all in one day. God has hidden some gold in your wife. As you know, gold is not easy to find. You may have to dig out a lot of dirt before you can find an ounce of gold. So, do not throw her out because you did not find the gold in a year or two. Notice the above verse that says, "He will have no lack of gain." It is in future tense. It does not say, "He has no lack of gain."

256

We need to love our wives as Christ loves the Church. What makes the Church special is her relationship with Jesus. Without Jesus, the Church has no life. It does not matter how expensive the building or the equipment. It is the same in a marriage relationship. He allows the Church to err and make plenty of mistakes because He knows that, at the end, He is going to have a glorious Church that has no spot or wrinkle. A spot refers to the mistakes of yesterday. A spot comes on a cloth when something falls on it but, though you wash it, it does not come out. A wrinkle means wear that comes by use. When you use a dry-cleaned cloth, after an hour there will be wrinkles in it. Each day we need to forget what happened on the previous day (the spots and wrinkles) and have a fresh look at life and each other.

> Proverbs 31:23 says, "**Her husband is known in the gates**, when he sits among the elders of the land."

Her husband is not just any guy. He is a leader and a well-known person in the gates. In the old times, gates meant the seat of government where decisions were made for the citizens and the community. I am not saying every man needs to be part of the government to marry someone. This refers to his character and quality. Not just anyone could sit at the gate; it was reserved for the wise and the prominent. They are part of the *ecclesia*, the called-out ones. It is almost like being a king.

I was thinking all this time that he became famous because of her. The Holy Spirit told me, "No, she is who she is because of him," just like we (the Church) are what we are because of Jesus. If your wife is not any better now than before she was married, that means, men, you are not doing your job. Let me be honest with you, I did not know this truth when I got married. So, don't think that I was born with this kind of revelation. It took me a long time. I am just beginning to practice it, so you have hope.

> Proverbs 31:28 says, "Her children rise up and call her blessed; her husband *also,* and **he praises her**."

The above verse says her children call her blessed. If the children are to call their mother blessed, they might need to hear someone else calling her that. I believe it is their father, her husband. Husbands, when was the last time you really blessed your wife? I know you bless her when you pray, that is not what I am talking about here. Look into her eyes and speak blessings and life into her on a consistent basis. We are all waiting for our wife to become a virtuous woman to say something nice to her, to love her, or to bless her. No, if she automatically became that, then she would not need your blessing. She needs your blessing now to become what God created her to be.

The rest of the verse says, "He praises her." Wow, can you believe that? This is Old Testament, where the law says you are to stone a woman if she does something wrong. Here we see a different kind of husband - one who praises her. When your wife does something for you, or around the house or for the children, praise her. To praise means to appreciate, compliment, and say something positive. Do not be ashamed of it; it is the Bible. You will be amazed by the return you receive from your investment.

The Church is considered the bride of Christ. He has been working on her for more than two thousand years to prepare her and present her without spot or wrinkle, but there is still a long way to go. Thank God, Jesus is not like some of the husbands of our time, where they throw their wives out because they are not doing everything right within the first six months of the marriage.

4) GIVE MORE IMPORTANCE TO CHARACTER THAN MONEY, TALENT, OR BEAUTY

Though God can override and change anything, we need to give more importance to character than talent or beauty. When God decides to use someone, He looks at that person's character. There are so many talented people on this earth, but very few possess good character. Do not be enticed by the external; be attracted by the heart of a person. Many people work from the outside to the inside, but God works from the inside out. If you can love the inside of a person first, then your relationship will be secure. If you love the external first, there will not be any stability because external things are temporary.

5) MAKE SURE THE PERSON IS ALREADY DOING WHAT THEY ARE PROMISING

Many get into marriage believing the promises of their spouse. Often, those good intentions do not come true. At the height of emotional euphoria people will promise you anything, but do not base your life on those promises. They are not promises but wishes they may never keep. Again, there are exceptions to the rule. God can use and change anyone. God can change the direction of a person's life at any time. You might not even be dreaming about ministry now, but ten years from now He can call you to be in ministry or call a minister to do business.

Make sure the person is a believer. Do not expect to win the person to Christ. That is not a reason to be married. In fact, if you are a believer, the Bible does not permit you to marry an unbeliever. Believe me, the devil will bring all kinds of reasons and excuses to go against the Word. Do not fall into the temptation; overcome it by speaking the Word of God.

6) A PERSON NEEDS TO BE HAPPY BY THEMSELVES

If you are not happy being by yourself, then you are not ready for marriage. Many people think that if they get married to the right person, then they will be happy. Let me tell you that if you are not happy with yourself, it does not matter who you marry, you will not be happy. We have all thought at various times, "If I could be somewhere," or "If only that would happen," or "If I were with this person," or "If I could have that, then I will be happy." Those are all wrong wishes. God wants you to be happy just being with Him. We are all waiting for someone to make us happy. It will not happen. And, if it does happen, it will be temporary. The secret to true happiness is having the right kind of relationship with God and discovering who you are in Him. Until then, you will be searching for happiness but will not find it anywhere.

When you are happy all by yourself, doing nothing, and discover the joy that has been deposited in your spirit by God and learn to exercise it any time you want, then you are ready for life. It may sound crazy but let me tell you, this is the truth. Adam did not go to God complaining and whining to Him for a wife. It was God who took the initiative, and He will do the same for you when He thinks you are ready. You are ready when you stop complaining and pushing God for something. I have seen men and women who are desperate and anxious because they are not married yet. They are dating and chatting and getting into all sorts of entanglements and, when the right person comes, they are already in a mess. Chill out and learn to be happy. He will bring the right person at the right time.

THE PURPOSE OF MARRIAGE

TO REVEAL GOD AND HIS NATURE

Why is family life attacked more than any other area of life on this earth? Why does Satan hate marriage? If God initiated it, then why is it sometimes the most difficult thing we ever experience in life? If God ordained this, what is the purpose of it? God created man to represent Him on this earth. That is why He created us in His image and likeness. Those who see us should see our Father.

When God created Adam, he had both masculine and feminine traits. God portrays Himself as a father and mother in His Word. He is a father to the fatherless. One of His names mentioned in the Bible is El-Shaddai, which means

All-sufficient One, or One with many breasts. If man was just a male, he could not exemplify the fullness of God's image and likeness.

God took the feminine quality out of Adam and made a separate person called woman. To join them together again as one, He instituted marriage on this earth. Man or woman all by themselves could never reveal the complete nature of God. Only when they are joined together and become one, and work together in one spirit, soul, and body, will it be revealed. The avenue through which an adult male and female come together and join with each other in spirit, soul, and body is called marriage.

The main purpose of marriage is to reveal the nature (image and likeness) of God to the world, and to our children. Otherwise, the children would have no way of knowing what God is like and what is His nature. The devil hates that. He does not want anyone to know God. More than that, he does not want anyone to know that God is good. He wants people to think that God is evil, angry, cruel, mean, and judgmental. The easiest way to do that is to attack the very thing God put on this earth to reveal Himself; family life.

Think about everything that goes along with a marriage these days: The ring, selection of the dress, cake, food, dance, venue, honeymoon, etc. They are all good but people miss out on the priority. Then, after six months the storm comes, but the relationship has no foundation to withstand it. The cake, the dance, the ring, and the honeymoon will not sustain you through storms. We have made the least important things the most important and given the most important things the least attention. We live in an upside-down world. The Church is here to put things in the right order. Unfortunately, the Church is functioning upside down too; we have adopted everything that is of the world when, in truth, we are supposed to change the world.

You might think that God established the Church to reveal Christ to the world. Well, that is true, but what is the Church made of? The greatest assets any church can have are healthy families. Through them, Christ is revealed to the community more so than the preaching of the pastor or singing of the choir. Paul told the Thessalonian church that he was like a father and mother to them.

> 1 Thessalonians 1:7 says, "But we were gentle among you, just as a nursing *mother* cherishes her own children."

> 1 Thessalonians 1:11-12 says, "As you know how we exhorted, and comforted, and charged every one of you, as a father *does* his own children, that you would walk worthy of God who calls you into His own kingdom and glory."

POSTERITY

When an adult male and female are joined together by God, He blesses them to bring forth children who will; in turn, represent Him on this earth. God blessed us to be fruitful and multiply on this earth and fill the earth with His glory and knowledge. How will that happen? It will happen when people on earth are born again and represent God on this earth. We have a big job ahead of us.

In order to bring about that posterity, God ordained sex. Sex is the most spiritual act a married couple can experience. Through it, they are entering into the process that brings forth a spiritual being (human) to this earth. It is an act of creation. But, the devil has perverted sex into a fleshly, lustful act that is just for physical pleasure. It is his desire to pervert anything that God made good.

SEXUAL FULFILLMENT

God created sex and, in the context of marriage, it is a good thing. The devil brought lust. Now, people do not wait until they are married to fulfill their sexual desire. The enemy has perverted it through lust and people have sex with anything and everything that moves on the earth. It is not God's will to have sex before marriage or outside of marriage. It is a holy act, where a husband and wife join with God in creation. It should not be taken lightly or just as something of the body or flesh. It is a spiritual act where two spirits join together to create another spirit being. Thank God for the pleasure and fun that goes with it!

We live in a culture and time where the place of sex is elevated and its purpose is exaggerated. Because of that, very few enjoy sexual fulfillment. Adam did not ask God for a woman to fulfill his sexual desires. True fulfillment only comes when it is done the way God originally intended.

The spiritual influence you are under when you have sex determines the quality of the seed you will produce (1 Corinthians 7:14). We can produce righteous seeds or wicked seeds on this earth. We see that throughout the Bible. Abel was a righteous seed, but the Bible says Cain was from the wicked one (Matthew 23:35; 1 John 3:12). God told Eve that He would put enmity between her seed and the serpent's seed. Both seeds are born through women.

WARFARE

When man and woman come together as husband and wife, we become a formidable force to withstand the enemy. We are not supposed to fight with, or apart from, each other. That is what happened in the beginning. The serpent came

261

to Eve. Instead of Adam protecting her and both fighting together, they acted independently; the woman yielded to the serpent and man gave in to the woman and ate the fruit. Another reason the enemy attacks the marriage is because he knows that, if he can divide them, he can defeat them and hinder their progress. That is why the Bible says that one can put a thousand to flight but two can put ten thousand to flight (Deuteronomy 32:30).

The Bible also says that if two of us agree on earth and ask God anything, He will do it for us (Matthew 18:19). The reason we do not see many answers to our prayers is because of the lack of unity. Unity and agreement should start in our family life; only then will it manifest in the Church.

TO HEAL US

That might sound strange, but it is the truth. Isn't marriage supposed to be fun? You might say, "I did not know it was a hospital!" Welcome to the real world. Everyone needs to be healed of some emotional defects or hurt in their life. As the old proverb says, "Birds of a feather flock together." Emotionally sick people are attracted to those who are emotionally sick. Initially, they will not realize this; they will think they found the perfect person on this earth.

Those who are wise in heart realize it sooner. God in His infinite wisdom will put together two people who would bring those exact wounds and defects to the surface. If you are married and cannot stand each other, it is because you are bringing the worst out of each other. The bad has to leave before you can bring the best out of each other. If you hang in there and work on your issues, you will see the light at the end of the tunnel.

This is why the Bible says that by wisdom a house is built and by understanding it is established (Proverbs 24:3). When conflict arises, a great deal of wisdom is required to understand the reason. Unfortunately, many people wound each other further instead of helping each other to be healed.

Your spouse is like a mirror. What you see in them as a problem is a reflection of an issue in your own heart. The Bible says, "As in water face reflects face, so a man's heart reveals the man" (Proverbs 27:19). God uses another person's heart to reveal what is in our own heart. Unfortunately, some think all the problems are with the other person. It is a deception.

It might seem unbearable for a few months (maybe years). You will aggravate each other so much that you will feel like you want to kill your spouse, or even wish they were dead. I am just being honest with you, this is real life and it's a fact. Saying "Hallelujah" and "Praise the Lord" will not solve such issues.

In most cases, God puts together two opposites, not opposite in calling, but in personality. There may seem to be very little in common between you and your spouse. You might wonder what in the world you were thinking when you said, "I do." Welcome to God's repair shop. He knew exactly what needed to change in your life to enable you to walk in His purpose, and He knew exactly what needed to be done to bring it about. When you get sick and go to the hospital for surgery, you cannot tell the doctor which tools to use or where to cut. Sometimes he has to cut you open and get the tumor out so that you can be healed. If the doctor won't make the cut and instead puts a bandage on top of that tumor, eventually, it will kill you.

That is what happens in many marriages. You both cut open the wounds first. Many quit and run away when they see the wounds in the other person. They think that if they leave this person and find someone else, they will not have those wounds. Surprise, surprise, they will have the same tumor but in a different part of the body, or a different type of tumor, that's all. I am speaking spiritually here. So, you need to stick your feet in the ground and get the tools you need. You may need to go to the right 'doctor' who has the right tools, and with their help, you and your spouse will be healed.

I am not talking about abusive situations. If your spouse is physically and emotionally abusive, then you do not need to endure it unless the Lord tells you to stay. Or, if they have a problem with addictions that are out of control, you need to seek professional help as early as possible. Delaying or avoiding dealing with our issues does not solve the problems, but confronting and dealing with them rightly does.

TO FULFILL YOUR PURPOSE

You do not have everything that it takes to fulfill your purpose. God will bring a person into your life that has the exact qualities you do not have. In the beginning, it might be irritating but, if you learn to work together, you will see the differences actually complement rather than contradict. In most families, one spouse will be good at managing money and the other is good at spending money. Imagine if they were both spenders, they would be financially broke in no time.

One spouse will be more disciplined and orderly than the other. One will be good with people and more social, and the other will be reserved. One will be more spiritually sensitive than the other. When you accept the differences of your spouse and put them where you have the weakness, you will get a perfect team. Do not get mad at each other because your spouse is not as disciplined as you are, or does not manage money as well as you. That is the reason God put you in their life. You need to make room for each other to grow without controlling or condemning. It will take time and may not happen in a month or a year.

COMPANIONSHIP

Everyone is looking for companionship. For someone who will understand them, with whom they can share their deepest feelings. One of the main purposes of marriage is companionship. We all desire to be intimately connected with someone. God provided the opportunity for that in marriage. You may say that you and your spouse are not connecting and have nothing in common—but the guy or girl at work, on the other hand, you were made for each other. That is a fantasy. You have heard the old saying, "The grass is always greener on the other side of the fence."

Once you cross the fence, you will know there is not much difference. The Bible says in Ecclesiastes 4:8a & 9-12, "There is one alone, without companion… Two *are* better than one, because they have a good reward for their labor. For if they fall, one will lift up his companion. But woe to him *who is* alone when he falls, for *he has* no one to help him up. Again, if two lie down together, they will keep warm; but how can one be warm *alone?* Though one may be overpowered by another, two can withstand him, and a threefold cord is not quickly broken."

12 WRONG REASONS TO BE MARRIED

1) AGE

Many people make the mistake of getting married because they think they are getting old. Just because you are 20, 30, or even 40 is not the reason to get married. There is no particular age mentioned in the Bible for marriage. You should get married when you know you are ready and when you find the right person.

2) SEXUAL SATISFACTION

Though God designed sexual desire to be satisfied within the marriage relationship, it is not the primary reason for marriage. If you marry for this reason, you will regret it later. Before marriage, you will feel like sex is the centerpiece of marriage, but you will soon discover that it is not. You can't stay in bed all day long and all night with your partner! It is just one important element of married life.

It is true that most human beings have sex drives and they long for the fulfillment of their sexual passion, but that should not be the reason for marriage. God never intended for people to get married to satisfy their sexual desires. For a person who is focused on finding or fulfilling their purpose, sexual passion is not a pressure that leads them. Joseph is the best example of that. He was more focused on God and his purpose than the temporal gratification of his sex drive. When we are not accomplishing anything and do not have a vision for our future, the temptation for sex will feel overwhelming.

I have a word of advice for my younger brothers and sisters here. The Bible says our longevity is eighty years old. For the majority of that life, you are going to live with a man or woman with whom you can have all the fun you want. If you hold the gun and be patient for the first part of your life, the latter part of your life will be better. But, if you play around now, you are going to pay for it later. It is better to pay now and play later.

3) MONEY

In many cultures dowry is a common practice and people think that if they get married they will get some money. Money should never be the reason for marriage. Some get married because they find a person who is rich and they think that if they marry that person their financial problems will be over. Wrong reason! It is true that we need money to survive on this earth. Money is attached to your purpose, not your marriage. If God decides to do that, it's okay, but that should not be your intention.

4) BEAUTY

Finding someone attractive is not a reason for marrying that person. There are many beautiful people on this earth but you cannot marry them all. It does not matter how beautiful the person that you are with is, you will see someone who is outwardly more beautiful sooner or later. The Bible says beauty is vain and charm is deceitful, but the woman who fears the Lord will be praised (Proverbs 31:30).

5) JOB OR EDUCATION

Some look at the job or education a person has and think that person is the right partner for them. Do not make this mistake. Education and job are not the reasons to marry a person. Your purpose is.

6) FAMILY OR PROMINENCE

Some people think that just because they met someone related to somebody who is popular or prominent in the community, they will be influential. This is another wrong reason to get married. Others think that if they marry someone whose parents are rich or influential, they got a good deal. Do not be deceived my friend: you are heading for trouble.

7) SEXUAL RELATIONSHIP

Just because you had sex with someone is the wrong reason to get married. It is true that the Bible does not allow sex before marriage, and it says in the Old Testament that if a man has sex with a woman he has to marry that person. God forgives sins you committed in ignorance, and mistakes. Don't let guilt make you feel like you need to marry that person because you had sex. The Bible gives advice to people who are in that type of situation, which is often to "run" (1 Corinthians 6:18; 2 Timothy 2:2).

I have seen people who cohabitate before they are married. Once they get married, the fun they had living together runs out of the door. So, they begin to fight and end up in divorce.

8) MINISTRY

Some people think they need to be married if they are in ministry, or to be effective in ministry. It is true that we will be tempted sexually, but we need to ask God for His grace to overcome the temptation. We should not marry until we find the right person.

Is there a perfect person that each person is meant to marry?

Yes, there is, but the truth is there is more than one 'perfect person' out there. God will bring you another right person if you missed one earlier, as He brought Eve to Adam.

9) FAMILY PRESSURE

In some cultures, when their children reach a certain age, the parents and relatives start pressuring them to get married. We should not get married under anyone's pressure or influence. Again, there is no particular age mentioned in the Bible for marriage. You should marry when you know you are ready for it. It's a major milestone in life. Your parents or relatives will not be there to help you when you need them. You will have to face life.

10) DEPRESSION/ADDICTION/ STRESS

In my culture, when a single person is having emotional problems like depression, loneliness, substance abuse, etc. people advise that person to get married and tell them that his or her problem will be over once they get married. Doing that is adding fuel to the fire. That person cannot take care of themselves and marriage requires them to take care of another person and their problems. Imagine what would happen to that person. He just received a double death sentence!

11) FALLING IN LOVE

These days, many get married because they feel they have fallen in love with each other. Naturally, when you fall, you will not stay there for too long. Sooner or later, you have to get up. That is what happens to people who get married because they fell in love. They 'get up' or 'wake up' from that fall. After a few months, they realize that the love they felt was not real and disappeared like vapor. Life gets dry and irritating. Before, you did not think you could be away from each other for a minute; now you can't stand being together for a minute!

If, after considering all of the other factors of marriage and relationship, you fall in love, it is good. Falling in love should not be the primary reason for marriage. The feeling of falling in love is a temporary emotional high, just like someone feels while they are drunk. It is the result of the chemical reaction happening in your brain. When the effect of the liquor dies down, they come back to 'normal.' Then, they do not remember what they did or said while they were under the influence of it.

12) PROPHETIC WORD

In some charismatic circles, people prophesy to each other about whom they should marry. That is pure witchcraft. People run after prophets and prophetesses for a 'word' to find their life partner. I have a 'word' for you, please read the Bible and follow what it says and your life partner will show up. I have known a few who got married because of a prophetic (I call it *pathetic*) word and destroyed their lives and calling. I have also seen people walk around saying God told them so and so is supposed to marry them and, if they do not, they are disobeying God. If someone is supposed to marry you and God spoke to you about it, then He will speak to the other person also. You do not need to manipulate that person or God.

I have also seen people who got married because their "spiritual leader" told them to do so. I do not recommend it. I am not saying God cannot or will not speak to us through someone about who we should marry but, if He does, it will most often be a confirmation and not a command.

THREE WRONG REASONS MEN GET MARRIED

1) THEY ARE PHYSICALLY ATTRACTED TO A WOMAN

Men are visual beings. That means what he sees influences him. When he sees the legs and breasts of a woman, he tends to forget everything else and begins to desire to have sex with that woman. He will pursue that woman and, if the woman responds to his desire, he falls in love with her. I just want you to know there is not one bit of love involved in this. He is lusting after that woman and is after what he can get. He will say nice words and buy flowers and gifts for a while, but the destination in his mind is sex. The woman believes everything the man says and falls for him. Let me tell you ladies, if a man's primary intention of having a relationship with you is to have sex, flee from that person and never look back.

So they fall in love and many end up in marriage. Within three months, all the love he felt toward her vanishes. Do you know why? Because he noticed that there are other women out there with skinny legs and bigger bumpers. Then he regrets what he did and neglects the woman whose life he just ruined.

2) THE MAN NEEDS A MOTHER

Some men enter into a marriage relationship not to have a wife, but a mother. They are emotionally immature and want someone to do their laundry, clean their house, cook their food, and nurture them like a baby. I know many men who stay at home living off of their wife's income and talk like they are in charge of the whole world. Many men did not receive the love and care of their mama because she was working, or absent from their lives. Now they act like grown-up babies.

Men, I love you, but I want to tell you that it is time to grow up. God did not create you to live off your wife's income. Your wife is not your mother. She is your companion and helpmeet. You need to love, protect, and provide for your wife and children. She is there to help you fulfill your purpose: not feed you.

Everybody is looking for someone to love them unconditionally and accept them as they are. There is a child in each of us looking for love and nurturing, which most did not receive as children. So, when someone of the opposite sex shows that kind of love and care, we feel attracted to that person. But that is not the right reason to be married.

3) THEY WANT TO BE A SAVIOR

There is another reason some smart men get trapped and get married. They see a woman who has a lot of issues: low self-esteem, a broken heart, or had a messed-up childhood, addiction and, all of a sudden, this smart guy feels like a savior. He begins to spend time with that woman, helping her recover from her mess. Sooner or later, that relationship ends up in places neither of them expected or wanted, and they get married. The man feels compassion for the woman and thinks he can save her from her pain if he marries her. Whatever reason you may have, my brother, what I would say to you is "run" as fast as you can and do not look back, before you get tangled.

You are not the savior of anyone, my friend. There is only one Savior and His name is Jesus. You cannot rescue anyone from anything, and you cannot change anyone's life. You can give advice and encouragement to anyone within boundaries but only God can change the heart of a person. Do not waste your life trying to save someone. I have seen many smart guys become trapped this way. When I see their wife, I wonder how on earth they ended up together.

You cannot change yourself so how are you going to change someone else? It is time for us to learn from other people's mistakes.

At the same time, if you are waiting for the perfect woman to marry, I also want to tell you that she does not exist. Many times, God will bring the right woman to you, but she may not have all the qualities you need (I am not talking about physical things) right now. She needs to be cultivated. It will take a lot of love, patience, and nurturing before you begin to see any result. The number one thing is to make sure you hear from God before you make a final decision. There is always hope for the future. Whoever (and for whatever reason) you are married to right now, it is God's will and, if you yield to the process, He will work it out for your good.

THREE WRONG REASONS WOMEN GET MARRIED

1) ENTICED BY A MAN

Many times a woman gets enticed by a man and what he says, and does not think beyond it: then she makes a permanent decision based on those so-called promises. Some men have no intention of keeping those promises and are just using those words to seduce the woman to get her to do what he wants her to do.

2) FALSE EXPECTATIONS

When a woman sees a man who is smart and handsome, what comes to their mind is the picture of an all-powerful knight in shining armor who will do anything for them: rescuing them from trouble, getting them everything they want, and the list goes on. You and I know the reality is far from that picture. Most of those expectations were created by Hollywood and Disney movies, or by other fairy tales.

3) FOR A FATHERLY RELATIONSHIP

When a woman does not receive love and acceptance from her father while growing up, she will fall prey to men who pretend they want to take care of her.

That is why some women marry much older men. It's like they are married to their father. That is not God's will for them. God wants to heal your heart from every wound and any abuse you experienced from your father.

Women who were abused by their father will have a hard time trusting God or having a healthy relationship with Him and their husband.

HOW AND WHY DID GOD CREATE WOMAN?

When God created Adam, He formed him from the mud of the earth and breathed into his nostrils. When God made the woman, He did not do the same. Instead, He took her out of the man. Before, the qualities of man and woman were in one person—Adam. God separated the woman from Adam and made a new person.

Man was created to fulfill God's purpose, and woman was created to help man do it. When God made Eve, He did not take her to a shopping mall first. He brought her in front of the man. Her purpose is connected to man from whom she was taken. Her protection and security come from the relationship she has with her man. Her life did not start in a shopping mall; she must discover her identity and purpose as she relates to the man.

We live in a rebellious world where people rebel against anything that is of God. We live in a world where people think man and woman are the same and capable of doing the same things. That is not what the Bible says. A woman is not physically capable of doing what a man does (with some exceptions). That is why we do not see many women on the construction site or in a mine. Man and woman, though they are spiritually equal, were created emotionally and physically different. A man cannot endure what a woman can endure; that is why God gave the womb only to the woman.

For the world to straighten out, the men need to be straightened out first. Men think women are the problem. They are not the problem. The real problem is how we treat women because of our own pain and ignorance. Life started with the man, not the woman. If anything has gone wrong with the woman, man is responsible for that. God did not call Eve when He came down to the Garden; He called Adam. He was the one to whom God had given authority and dominion on the earth. Woman came to help him exercise that.

That is why Jesus selected only men as His disciples, not because He did not like women. He knew that if He could fix the men in a society that would fix the women, not the other way around. Dear men, please understand that the future of your family, church, and nation depend on you. The reason women are not willing to submit is because the men have not treated them right. Generally, men think that if the women submit, then they will be nice to them or love them. No, it's the other way around. When you love them and are nice to them, they will submit in response. The reason we cannot love them and be nice to them is not them, but the hurts and wounds that need to be healed in us.

A woman needs to feel that she is protected and secure. Women were not created to work like men, but to be an emotional companion to a man. When God created us, it was to Adam that He gave the Garden and told him to till and guard it. When He created the woman, God did not say anything to her but brought her to Adam. When God pronounced curses after the fall, He did not say anything related to work to the woman. There are many women who would love to stay home and be a wife and mother. For these, that gives them joy and fulfillment.

One of the reasons marriages are falling apart is because the woman has to work to support her family. She becomes more vulnerable to the temptations of the enemy while she is alone at work, just like the devil came to Eve.

If there is something wrong with a product, do not try to fix the product. Fix the mold that manufactured it, and the defect in the product line will disappear. Woman came out of man. If women are to be healed from their defects, then men need to be healed first. When we are healed, we will have perfect men and women on this earth. Dear men, I want to give you the simplest piece of advice anyone could give; stop trying to fix your woman. Fix yourself and, as a result, she will automatically be fixed. When I tell you to fix yourself, I mean submit to God's process. I know that we cannot fix ourselves; only God can do it. Amen.

CHAPTER 16
14 REASONS MARRIAGES FAIL

CHAPTER 16: 14 REASONS MARRIAGES FAIL

1) A LACK OF UNDERSTANDING OF GOD'S ORIGINAL INTENT

God initiated marriage on this earth. Adam was created in God's image and likeness and God brought all living creatures to him to see what he would call them. Adam named all the animals and creatures God made, but he could not find a suitable mate among them. Every other creature had a mate but Adam was a single man. God did not create Eve to fulfill Adam's sexual desire. That is the reason many people get married today: to have sex. Adam needed someone to relate to on his level, to share with, and to have an intimate relationship. God said, "I will make him a helper comparable to him" (Genesis 2:18).

Whatever reason people get married, if it is other than the original reason God intended, it will fail or will not be fulfilling. One day I became frustrated and asked God why so many marriages fail. Why do so many people seem to marry the wrong person? I see men and women who are called to the mission field married to someone who does not want anything to do with missions or ministry. There is nothing more frustrating than that.

God spoke to me and said, "Son, I intended marriage to be the most joyful thing on this earth. But, if it is not done my way, it could become the greatest source of pain." Whatever God intended for good, the devil will try to mess up and use to create pain. In turn, we will blame God for our pain and that will make the devil happy. Marriage could be the best or worst thing in your life.

People get married for all kinds of reasons, sometimes for the most stupid reasons. God intended marriage for companionship.

2) MULTIPLE 'MARRIAGES'

God intended the sexual relationship only within the context of marriage. When you have sex with a person you become "one" with that person in spirit, soul, and body. That is called marriage. The Bible says man shall leave father and mother and be joined to his wife, and they shall become one flesh (Genesis

2:24; Matthew 19:4-6). When you join yourself with a person in a sexual relationship, you become one with that person (1 Corinthians 6:16). That means there is a connection that takes place between the two physically, emotionally, and spiritually. God intended for this to happen in each life with only one other person. It is impossible to have true intimacy with more than one person at a time.

We live in a society where people have or have had multiple sexual partners. When these people get married, they do not feel intimacy with their husband or wife. It is because they are already 'married' to someone else. Their soul and spirit are tied to someone else, and they are trying to become one with their husband or wife. It will not happen until you break the "soul tie" from all previous partners in order to have intimacy in your marriage. This is a painful process.

No one can love two people and be committed to both of them in the same degree at the same time. Just like Jesus said that no one can serve two masters, no one can love two people at the same level. Your heart is wired that way by God. Once you have a sexual or soul tie with a person, unless it is dealt with, you cannot have an intimate relationship with another person.

3) NO LEAVING: NO CLEAVING

God said that a man shall leave his father and mother and cleave unto his wife, and they shall become one flesh. When you get married, your relationship with your husband or wife is the most important human relationship. There has to be a healthy separation from parents and others when a man and woman marry. I have seen many men marry their wife and take her to their parents' home. In a few months, war breaks out between his parents and new wife. The man, instead of siding with and supporting his wife, sides with his parents and attacks his wife. There is nothing more cursed on this earth than that!

When you are married, you are not your Mama's boy or Daddy's girl any longer. You do not belong to your grandparents. You belong to each other (husband and wife). There has to be a healthy detachment from your parents in order to form a new family. It may take a while to feel that detachment because your parents have been the most influential people in your life. So if it does not happen in a month or two, be patient and work on it one day at a time.

4) A LACK OF UNDERSTANDING ABOUT THE DIFFERENCES BETWEEN MAN AND WOMAN

Most people are aware of only the physical differences between male and female. Man was created in the image and likeness of God. Woman was taken out of man. They are not the same. There are physiological and psychological differences between a man and woman. Men and women need to understand this before they enter into marriage.

In most marriages, men and women are trying to change each other to make the other person like them. They see the difference and they do not know what to do with it. They perceive it as something negative and begin the attempt to change the other person. We need to know that differences are complementary and God-intended. They are not negative.

Men and women think differently. It has been said that each woman has twenty to twenty-five thousand words to speak a day and each man has only ten thousand. A man's strength is in his muscles and a woman's strength is in her words. Be sure to use these properly and wisely.

Through wisdom a house is built and by understanding it is established (Proverbs 24:3). It is very important that we receive God's wisdom and found our marriage on it.

5) LOVE AND RESPECT

The Bible commands husbands to love their wives as Christ loves the Church. There is no command to wives to love their husbands. Instead, it commands them to submit and respect their husbands. For most men respect is their number one need. For a woman love and affection is her number one need.

How love and respect are interpreted also varies from person to person. We need to discover that about each other through sharing and spending intimate time together.

6) LACK OF VISION

Every marriage needs a vision and purpose. It is better for a man and woman to get married where they can complement each other. God puts two people together for a purpose and it is not to kill each other! Husbands and wives need to talk to each other and come up with common goals and work together to achieve them. When they work together on these, it deepens their intimacy and oneness. Before you get married, make sure your purpose and vision for life complement each other. Otherwise, you will have conflict down the road.

7) LACK OF MUTUAL SUBMISSION

Another misunderstanding men have is that their wives have to submit to them all the time, and they do not need to submit to their wives. The Bible says we need to submit to one another (2 Peter 5:5). No one is right all the time. God put in our wives something we need. Wise men tap into it, and they are more blessed than the others. A family in which the husband demands the submission of his wife without question will be like a funeral home. It will be very quiet and feel like someone is dead. In fact, that is the truth. The wife is alive physically but emotionally she is dead. In a matter of time, she could become sick and pass away physically too.

Submission is made of two parts: the prefix "sub" and the word "mission." When you submit to someone you are joining the "mission" of that person. You are coming alongside of that person to encourage, uplift, and support. The house of the righteous should be the most joyous place on this earth. The Bible says there are shouts of joy in the house of the righteous (Psalm 118:15).

8) PAST HURTS AND PAIN

We all enter into marriage with a personal and a generational history. When you get married you are not just marrying that person, you are marrying more than six thousand years of history that comes with that person. Some call it 'baggage.' Before we get married, we may have no idea what is in each of our bags. They are full of skeletons and carcasses. Once we begin to live together, those hurts (skeletons) and that pain (carcasses) will begin to surface, and we will not know what to do with it or how to handle it. We will think the problem is with our spouse and try to blame him or her. Usually, a spouse is blinded to his or her own hurts and only sees the hurts and weaknesses of the other. They will begin to try to change the other person only to see that it causes more harm than good.

We face and react to the issues of life based on the hurts and the belief system that was formed in us while we were growing up. We see the world and our spouse through those glasses but are not able to see or receive truth. Everyone is brought up with some kind of dysfunction. Our parents were not perfect. If we are not careful, we can carry that baggage into our marriage and it will manifest at times we do not expect. Then we ask ourselves, "Where did that come from?" I believe God uses marriage to get that baggage cleaned and healed.

I have seen that a majority of the problems we face as adults are rooted in our childhood hurts and abuses. Recently, I read something by Dr. Paul Hegstrom that said, "In 25 years of research close to 98% of the issues couples deal with are rooted in childhood wounds each of them suffered below the age of 11." Many times as adults we deal with the symptoms (the fruit), and do not recognize the root. It is important that people seek help for their emotional healing instead of blaming their problem on someone else.

As a result of those wounds both husband and wife may begin to daydream that if they were married to someone else they would not have any problems. Keep in mind that there are hundreds of married people in churches and at the work place who are facing similar problems and dreaming the same daydreams, wishing they were married to someone else. They easily fall prey to the lust of the flesh, 'fall in love' and end up having an affair, without knowing they will soon face the same enemy (problems) they tried to run away from in their previous marriage. Statistics show the divorce rate is higher among second marriages than first. God have mercy.

Children are supposed to receive love, acceptance, appreciation, and feel protected while growing up. When they do not receive these they grow up emotionally dysfunctional and, though an adult, their inner child is still yearning to receive those four things. When people get married they, knowingly or unknowingly, begin to expect or demand those things from each other. Neither is able to give them and trouble begins.

9) UNREALISTIC EXPECTATIONS

We all had certain expectations about our future spouse before we were married. Those expectations were not based on reality. When those expectations were formed, we did not take into consideration the weaknesses or defects of the other person. We drew the picture of a perfect person in our imaginary world, but when reality sets in and we are faced with the defects, we get irritated because it does not fit the picture we drew in our mind. Many enter into marriage thinking that, once they get married, all of their problems are going to be over because someone is going to take care of them and make them happy all the time. Well, both spouses enter into marriage expecting to be taken care of, and neither of them wants to take care of the other. The marriage becomes a battlefield, each demanding the other do the things they want.

I have found that the root of some of the problems we have in marriage is found when we treat our spouse with those unrealistic (perfect picture) expectations we made up in our heart. When we formed that perfect picture, we did not leave any room for weaknesses. Weakness was out of the question. When our spouse does not meet those expectations, we either try to make them fit into that frame or resent them because they are not functioning as we think they should. The solution is for both to go back to the drawing board, delete that unrealistic picture, and begin to draw a new picture together. It takes a while to figure out that the way to get our needs met is to meet the other person's needs first. When we sow good things into our marriage, we will begin to reap good things.

10) CURSE

God created men and women (husbands and wives) to work in unity, to subdue and take dominion over the earth. As we see in the book of Genesis, when man sinned God pronounced curses on both man and woman. He said to the woman, "Your desire shall be for your husband and he shall rule over you" (Genesis 3:16). What does that statement show? It shows man and woman fighting for dominion over each other. After the fall, because we lost the dominion over the earth, men and women began to fight to dominate each other. Woman's desire for her husband means she is trying to control him and take his place. Man, in turn, dominates using power and pressure.

In case you do not know, you have been redeemed from that curse by the blood of Jesus. He has redeemed us from the curse of the law by becoming a curse for us. Husbands and wives are supposed to work in unity, fighting together to subdue and take dominion over the earth. Believe this and declare it over your marriage and family; you are redeemed from the curse. It's not a question of who is the head and who has more authority. The real question is: Are you fulfilling God's purpose? Are you exercising your dominion over anything? If not, there is disunity. Where there is disunity in marriage, the husband and wife are still operating under a curse.

11) MISUNDERSTOOD LOVE

Love is one of the most misunderstood subjects on this earth. Love, acceptance, and appreciation are the fundamental emotional needs of every human being. Very few of us received them while growing up. When people get married, deep down in their heart they are longing to receive these three from their spouse. When the sexual passion dies down and the romantic love vanishes, couples do not know how to give love, acceptance, and appreciation to each other. The only time we received that when we were little is when we did something good. We all want to receive them but most do not want to give it first so we start to fight and demand that our spouse first give that love, acceptance, or appreciation to us. The truth is that if we want to receive something, then first we should give.

12) NO CONNECTION IN THE SPIRIT

Man is a spirit being, and marriage is a union of two spirits (in fact, it is the union of three spirits: two human spirits and the Spirit of God). The way you know if someone is the right person for you is if there is a spiritual attraction between you and that person. Spiritual attraction is the attraction of two destinies that are supposed to merge and become one powerful and unstoppable force. God designed it that way. He designed people in a way that not everyone complements your purpose, but there are some out there who are just the right fit for you. The truth is, only those who live and walk in the spirit will get attracted in the spirit first.

These days most start with a mere physical attraction, then they enter into sex but their spirits are not connected. They were never meant to be connected so there will not be any real unity between the two, though they might be married for many years. Their marriage will hang on mere sex, or material things, and what the flesh can bring forth. As time goes by they will start fighting for more sex or material things because there is nothing else to sustain the relationship.

You know what the flesh brings forth; it brings forth death. It will slowly kill your life altogether. That is why the Bible says to flee from immorality and fornication, it does not say try it out for a while, and then stop if it doesn't work. If someone asks you for sex before marriage, the answer is simple—FLEE! If some woman is willing to give you sex before you are married, the response has to be—FLEE! Remember Joseph.

13) INDIVIDUALISM

We live in an individualistic society, where no one wants to be accountable or submit to anyone. This is one of the major reasons for divorce. The song of the day is "I, me, mine, and myself want to have fun." Everything in God's Kingdom works under authority. The reason Lucifer fell is because he wanted to be independent. He decided to rebel against the authority structure he was under.

Adam and Eve fell because they made a decision without including God. Even the Almighty, though He is limitless, chose to submit Himself to His Word. The devil cannot submit to anything or to his own word because he is a liar and the father of lies.

Have you ever wondered why there is perfect unity between the Trinity? Though they are equal, they work in perfect submission. The Son will not do a thing or say a word except what He sees or hears from the Father (John 5:16; 6:38; 8:28). Do you think Jesus was a real person with a will and passion like we are, or was He a robot who did things by the push of a button? He is the example of a perfect human being. He came to show us how life is supposed to work on this earth. Everyone who desires to be like Him will act like Him.

281

The Spirit will not say or do a thing on His own unless He hears it from Jesus (John 16:13-15). Though they submit to each other, it does not diminish their identity as individuals or reduce their freedom and authority. The reason they can submit that way is because they are so secure in themselves and their love and respect for each other is deep. Insecurity and fear causes us to rebel against authority.

Though we are created as free agents, we are not supposed to work independently. Everything God created depends on each other for their sustenance. That man and woman were created equally in the spirit does not mean we do not need to submit to each other. Many men misunderstand submission and confuse it with domination. There is a big difference between the two. Submission is when someone willfully chooses to work under God-given authority. Domination is demanding submission by fear or force.

In the family structure, Christ is the head (authority) of the husband (man) and the husband is the head of the wife (woman) (1 Corinthians 11:3; Ephesians 5:23). God has commanded the husband to love his wife as Christ loves the Church and the wife to submit to her own husband in everything (Ephesians 5:24-25). This is a command from the Lord not an option based on which culture you live in. Notice the two phrases when it says to the husbands to love their wives "as Christ loves the church" and wives to submit to their husbands "in everything."

Many times, husbands and wives wait for the other to do their part first in order for them to love or submit. The above command is not given with an "if," meaning, if the other party does his or her part, then you do it. No, it is directly given to husbands and wives regardless of what the other person may or may not do. The real question is whether you as a person walk in obedience or in rebellion to Christ.

As long as a man walks in obedience and total submission to Christ, whatever he does and wherever he goes his wife is supposed to submit to him and follow him without any question. A woman has to be secure in the Lord and fully trust Him for this to happen. Otherwise, she will rebel and fight for her independence saying, "I am also created equal as you are and want to live my own life in my own way." This is done out of ignorance. I have seen both domineering husbands and wives. They operate under a curse and never prosper.

When a man and woman receive the revelation of the Trinity and how they operate, they will have a family life that is peaceful and heavenly. Many of us forfeit the blessings of the Lord from our family life because of strife and disunity, which comes from a lack of understanding. Family life is supposed to be an enjoyable thing, not a place for stress and strife. When a woman trusts the Lord and knows her husband is looking after her and what is the best for the family, she should willingly submit to her husband.

The Bible says that even if the husband walks in disobedience to God, if he has a godly wife, she can win him to obey God through her chaste conduct.

> 1 Peter 3:1-6 says, "Wives, likewise, *be* submissive to your own husbands, that even if some do not obey the word, they, without a word, may be won by the conduct of their wives, when they observe your chaste conduct *accompanied* by fear. Do not let your adornment be *merely* outward—arranging the hair, wearing gold, or putting on *fine* apparel— rather *let it be* the hidden person of the heart, with the incorruptible *beauty* of a gentle and quiet spirit, which is very precious in the sight of God. For in this manner, in former times, the holy women who trusted in God also adorned themselves, being submissive to their own husbands, as Sarah obeyed Abraham, calling him lord, whose daughters you are if you do good and are not afraid with any terror."

Husbands need to make sure they honor their wives through words and deeds (1Peter 3:7). Individualism will not bring anything good to a family or a society. Everything God created, both living and non-living, works under some form of authority structure and depends on others. The Bible says that all authority is from God, and whoever rebels against authority rebels against God (Romans 13:1-2).

14) DIFFERENCE IN REALITIES

Reality is your perception and understanding about an area of life. This is based on your current knowledge and experience about that area. Every individual is at a different level concerning his or her knowledge and experience. Subconsciously, people think that what they know is the ultimate and there is nothing more out there. It is actually a deception. In fact, we know that there is always more to learn and that different ways of doing things exist.

When people get married, they need to know that they are coming from two different families, different geographic areas, and sometimes even different cultures. Each family has a different culture. When I say culture, I mean the way we think and how we do things, and the shared perspective about the world we live in. Siblings who were raised up in the same family or even twins when they are grown do not necessarily share the same values or form the same mindsets. I call it a reality. What is a reality to me may not be your reality. You may not be able to comprehend that there is more out there.

When two individuals come together to form a family and a future, there will be a clash of these realities or cultures. Both might feel like they are from two different 'worlds.' Yes, they are coming from two different worlds. Both husband and wife need to understand this and work on their 'realities' and always be willing to learn more and try different ways of doing things; they should even be willing to do something new that they never did before, instead of just trying to defend their own perspective.

PART IV

CHAPTER 17
THE PROCESS OF MAKING
GOOD DECISIONS

CHAPTER 17: THE PROCESS OF MAKING GOOD DECISIONS

S ince this book is about decisions, we need to know how to make good decisions. The decisions we make today create our tomorrow. Where you are in life is the result of the decisions you made in the past. We cannot blame our circumstances, or others, for where we are in life or for the decisions we made. They were our choices.

Life is a total sum of the decisions we make. Some are temporary while others are permanent. Success in life depends on how informed you are before you make a life-altering or major decision. There are three kinds of decisions that we make in life.

1) PERMANENT DECISIONS

These are turning-point decisions, which have the power to make or break your future. This book is about permanent decisions. Life on this earth works in seasons. At the beginning of every new season, you will need to make at least one key decision.

2) TEMPORARY DECISIONS

These are decisions you make in everyday life; when to get up in the morning, what to have for breakfast, from which store you should buy something, etc. Though these are temporary decisions, they can also be life-altering decisions.

3) INDECISION

There are some people who will not make any decision at all when the time comes. They have no direction in life and want someone else to make all of their decisions for them. They may be too scared to make decisions because of past mistakes. They spend almost all their life afraid of making decisions.

10 REASONS PEOPLE MAKE POOR/WISE DECISIONS

Before we make a permanent decision, there are certain things we need to know. The quality of a decision is based on the knowledge you have about that particular thing or area of life. We need to know the purpose. The consequences of a decision and how long you have to live with the result need to be taken into consideration. The quality of life you have right now is based on past decisions.

Once we make a wrong decision, our life will move in the wrong direction. It will be like taking a wrong turn while we are going somewhere. The longer we go in the wrong direction, the longer it will take to get back to where we missed the point. Once we make a wrong decision, depending on how major the decision was and the results of that decision, the longer it will take to restore our lives.

The Bible is full of examples of people who made good and bad decisions. We do not need to go far. We are surrounded by people who have made great and poor decisions. If decisions are that important in our lives, we need to learn how to make good ones. We need to know the things we need to take into consideration before we make a decision.

The Bible is the standard by which we must draw our moral and social values. It is the foundation for our life and conduct on this earth. When we make a decision, we first need to make sure it balances with the written Word of God. If the choice you are going to make is contrary to what the Bible says, then you can be sure that the result of your choice will be negative. Before we make a decision, we need to be sure of what the Bible says about that particular situation.

That is why the Bible says to store God's Word in our heart, and to keep it in the center of our heart (Proverbs 3:3; 4:20-21). Never let it depart from our sight. Any decision you make based on the principles of the Bible will be good; even if it causes you pain or initially seems like the wrong choice. The opposite is also true. Any decision you make outside of God's counsel will tend to lead to failure and will bring forth negative results, even if it seems to go well in the beginning.

When you make a decision, so many things play out in what led you to make it. Following are some of the reasons people make poor or wise choices. Your current knowledge about the situation, your need, your emotional well-being, spiritual influence, circumstances, experience/past, your vision for life, financial situation, peer/family pressure, are only some of the ingredients that play a role in decision making.

1) YOUR CURRENT KNOWLEDGE

When you make a choice, how much you know about that situation, subject, or person plays an important role. Many times we say, "Oh, I did not know that." Or, "I wish I had known that." Sometimes, we gain the knowledge when we have to pay the consequence for the bad choice we made. Gaining knowledge is very important in life and you need to make that a life goal. Before you make a decision, find out every piece of information possible about it. Ask people who have made such choices before because you can learn a lot from the experience of others. As I said in the beginning of this book, consult your three friends first, especially if it is a permanent decision.

2) YOUR NEED

The second thing that plays a role in making a decision is your current need, or the things you perceive as *needs*. Many times, what we think is a need may just be a want.

Advertisements and sales people are experts in this. They know how to present a product and make it look like you need it, though you wouldn't need that in a million years. So, we spend money we do not have for something we do not need. That is one of the reasons people never get ahead in their finances, because there is always something that appears to be a need. Do not follow your feelings when you make a choice, follow your spirit.

3) YOUR EMOTIONAL WELL-BEING

We are living in a world of feelings. We often say, "I feel this," or, "I feel that." I want you to know that you are not what you feel. Not all of your feelings are from God. You cannot trust your feelings; they change every millisecond. Some people have healthy emotions and others have crazy emotions. Sometimes, our hormones play a role in how we feel. Other times, what we went through in life, the pain, hurts, abuses, and neglect, have affected the make-up of our emotional life. Our life is always a reflection of our emotional set-up. We see life and others through those glasses.

Your emotional well-being affects the decisions you make in life. People with healthy emotions make healthy choices and vice versa.

4) SPIRITUAL INFLUENCE

As I mentioned before, we are spirit beings and are constantly influenced by the spirit world. The first decision man ever made on this earth was influenced by the spirit world. Adam was influenced by the devil and the kingdom of darkness and it was a wrong decision. We are still experiencing the consequences of that first decision. So, please make sure you are under the guidance of the Holy Spirit and not any deception when you make a choice.

The Holy Spirit and angels will never lead you to make a decision contrary to the written Word of God. Even if you hear the Word, you need to recognize the source of it. The devil speaks God's Word. Most of the time, when the enemy comes to deceive Christians, he comes with the Word taken out of context. Most people fall prey to his deception because they know they should never disobey God's Word. We need to have the wisdom of God to understand the context of the situation, like Jesus did when He was tempted by the devil. I believe the highest level of spiritual warfare is the warfare of the Word of God. That is why the Word is called the sword of the Spirit, which is the only offensive weapon God gave His children to use against their enemy.

5) CIRCUMSTANCES

Another reason people make impetuous decisions is because they are influenced by their circumstances. We see commercials, get bombarded by e-mails, and receive mass-mailings about deals that last only 24 hours or less. The purpose is to pressure you to make a decision. Let me tell you, there will always be another deal available if you miss one. So, do not be enticed by "deal makers." If they are not offering that deal more than 24 hours, that means there is something wrong with what they are trying to sell and the product may not last more than 24 hours (at least the excitement). It is not worth having. You do not need to use such schemes to sell a quality product. Any product that is of quality has been around and on the market for years. Some people get married this way. They see someone out of the blue and decide to get married on a whim. I have even heard that there are drive-thru marriage ceremonies these days!

6) PERCEPTION

Your perception is formed by your experience, past history, and knowledge. Some people repeatedly make poor choices. It's almost like there is a default setting in their brain to make the wrong choice. You need to break that cycle.

If you were abused and grew up in a dysfunctional family (most of us), there is a greater chance that you will make poor choices when it comes to life's important decisions. Make sure you receive healing for all of those defects. I think the second time around people should be smarter but, unfortunately, many are not.

7) YOUR VISION FOR YOUR LIFE

Your choices in life are determined by the vision you have for your life when you make that choice. People make frivolous choices without thinking about their future. Jesus said that when you decide to build a tower, make sure you *sit* (not standing or in a rush) down and consider if you have the resources to complete the project. Otherwise, those who see it unfinished will ridicule us (Luke 14:28-30).

When you make a permanent decision, always take your future into consideration. Once you make that decision, it can alter your future; because it is permanent you have to live with it.

8) FINANCIAL SITUATION

Your financial status affects your decisions. If your income is fifty thousand a year, you cannot afford to buy a million dollar house. That goes along with all other areas of life. People fail to consider their income and end up in disaster when they spend more than what their income can sustain. Always do the due diligence before you make a financial decision.

9) PEER/FAMILY PRESSURE

Some people make choices because of pressure from their family and friends. Well, if your decision is going to affect the rest of your life, you should not give in to the pressure of anyone. They will not be there to experience the consequences. God made each individual differently and their needs are different. No one has the authority or the right to force a person to make any decision. It is ungodly.

10) WISE DECISIONS

Wise decisions are those we make after we pray and think through all possible options. Take as much time as is necessary before you make destiny decisions. A person who is hasty always ends up in trouble.

Proverbs 19:2 says, "Also it is not good for a soul to be without knowledge, and he sins who hastens with his feet."

293

God sent His Holy Spirit to be in us and with us. One of the responsibilities of the Holy Spirit is to lead us into all truth. Before you make any decision, ask the Holy Spirit for His help and guidance. If you do not hear from Him, wait until you hear. He knows about your life and your future better than you know about them. Do not think your life is in your hands. No, it's not your life; God gave you your life as a gift and sent you to this earth to fulfill His purpose.

CHAPTER 18
A WORD TO PARENTS

CHAPTER 18: A WORD TO PARENTS

Many people's lives get messed up not because they do not go to college or a church. Their lives get messed up because they do not receive what they are supposed to receive from their parents. We are all products of how we were brought up in a family, or without a family. One-third of American children are being raised without a father (LifeSitenews.com). Most of us grew up in a dysfunctional family. I myself grew up in one.

As adults, our upbringing really affects the decisions we make in life, which is why I am prompted to write a few words about parenting. What I am sharing with you here is what the Holy Spirit has taught me. I am not a perfect father, nor an expert in the area of parenting. I know that and my children know it. When I am wrong, I ask my children to forgive me. As I shared before under the title of Ultimate Purpose, the ultimate purpose of parenting is to reveal the heart and purpose of the Heavenly Father to our children, to manifest Christ.

It is not an easy task. Naturally speaking, it is an impossible task. I have not seen a perfect father or mother, except the heavenly Father. But, most of us grew up with fathers who represented anything but the true nature of our heavenly Father. You might have been abused, neglected, rejected, criticized, or forsaken by your earthly parents. If so, it is difficult to picture in your heart a God who loves and cares for you.

Parents play the most important role in a child's life. We are not just providers who put a roof over our children and food on the table. You might provide a good education, too. That is not all there is to parenting. Those are just the basics. Our children need much more than a roof over their head, food on their plate, and clothes to wear to school every day.

I have read that the first five years are the formative years of life. A child's outlook on life and their concept about God and life will be formed during those years. The rest of the years are just building on that foundation. The roots of the majority of the problems we face in adult life, marriage, finances, etc. are found in the childhood years of our life. We are just dealing with the fruit of it now. Dealing with fruit will not solve the issue. We have to go to the root. As long as the root remains plunged into contaminated or polluted soil, it will produce bad fruit.

We learn almost everything from our parents through watching them: how to treat others, how to communicate, how to relate to the opposite sex. Our values of life, worldview, and spiritual foundation are all learned at home. As parents, we need to prepare our children in these areas and many more. It is a complicated responsibility.

Whatever wounds and dysfunction you inherited from your parents, you need to get healed from them. The fundamental emotional needs of a human being are to feel loved, accepted, appreciated, and protected. When we are growing up, our parents are supposed to pour these into us. Instead, most of us grew up in homes where criticism, abuse, neglect, and rejection were poured into us. That does not take away our need to be loved and accepted.

Most people grew up with a void in their heart because the need to be loved and accepted was unfulfilled. The reason God put parents on this earth was to convey the love of God and represent Him to their children. A child has no way of knowing God when they are little, and the people they are around the most are their parents. Parents are like God to their children. We stand in the place of God to a child. Whatever we say or do is equal to God saying or doing it to them.

We know (some may not) that God is a perfect Father. God has both fatherly and motherly qualities (nature) in Him. In the Church, the closest office among human beings God put on this earth to represent Him is the call and function of an apostle. Look at what Paul says.

> 1 Thessalonians 2:10-12 says, "You *are* witnesses, and God *also,* how **devoutly** and **justly** and **blamelessly** we behaved ourselves among you who believe; as you know how we **exhorted**, and **comforted,** and **charged** every one of you, as a **father** *does* his own children, that you would **walk worthy** of God who calls you into His own kingdom and glory."

The major qualities of a great father are mentioned in the above verses. Parents form the first image of God in their children. Depending on whether it was positive or negative, when a child grows up they relate to and view God based on their experience with their parents. That is why parenting is so important.

As I said earlier, man is a three-part being made of spirit, soul, and body. Each of these parts needs to be nurtured if a person is going to properly grow. Many parents nurture only one or two parts of their children. Some take care of them physically, and others emotionally, but neglect the spiritual life. Others take care of them physically and spiritually but neglect the emotional aspect of life.

Just like our body needs vitamins and good food for its proper growth, our soul needs emotional vitamins and minerals for proper growth. Unconditional love, acceptance, affirmation, validation, approval, feeling protected, and appreciation are some of those vitamins and minerals. When a person grows up without receiving those from their parents, they will definitely be dysfunctional as an adult in one (or more) area of their lives. To compensate for those malfunctions of their soul, some grow up to be overachievers while others become underachievers. Many turn to various forms of addiction. Trying to cover up their feelings of shame and inadequacy, some children become extremely extroverted while others become unusually introverted.

Based on the above scripture and by the revelation of the Holy Spirit I am going to explain in a nutshell some of the responsibilities of a father and mother in the following lines.

RESPONSIBILITIES OF A FATHER

1) LOVE

Children need to know that they are loved. Every parent says they love their children, but the question is; do the children know it in their heart? If they are not *feeling* that in their heart, parents are not *expressing* their love enough. You need to make sure that you are expressing your love to them in words and deeds. You might be working 80 hours a week to provide for them but at the end, if they do not feel you love them, all the work you did was in vain. If we fail to show them our love, later when they are released to God they will have a difficult time receiving His love or knowing that He loves them.

2) ACCEPTANCE

Children need to know that you accept them unconditionally, not based on their good behavior, the grades they earn in school, or their achievements. God accepted us in Christ Jesus, not based on what we did or do.

3) PROTECTION

Children need to know that they are protected by their father. If we do not give them that assurance, they will not believe God will protect them. It will take them a long time to realize that God will protect them. When they feel they are protected, they feel secure enough to face life.

4) PROVISION

Most parents in the West are good at providing for their children materially. Provision has different levels. Do not create a picture in their heart that God is stingy with us. He is very generous toward us, depending on our personal belief and faith.

5) APPRECIATION

We all need to feel appreciated. Look for creative ways to appreciate your children, even for the little things they do. You cannot overdo appreciation. I do not think we can appreciate our children too much. The better question is: Are we doing enough? When we appreciate our children, it creates in them a sense of worth. Let them feel how valuable they are, rather than feeling they are an inconvenience to what we want to do. Something good happens to a child when they hear from their father they have done a good job, or that they are good at something.

6) CORRECTION

We are also good at correcting our children. Sometimes though we do not do it in the right spirit and that can hurt their soul and spirit. Do not try to correct everything in a child. Sometimes, we try to treat our children based on our level. That means we expect them to behave and do things like we do. They can't. We need to always keep in mind that they are children and, as long as they are children, they are going to do certain things that may irritate us.

I have seen certain behaviors in my own children, certain things they like or habits that change over time. I used to jump up and down when they did something wrong. God said, "Chill out, My son. You did the same thing when you were a kid. Do not get upset with them all the time."

7) TRUST

We need to trust our children, and they need to know that they can trust us without question. Keep in mind that all these qualities I mention here are qualities of God we are trying to instill in our children. So, what we do determines how they view God when it is time for them to take their relationship with Him personally and seriously. If they cannot trust their father, they will not trust God for anything.

8) WORTH

Human beings are the most precious of all God's creation. We are of great value and importance. We are not just people passing by and doing nothing. The future of the earth depends on us. Children need to know how valuable they are. There may be times they feel like an inconvenience, or an expense, and it is our job to show them they are treasured.

9) PURPOSE

A father needs to instill the hope of a bright future in his child's heart. Mothers focus mainly on taking care of the immediate needs of a child (food, clothing, school, and other daily necessities). That is what they care about and pay attention to, and there is nothing wrong with it. A father always looks ahead and wants to prepare his children for the future. There is a prophetic element attached to fathers because they are the priest, prophet, and king of the family.

There is a prophetic element to all of our lives; we call it the future. God is a prophetic God and everything He does has a prophetic touch. A father needs to exemplify that to his children. Whatever God does, He thinks generationally.

The reason most people do not understand or know their purpose is because their father did not instill this quality in them. Many are growing up without their father around them. May the Lord help this generation.

> The Father says, "For I know the thoughts that I think toward you, says the Lord, thoughts of peace and not of evil, to give you a future and a hope" (Jeremiah 29:11).

10) IDENTITY

A father is supposed to assure his children of their identity, both their spiritual and sexual identity. Many are not happy with the way they were born. Girls are not happy because they are girls, and boys are not happy they were born boys. They want to change their sexual orientation because they were not blessed as a girl or a boy by their parents when they were little. Sometimes, parents talk to children as if they wish they were the opposite sex. It puts a question mark on their identity. Please do not do that.

We live in a world where boys look and act like girls, and girls look and act like boys. We have an identity crisis. This crisis can only be addressed and healed by assuring these fragile hearts through fatherly love. I believe one of the reasons men

301

want to be with men and women want to be with women is that no one affirmed their identity and sexual orientation. They may have been abused by one of them while they were children so, when they are older, they may gravitate toward the opposite gender of the person who abused them.

We also need to instill in our children their spiritual identity as children of God. They need to know that God loves them and ultimately they are His children. He gave them to us for a season, to train them in His ways and to kick-start their spiritual journey.

11) AFFIRMATION

Affirmation goes along with identity. We need to affirm our children's gender, ability, looks, character, sex, and creativity. We need to show them that they are accepted just the way God created them. God put every quality in them that is required to fulfill His purpose. God never makes a mistake.

12) FORM THE IMAGE OF OUR HEAVENLY FATHER

A father portrays the heavenly Father to his children. Whatever he does creates a corresponding image of God in the child's life. This is very important and the key role of a father. Most of us had fathers that were raised by parents who were not born again, and they did not have a healthy image of God in them. This has been going on for generations and we need to bring a change. One of the main reasons people fear or resent God is the distorted image that was formed in them while they were growing up.

13) SHOW LOVE AND HONOR TO THEIR WIFE

Children learn how to treat others by seeing how their parents treat each other. Fathers need to show love and honor, in both word and deed, to their wives in the presence of the children. This works both ways between husbands and wives.

14) PROPHETIC BLESSING

The final thing a father needs to do for his children is to speak over them a final prophetic blessing. We see this throughout the Bible. Fathers spoke over their children prophetically concerning their future, acting as the mouthpiece of God. Whatever he spoke, it was as if God spoke it. There was no annulment later. As I shared with you earlier, parents represent God to their children. It is a serious responsibility. Every father must do this for his children as the Spirit of the Lord leads them. You do not need to wait until just before you die to do this. The earlier you do it the better it will be for your children.

Every child needs to be blessed at four different stages of life and I will explain this later in this book.

RESPONSIBILITIES OF A MOTHER

1 Thessalonians 2:7-9 says, "But we were **gentle** among you, just as a **nursing** *mother* **cherishes** her own children. So, **affectionately** longing for you, we were well pleased to **impart** to you not only the gospel of God, but also our own lives, because you had become **dear to us**. For you remember, brethren, our **labor and toil**; for laboring night and day, that we might **not be a burden** to any of you, we preached to you the gospel of God."

Isaiah 66:13 says, "As one whom his **mother** comforts, so I will comfort you; and you shall be comforted in Jerusalem."

The major qualities of a mother are mentioned in the above verses.

1) NURTURING

Mothers are good at nurturing. What does nurture mean? The online dictionary says, "to feed and protect: to support and encourage, as during the period of training or development: to bring up; train; educate" (Dictionary. com). Wow, that is a great responsibility! Usually, mothers are more involved with the children's early education and training. Fathers might be at work while mothers take care of the home. Many mothers, unfortunately, do not train their children. They need to train and instill in them that their father loves them (though he may not be a perfect father and has plenty of weaknesses). They need to train them in the ways of God. As the Bible says, "Train up a child in the way he should go, and when he is old he will not depart from it" (Proverbs 22:6).

Whatever you teach and train them; know that it is going to stay in them when they get old. So, make sure you are training them in the right things and not dancing to their tunes all the time.

2) CARING

Mothers, and women in general, are excellent at caring. Most caretakers and nurses on this earth are women. They need to take care of children's spiritual, emotional, and physical needs, not just one. Make sure they get a balanced diet for their spirit, soul, and body. Children have an amazing capacity to learn. Many times parents suppress that capacity because they are little. That is what our parents did to many of us. Please do not do that with your children.

3) LOVING

Both father and mother need to show and express love to their children. As I said before, most parents love their children in their heart, but I encourage you to express it with your words as much as you can, and follow those words up with loving actions.

4) COMFORTING

When a child gets hurt, they usually run to their mother because children know mothers are good at comforting, and fathers are good at correcting. We need to know when they need to be comforted, and when they need to be corrected. They need to be comforted first; correction comes later.

5) HEALING

A mother's touches, caresses, and hugs have healing power. Sometimes when children cry (for whatever reason), all they need is to be held by their mother and they will stop crying. Humans need to be touched, especially women. If they do not get that, they wither away. Mothers, make sure you pour into your children healing words and touches.

6) FEEDING

I do not need to explain this in detail. Thank you, mothers, for feeding your children. It starts from the time they are born and does not end as long as they live. In fact, children come with an open mouth, hungry to be fed. One thing to be sure of is to feed them the right foods. We live in a world of junk food. Most eating habits are formed while we are young.

7) SHOW RESPECT AND OBEDIENCE TO THEIR HUSBAND

After the children are weaned, a mother's job is to release them to their father, constantly affirming to the child the love and care of the father, even without his awareness. The father in turn, trains the children and releases them to God, consistently affirming the love and acceptance of their heavenly Father for them. Mothers need to teach their children how to honor their father. This only happens in mature households. We see in the Bible mothers like Hannah, Elizabeth, and Mary, the mother of Jesus, doing this. Once the child was old enough to relate to

God, they released them to Him. Hannah brought her son Samuel to the house of God after he was weaned. Their sons grew up to be extraordinary people on this earth.

When Jesus' family came to visit the temple when He was twelve years old, He chose to stay back in Jerusalem (in the temple) talking to the leaders. When his parents found Him after three days and Mary expressed her concern, Jesus replied, "Why did you seek Me? Did you not know that I must be about My Father's business?" (Luke 2:49-50). But they did not understand Him. In other words, He was saying, "Mother, sooner or later I have to make a transition to do what My Father wants me to do rather than just being your child forever."

God gives our children to us for a season with the intention that we will have the goal of raising them then releasing them to Him when they are able to know Him personally. By then, the parents should have painted a healthy picture of God for them through the lives they modeled. Although parents will be related to their children forever, our responsibility toward them changes with age. Parents need to bring their children up in such a way that, after a certain age, the parents are willing to release them to God.

We do not get very much time to do what we need to do for our children. With all of the distractions that are around us, most of our time is spent on things that are of no value. In modern homes, TV (or some other form of media) trains children more than parents. Everything we do with them and to them has to be very intentional and geared toward training them for their future. Once the time is up, we cannot go back and start over.

> Deuteronomy 4:9 says, "Only take heed to yourself, and diligently keep yourself, lest you forget the things your eyes have seen, and lest they depart from your heart all the days of your life. And teach them to your **children** and your grandchildren."

When and how are we supposed to teach our children? Twenty minutes, once a week, on Sunday mornings? Let's see what God has to say.

> Deuteronomy 6:7, "You shall teach them diligently to your children, and shall talk of them when you **sit in your house, when you walk by the way, when you lie down**, and **when you rise up**."

Wow! No wonder we have so many challenges with our children these days! Our priorities are totally messed up. We are living in an upside-down world. What is most important has become the least important, and what is the least important has taken the place of the most important. Do you know what most parents talk about these days when they sit in their house, when they walk by the way, when they lie down and when they rise up? Sports, pets, and movies. Many parents make sure their children get to visit Disney World and other recreational places, watch all the new release movies, and read all the fun books. I am not against any of these fun things, but make sure the priority is right. That means that, if they are to prosper and become everything they need to be, our children must spend more time being taught the ways of God than sitting in front of media.

Who said kids are too young to pray, fast, or memorize the Bible? There is a lie of the devil that is going around today that says kids are too young to do or understand spiritual things.

Did God make a mistake when He said to teach and train our children His Word and His ways (not games) when they are little? If a Jewish child can memorize the first five books of the Bible (that is 187 chapters and 5,852 verses) by the time they are thirteen, we had better wake up, Church! No wonder they are successful! He did not tell the priests in the temple to do it, but the parents to teach their children!!! I know many adult believers who have been in church for decades but still struggle to find the right book and verse in the Bible.

Muslims do the same with their children. That is one of the reasons you do not see a Jewish or Muslim kid at the park or on a field playing in the evening. I have heard many Christian parents say their biggest dream is to take their children to Disney World before they are thirteen!! That is good: but have them recite the five books of the Bible (I would say at least the four gospels) before you book the flight! ☺

Our kids sit quietly and with full attention (glued) in front of a movie screen for two hours, but they cannot do the same in church for an hour? Our kids can play adult games and sports before they even reach thirteen (football, soccer, wrestling, skiing, skating, etc.) and break their ribs and bones, but they are too young to pray for 15 minutes? Are we raising a godly future generation or zombies?

Parents make time to take their children to all these places and games, but they do not have time to pray or read the Bible with their children! They will sit and play their newly bought game or toy for hours forgetting to eat or even to drink water, but they are too young to fast a meal?

They ride on roller coasters for a whole day and make their brain like a smashed potato, but they are too young to stand and worship in church for 20 minutes? They read stories and other fiction books, which have hundreds of pages, without any struggle but they are too young to read their Bible?

I know kids (Christians) who know the names of every football player and team nationwide, but they do not know the names of Jesus' twelve disciples.

Excuse me: Are we blaming the government for our problems? Where did all this begin? In school or in the family? I would say in the family. Let's go back to God's drawing room and follow His blueprint instead of trying to invent our own or playing the blame game.

I grew up in a home where we had three family prayers every day. I mean *every* day. Rain or shine, every morning at 5:45am my father started the family prayer. We did not have any choice; we had to get up and join the rest of the family at any cost. Then in the evening before we did our homework, all of the children (there were four of us) would sing, read our Bible, and pray. The third one was after we had dinner, just before we went to bed. Then I read the Bible every day before I went to school. I came home to have lunch and before I went back to school, I read the Bible again.

All of the revelation of the Word that I receive today is from the seed that was sown into my spirit in those days when I read the Bible. Though I did not understand a thing that I was reading, now I am glad that I did it. I would not trade that for the whole world, not even for a million hours of fun movies and games. Though it was not done perfectly, it drilled in me some of the discipline, order, and consistency that are essential for life and created in me an awareness of God and a love for His Word that will last for the rest of my life. The foundation of my life was laid during those days.

When I was eighteen I received the call of God from my heavenly Father, and I left my house to follow Him. When I say, 'the call of God,' there was no dramatic experience. It came to me as a desire in my heart. After twenty-three years of walking with Him, I have never looked back to wish I had done something different with my life. If I had one more chance to do things all over again, I would still choose to follow my heavenly Father. The only things I would do differently are: I would not wait until eighteen and I would not back away from anything He told me to do because of fear.

When a child reaches the age where they are able to relate to God for themselves (it is a gradual process), parents need to trust God with their children. Make sure you do your job well before that. By the time they reach that age, they should have a healthy image of God in them and be ready to accept Him into their lives as their Father, trusting in and following Him wherever He takes them. The foundation has to be laid right; otherwise, they will have unnecessary challenges.

What parents give to their children is just like an appetizer before the real meal. The love we yearn for, acceptance, forgiveness, and everything else we need, can only come from God, not from any human. That is the number one reason for challenges in most relationships. Most try, or expect, to receive from people what only God can give. Once we receive these from God our human relationships become fulfilling and enjoyable.

For a person who is not happy with himself or herself, no one or no thing can make them happy. They will blame or project it on others but the real problem lies within. When they are at peace with themselves, they can have peace with others. Lord, help us.

Most people do not want to follow God because they do not have a healthy image of Him. It was not formed while they were growing up so they do not want anything to do with Him. Unfortunately, most of us did not grow up with a healthy image of God, or ourselves. The foundation was not properly laid. In some cases there was no foundation at all. Instead, many developed a survival mentality. They do not know why they are on this earth or where they are going from here. Children come out of their homes without knowing their purpose or possessing any sense of worth. As a result, they are influenced by others and make wrong choices. Many lives end up a big mess.

We live in a society where parents have no time to spend with their children. They are working hard day and night, thinking they are working to provide for their family. Well, provision is only one of the needs they have. Many others are growing up in single-parent homes, where children are torn apart and attacked by the enemy without proper protection.

Most of us grew up in homes where we received some of these elements. I grew up in a home where my father provided for me, but it was the bare minimum. So, I developed this image of God as a God who only provided just enough to get by. My father was not there to protect me and never expressed his love to me. When a problem came, he never took my side. Instead, he always accepted my enemy's accusation and took his side. When I had grown up, I had a hard time believing God would protect me or love me. I did not know how to receive or give love. So, I took things into my own hands each time a challenge came up. It almost killed me.

My mother never comforted me. She cooked meals and cleaned the kitchen. So I did not know how to receive comfort from God when I went through hard times. Then, we come with our brokenness and unmet needs getting ready to marry someone. Whatever we needed to receive from our parents and did not receive from them, we are in search of to meet those needs.

The reason we enter into a relationship is based on what we did not receive from our parents. If I did not receive caring and nurturing from my parents, I will be most attracted to someone who is caring and nurturing. If you were not protected by your parents, when someone you think will protect you comes into your life, you will 'fall in love.' Know that both individuals have this issue and that is why opposites always attract.

There is a negative side to it, too. If you grew up in homes where trust was not developed, then you will have problems trusting other people. These people will have issues trusting their spouse. Two people enter into a marriage relationship expecting the other person to meet the needs that were unmet by their parents. There begins the problem.

When we find Jesus, whatever needs were unmet by our parents are supposed to be met by Him. We do not get healed from those issues because we do not know how to receive that healing from Him. It is unhealthy and unrealistic to expect another human being (our spouse) to meet those needs. When we get married, we are supposed to be at a healthy place where we are healed and willing to meet the other person's needs without expecting anything in return. When both spouses enter into a relationship like that, they can build a healthy marriage.

Most marriages end when one of the spouses realizes the other one is not going to listen or meet their needs and exits the relationship. But, if they work together and dig deep to find out their real needs, they can be healed and have a great marriage. I believe there is no need for any marriage to end in divorce. There is a solution to every problem that arises in your marriage. It will take some time, effort, and pain to work through the challenges, but there is always hope.

It is better for people to work out their pain and challenges before they get married so they can focus on building a future together. Otherwise, years will be wasted fighting and that strife lasts until they find the solution; sometimes it can take decades. The sooner you realize the problem and start working on it, the sooner you can be healed. Many go from one relationship to another thinking the next person will meet their needs. Soon they find out this one has more challenges than the previous one. If God has put you together (if you are married for whatever reason, God has put you together), there is always hope.

Sometimes, God puts people together who have totally opposite needs. He does that to reveal the wounds in their hearts so they can get healed. Many misunderstand and begin to fight with their spouse, thinking they are causing the trouble. Your spouse will seem irritating and drive you crazy. In truth, it is not your spouse doing that. It is your brokenness and the wounds that caused it. You are reacting to your spouse based on those wounds and that brokenness.

God knows exactly who to put together. He does it in a way that the other person reveals your weaknesses and problems that need to be dealt with. Many people think it was a mistake and that they made a wrong choice. No, you did not. You got exactly what you needed, so stop fighting; take your shoes off and stay a while and start working on it NOW.

CHAPTER 19
BLESSING THE FOUR
STAGES OF LIFE

CHAPTER 19: BLESSING THE FOUR STAGES OF LIFE

Many people live like they do not belong on this earth or they do not know where on this earth they belong. They have visions, dreams, and ideas, but they feel like they are missing something in their inner being. They do not know what it takes to get from where they are to where they want to be. You might be an adult who has grandchildren but inside you feel like a little child who is looking for their daddy.

I believe there is a little child in all of us who is looking for acceptance, love, and the approval of someone, especially our parents. If you grew up without receiving emotional nurturing from your parents, you will feel like a person who is left out and missing something. You might be one of the most talented people in the world, with the special revelation and calling to change the next generation, but feel like you do not have the "guts" to stand on your own feet.

You may not like yourself and your emotional maturity might be at the level of a child. People who started later in life might be way ahead of you, leaving you wondering when your time is going to come. You keep holding yourself back from moving forward because you are afraid to step out. There is a reason you are feeling this way. These are just the tips of emotional icebergs—or, worse yet, volcanoes—that are ready to erupt at the push of a button.

One of the main reasons you feel these emotions might be because you were not blessed when you were a child especially by your father. So, you are constantly looking for someone to hold your hand and take you where you need to go. Once you receive the healing for your emotions and receive the blessing that I am sharing in this book, you will be on your way to fulfilling your purpose.

When we do not receive the blessing, the enemy of our soul is busy putting his lies in our mind. In the place of blessing he puts fear, shame, rejection, and insecurity. We will not know how to interact with adults. We will not know what to do when problems arise. Below are seven symptoms or "feelings" a person will develop if he or she was not blessed while growing up.

1) I do not belong here

2) Nobody likes me

3) I don't have what it takes

4) I can't do anything right

5) Something is wrong with me

6) I am not good enough

7) Everybody else is okay except me

These "feelings" are lies the enemy caused you to believe in your heart. People with these symptoms tend to develop a heart condition that I call the "Orphan Heart Syndrome" (OHS). They will not use half of their potential in relation to their purpose. If you suffer from one or more of the above symptoms in your emotional life, know that there is a reason for it. One of the main reasons could be that you were not blessed (by someone with spiritual authority over you) when you were young. You might have received prayers and felt temporary relief but, sooner or later, you fell back into the same ditch. This is because in your heart you are not convinced that you are blessed. For that to happen, those lies about yourself that you believe in your heart need to be replaced by the truth of what your heavenly Father thinks and says about you.

I also found that even people who were blessed and had great parents while growing up can struggle with negative feelings about themselves. We live in a fallen world where the lies of the enemy are more prevalent than the truth of God. We need to always guard our soul and intentionally abide in the truth.

LIFE OF JESUS

The only perfect Son on this earth was Jesus Christ. What made Him perfect? He grew up in a dysfunctional family. He did not have a natural father. His mother conceived Him out of wedlock. You may say He was perfect because He was God. He did not live on this earth as God. The Bible says He emptied Himself and took on the form of a servant. The Jesus we see in the Gospels is Jesus in His humanity. We see Jesus in His divinity in the book of Revelation.

If you study the life of Jesus, there are things that took place in His life that made Him a perfect Son. Though He did not have a natural father, we do not see the insecurity, rejection, anger, or any other trait people develop when they grow up without a father. I saw something powerful in Jesus' life. The Bible is a book of blessing. I found that Jesus was blessed by someone at four stages of life, which all of us need if we are going to have confidence, purpose, and a positive outlook on life. If we bless our children in these four stages, they also will grow up as "perfect."

There is a reason for why you feel you do not belong in this world. There is a reason why you do not like yourself, or feel like nobody likes you, or like you are being rejected, or as if there is something wrong with you. It is because you were not blessed at the critical moments of your life, either by your parents or someone in spiritual authority (in the absence of your parents). If you are not blessed in the four stages of life, what is supposed to come easily in life, you need to fight for with your teeth and skin. What is supposed to take three months to accomplish will take thirty years. Jesus accomplished in three and a half years what most people will not accomplish in a lifetime. Do you see the difference? The difference is the blessing.

Most of us, instead of being blessed by our parents, were cursed without even knowing it. What brings a blessing, or curse, are the words we speak. As I mentioned earlier, parents are the first 'god' a child sees and experiences. You are in the position of God in their life. You can either curse or bless your child. It is so important that you bless them. The Bible says, "Death and life are in the power of the tongue" (Proverbs 18:21). In other words, curses and blessings are in the power of the tongue.

Many, unfortunately, think of blessings only as material things. So, they "bless" their children with new shoes or the latest computer game without ever giving them the real blessing. These children grow up to squander their life and the 'blessings' they received. Even if you do not bless your children with a lot of material things, make sure you give them your 'blessing.' It will only be a matter of time before they prosper and find all the blessings they need. What I mean by the blessing is giving them your favor, acceptance, unconditional love, and speaking life to them. I hope you understand what I am saying here.

You and I are not alone in this. Some of the great people God used in the Bible felt like a child inside. Solomon and Jeremiah are some of them. In 1 Kings 3:7, Solomon said, "Now, O Lord my God, You have made Your servant king instead of my father David, but **I *am* a little child**; I do not know *how* to go out or come in." Jeremiah said, "Then said I, Ah, Lord God! behold, I cannot speak: for **I am a child.**"

Paul said that when he became a man, he put away childish things (1 Corinthians 13:11b). There has to be a time in each of our lives when we are able to put away childish ways of thinking and doing things. It takes the revelation of the Holy Spirit to come to this understanding. May the Lord help all those

315

adults who are sitting on the pews feeling like children to put away their childish behaviors and perspectives, in Jesus' Name.

There is a difference between being childish and child-like. When Jesus said that unless we turn and become like a child we will not enter the Kingdom of God, He meant child-like, not childish. Unless we learn to believe, love, and forgive like a child, we will not enter the Kingdom of God (Matthew 18:3).

Each person needs to be blessed at four stages of life. We are born into a cursed world that is ruled by demonic forces. The devil does not like it when a righteous seed is born. He loses that much of a hold on this earth. The righteous seed has positive spiritual influence; they do not need to be in ministry or shout every day to make a difference. Just being alive, a righteous seed (born-again spirit) has some spiritual jurisdiction. The more righteous people there are in a city, or a nation, determines how much the demonic activity will be limited. Remember the story of Sodom and Gomorrah? Just being alive you make a difference on this earth.

Let me come back to my subject. You do not need to be born into a perfect family to be blessed. The four stages at which a person needs to be blessed are conception, birth, childhood, and adult life. Jesus was not born into a perfect family. When Mary conceived Jesus, everyone thought she was a wicked woman that got pregnant before she was married. You can imagine the stigma she had to endure from her own family and neighbors. There was no one from her immediate family to bless her or the child; even Joseph would not do it. We are going to see how Jesus was blessed in all four stages of His life. To bless means to speak well of, empower, give favor, and cause to prosper. In simple words, say something good to that person or about that person in their hearing.

CONCEPTION

Since no one in Mary's family would bless her and the baby, God put it in her heart to go and see her cousin Elizabeth. When Mary reached her home, the Holy Spirit came upon Elizabeth and she began to prophesy. Luke 1:42 says, "Then she spoke out with a loud voice and said, "Blessed *are* you among women, and **blessed *is* the fruit of your womb!**"

Blessing someone from the point of their conception makes them feel welcomed to this earth. A baby can feel and hear what is happening to his/her mother and certain things outside. Many children were not welcomed because their mothers were not happy they were pregnant. Some others cursed the baby even while it was in the womb.

One of the happiest days of my life was when we discovered that my wife was pregnant with our first child. If you were not blessed during your conception, someone can do it for you now. I will share about it at the end of this chapter. It does not matter what circumstances you were born into: within the context of marriage, out of wedlock, even the result of rape, the power of the blessing can reverse and break any curse.

I want to tell couples to do this as soon as you find out that the wife is pregnant. I want to tell the women who are reading that if you are invited to a baby shower, please make sure you bless the baby while you are having fun.

BIRTH/CHILDHOOD

The second stage in which a person needs to be blessed is at birth. The first thing God did to Adam after he came alive was to bless him (Genesis 1:28). God knew man could not function on this earth without a blessing.

If you study the Jewish culture, it has been set up so that they bless their children and each other. It is set up in a way that a child gets blessed at these four stages. Eight days after an infant is born, the parents bring the baby to the temple to show the priest and offer a sacrifice. Then, the priest is supposed to bless that child.

When Mary brought Jesus to the temple, God appointed a man, a father figure, to bless Him. The man's name was Simeon. He came to the temple, led by the Spirit, at the same time and saw Jesus and Mary. He took Jesus in his hands and spoke. Luke 2:28-35 says, "**He took Him up in his arms and blessed** God and said:

> "Lord, now You are letting Your servant depart in peace, according to Your word; for my eyes have seen Your salvation which You have prepared before the face of all peoples, a light to *bring* revelation to the Gentiles, and the glory of Your people Israel." And Joseph and His mother marveled at those things which were spoken of Him. **Then Simeon blessed them**, and said to Mary His mother, "Behold, this *Child* is destined for the fall and rising of many in Israel, and for a sign which will be spoken against (yes, a sword will pierce through your own soul also), that the thoughts of many hearts may be revealed.""

We do a similar thing in churches at baby dedications. They are designed to serve this purpose. What happened to Jesus as a result of the blessing? Please read the following verses.

> Luke 2:40, "And the Child grew and became strong in spirit, filled with wisdom; and the grace of God was upon Him."

> Luke 2:52, "And Jesus increased in wisdom and stature, and in favor with God and men."

PUBERTY

The next stage in which a person needs to be blessed is when they reach the age of puberty, or their teenage years. I do not see a particular verse that says Jesus was blessed at this time. But, in the Jewish culture there is a thing called 'bar mitzvah'. It is a great celebration, an event to bless the sons and daughters. I am sure Jesus received that. The Bible says His parents went to Jerusalem (temple) every year.

> Luke 2:41 says, "His parents went to Jerusalem every year at the Feast of the Passover."

ADULTHOOD

A person needs to be blessed when they become an adult. Parents (especially the father) need to bless their children every time they start a new season, or venture, in their lives—especially when they start their first job, business, get married, etc. When Jesus was thirty, He began His public ministry. While He was coming out of the Jordan River after the baptism, the heavens opened and the Father spoke a blessing upon His Son.

> Matthew 3:16-17 says, "When He had been baptized, Jesus came up immediately from the water; and behold, the heavens were opened to Him, and He saw the Spirit of God descending like a dove and alighting upon Him. And suddenly a voice *came* from heaven, saying, "This is My beloved Son, in whom I am well pleased.""

Every son and daughter needs to know that their father is pleased with them. That gives them an inner strength and confidence to go forward in life and overcome the obstacles and storms. Without that, we will feel alone and the enemy will take advantage of us. The blessing gives us spiritual protection and covering.

Jesus did not have to hang around for ninety years to fulfill His purpose. He completed His mission in three years and changed the whole world. It was not because He did not have any challenges, persecution, or obstacles. He knew He was blessed. He knew He was the beloved of His Father. That is the power of blessing.

In the Bible, we see fathers call their children to themselves before they die and speak a blessing over them. Why? Because that is a spiritual principle that God ordained. As long as we live on this cursed earth, we need all the blessing we can get. When there is no blessing, only curses are in operation. When I say blessing, it does not mean giving material things or money. That is what we normally look at as a blessing. The blessing I am talking about here is the *empowerment* and favor to get all those things you need, including material stuff.

If you were not blessed as a child or an adult, or at any other stage of life, talk to someone who knows how to bless. It is best if your father can bless you. If he is not around or is not in his right mind, ask your pastor, a mature Christian friend, a family member, an elder in your church, or anyone in whom you recognize the Spirit of God. You need to be blessed. Without it, nothing will go well. Nobody will know that you existed on this earth. May the Lord lead you to the right person.

3

CHAPTER 20
THE SEASON OF TOTAL RESTORATION

CHAPTER 20: THE SEASON OF TOTAL RESTORATION

What I (God shared through me) share in this book is the perfect scenario of life, the way life is supposed to work on this earth. This is the order God ordained for us. We see it in the Garden of Eden.

1) God created man (they had a relationship and that is the first decision)

2) God made a garden and put Adam in it to work and to guard it (that was his purpose, the second decision)

3) God made Eve and brought her to Adam (she became his wife, the third important decision)

We see the same order in the life of Joseph in the book of Genesis. His relationship with God and the dream he received from God were the foundation of his life. After the tests and trials, Joseph was promoted to the palace of Pharaoh, which was the place of his purpose. Thirdly, Pharaoh gave him a wife and Joseph lived a fulfilled life in Egypt.

Most of us were not correctly informed and did not know what we were doing when we made these major decisions of life. The majority of humans made the wrong choice in at least one of these major decisions. That is the root of most of the pain we experience. God never intended it to be that way. We have made a mess out of life. Most of us do not have the freedom to go back and reverse those decisions or their consequences.

There is one thing we can do, which I believe is one of the main reasons God made me write this book. We can teach our children and grandchildren about the ways of God, to prepare a generation who will know God and walk with Him all the days of their lives. Let us share with them not only our triumphs but also the bitter mistakes we have made in life so they will not need to walk through it and waste their precious years as many of us did.

After you read this book, you will have one of these emotions. First, you will be excited because you have found some keys that will help your life. Some will wish they had this book twenty or thirty years ago. Perhaps you've made all of these important decisions and are done with parenting. Or, you might be feeling regret, anger, or frustration arise in you, remembering all the wrong decisions you made and the consequences they brought to your life.

I was born into a Christian home and attended church all of my life. That did not make my life any easier. Though I received Christ when I was sixteen and discovered my purpose early in life, it has not been a smooth ride for me. Every person on earth thinks they go through the worst and their experience is the most painful of all.

I received a glimpse of my purpose and set out to make it all happen. Nothing happened when I wanted it to happen, though. A few times, I tried to help God make things happen faster and, as a result, I brought forth Ishmaels. It is not easy to live with an Ishmael in your life when it does not match the picture of the "promised son" in your heart.

There were times I thought I would not make it through life, I thought I would die of a heart attack or have a mental breakdown. I have been through water and fire as the Psalmist says but the LORD has brought me to a broad place. Then I understood the story of the man who brought his son to the disciples but they could not heal him. Later, he brought him to Jesus, and the father said that the spirit that was in his son tried to throw him in water and into fire to kill him.

> Mark 9:22 says, "And often he has thrown him both into the fire and into the water to destroy him. But if You can do anything, have compassion on us and help us."

The reason all that happened in our lives and we made the wrong choices is because the enemy of our soul does not want us to know God or fulfill our purpose. He comes to steal, kill, and destroy. The enemy tried to destroy your destiny by throwing you into water and fire. Water and fire represent trials and problems in our lives, but God has brought you out of water and fire.

Jesus cast out the spirit and the boy was healed. I want to tell you the good news, you might have gone through water and fire or you may be going through it as you read this book. Cheer up, the devil, unless you let him, is not strong enough to kill you or destroy your purpose.

Isaiah 43:2 says, "When you pass through the waters, I will be with you; and through the rivers, they shall not overflow you. When you walk through the fire, you shall not be burned, nor shall the flame scorch you."

Whatever decision you made and however much of a mess it has brought, I want to tell you that there is hope, and you can be healed and restored. I am not just saying that casually to make you feel better. I believe it with all my heart. I also want to tell you that it will not be easy; it might be gruesome and hard to go back and fix things, but it is possible.

It is up to you. There is hope and there are answers to all of your problems. God wants to heal your heart. Jesus said that He was anointed to heal the brokenhearted, open the blind eyes, and set the captives free. One day, I was so upset and asked Him, "Lord, how do you heal the brokenhearted? I see many people in church who have been hurt and broken. Why are You not healing them? Show me one person who is totally healed and set free."

I found that there are two ways Jesus heals and restores people. One is instant healing, which we all like and expect. But there is another way that is mentioned in the New Testament. It says, "You shall lay hands on the sick and they shall *recover*" (Mark 16:18). Recovering is a gradual process that happens over time. Many people never receive their healing because they do not see an instant change in their situation, lose heart, and stop believing for their healing. Emotional healing is a gradual process. Jesus did not wave His hands over the fishermen (His disciples) to become mighty apostles in three months. They had to go through a process that took years.

You might be divorced, maybe more than once. Or, maybe you waited all your life and have not found the right person to marry. What is left over might be a heap of disappointment and heartache. You may have been betrayed, perhaps by your spouse, the lover of your life. When you were married, you never thought such a thing would ever happen. You may have lost a child, or have a child that was born with birth defects. How do we cope with life's unexpected situations?

I am not an expert in ministering to these issues. I would tell you to seek some professional help. There is help available if you pray, seek, and never give up. God will restore your joy, even the lost opportunities and time that was wasted. Our God is a God of redemption. The Bible says there is plenty of redemption with Him (Psalm 130:7). He promised in His Word that the lost years would be restored to us.

> Joel 2:25-26 says, "So I will restore to you the years that the swarming locust has eaten, the crawling locust, the consuming locust, and the chewing locust, My great army which I sent among you. You shall eat in plenty and be satisfied, and praise the name of the LORD your God, who has dealt wondrously with you; and My people shall never be put to shame."

Some things the enemy has stolen; you need to take authority over them and declare their restoration.

> Isaiah 42:22 says, "But this is a people robbed and plundered; all of them are snared in holes, and they are hidden in prison houses; they are for prey, and no one delivers; for plunder, and no one says, "**Restore!**""

I got married thinking we were going to go around the world to preach the gospel, establish churches, and train pastors. I had no idea what I was getting into. I had no idea what was in me. What happened after my marriage began was just the opposite of what I expected. Welcome to the real world!

We could not live in peace more than three days at a time. We went through everything you can imagine, except physical death. We were reacting from the wounds and hurts of our childhood. What I found was that when a person goes through abuse or a trauma in their childhood, that person stops growing emotionally at that point. It becomes a roadblock and, unless it is removed and healed, that person is stuck at that moment in life. Even when they are thirty, or forty, the level of emotional maturity will be of the time when they were abused. I thought my wife was the problem, and she thought I was the problem.

We had to be healed in our heart and soul. Our marriage was not heaven on earth when we began. We both grew up in different cultures, different countries, on different continents, and in very abusive homes. There was only one thing in common between us: that was our abusive childhood!

A few days before we got married, the tragic Columbine school shooting took place in Colorado. One of the girls who died was a member of the youth group in the church we attended. Our church hung a huge banner in the main sanctuary, which said, "Triumph in the midst of Tragedy." When we got married in the same sanctuary, that banner came in the background of all the photographs of our wedding. I believe God put that there for a reason. Our marriage started out with tragedy but, with the grace of God, we triumphed.

Years went by in between, and we did not know what to do. We could not agree on one thing. I fasted and prayed. I cast out and bound every demon I could think of and still there was no breakthrough. I convinced myself I made the wrong choice marrying my wife. The devil came to support that idea, and I lived in torment most of my waking moments. I was in ministry, preaching the gospel. From the outside, everything looked fine. Inside, there was a volcano brooding; waiting to erupt.

God, who gives life to the dead and calls those things that are not as though they are, came to our rescue. We found the help we needed. He began to heal both of our hearts. After twelve years, for the first time, I found peace in my heart about my marriage. I saw the sun rising on our horizon. Before I could not love my wife because I did not receive any love from anyone while I was a child. I did not know how. How can you give something you never received? My idea of marriage had been distorted by religion and by the cultural background I grew up in.

I want to share with you *how* and *what* God used to set me free. There are three things God used in my life. One is Proverbs 11:9, which says, "The hypocrite with *his* mouth destroys his neighbor, But through **knowledge** the righteous will be delivered." This verse says that a righteous person is delivered through knowledge. If you are the righteousness of God (if you believe in Jesus Christ, you are), and you need deliverance in an area of life, then God will use or lead you to the right knowledge that will set you free.

> Hosea 4:6a says, "My people are destroyed for lack of knowledge..." Many precious saints and their families that I know are being destroyed for lack of knowledge. Again, Isaiah 5:13a says, "Therefore my people have gone into captivity, because *they have* no knowledge..."

Next is John 8:32, which says, "And you shall know the truth and the truth shall make you free." If you are bound in any area of your life, that means you are believing a lie from the enemy about that particular situation or area of life. The Spirit of truth will lead you to a specific truth you need to know and it will set you free from that bondage. The enemy will fight all he can to keep you in bondage believing his lie. The moment you discover the truth about a particular area or situation in your life, you are free.

And, the third tool God used to set me free is mentioned in Ecclesiastes 10:10, "If the ax is dull, and one does not sharpen the edge, then he must use more strength; **but wisdom brings success**." There is a wisdom that comes from God that gives you success in every area of your life. Many want to be successful but they do not know what will bring it. Wisdom brings success into your life. Therefore, love wisdom.

I would encourage you to pray this prayer every day. "Lord, please lead me to knowledge that brings deliverance, to the truth that sets me free, and to the wisdom that brings success in every area of life. In Jesus' name, Amen."

I found out that I was fighting against my own purpose. God put the woman in my life that I needed. I was stubborn and wanted my own way. When God made my purpose as clear as the sky above me, I did not want to see it because I had my own preconceived ideas about family, ministry, and how God should do things for me. I was afraid of men and what they thought. God set me free from all that junk, and I can guarantee He will do the same for you. Thank God for His goodness.

Now that we are healed, we are happily married and never regret the choice we made. We complement one another's purpose. I told my wife the other day that if I had to do it again, I would still choose her. She is a pearl of great price. In the beginning, I could not see the seed God planted in her. I was focusing on the tares and trying to pluck them out. I thought I was helping her. Now I know it is not my job, it is God's job. My job is to love her as Christ loves the Church.

The process you are going through is not an accident or a surprise to God. He knew what He was doing. I want to tell you to stop fighting His purpose and yield to His process. Yield to His Spirit and, at the end, He will use that experience to bless someone else. Let me tell you, the problems and mess we have now were made because of our own pride, rebellion, and ignorance. The devil will take advantage of it. That's all. He cannot do anything of his own authority. Make sure there is no hook in your life where the devil can hang his chain.

God has made everything beautiful and set us free from every bondage. Believe it first, and seek the knowledge that comes from God. It is not easy to find and recognize the truth when we are deceived by lies. First, those lies need to be exposed by the light of God's truth. Then, you need to admit it and repent. You are free. At first, the truth may make you upset or angry, and you may even resist it for a while, but the sooner you yield; the sooner it will set you free.

Proverbs 15:14 says, "The heart of him who has understanding **seeks knowledge**, but the mouth of fools feeds on foolishness."

Everything I wrote in this book is taught by the Spirit of God. May He use this book in your life, and in the body of Christ, to heal that which was made crooked, build back that which was demolished, and take back that which was stolen, in Jesus' Name. God straightened out the crooked places and gave me a new heart. I can tell you with confidence that it does not matter how hopeless your situation may seem; there is hope. You might have lost a loved one in an accident, by sickness, or in a war. I may not understand the exact situation you are in, but God is an expert in healing hearts and He is on your side. Just give Him a chance and some time. You will be amazed at what He will do. The season of total restoration has begun. Amen.

Acts 3:20-21 says, "And that He may send Jesus Christ, who was preached to you before, whom heaven must receive until the **times of restoration of all things**, which God has spoken by the mouth of all His holy prophets since the world began."

If this book has blessed or impacted you in any way, would you please take a minute and let us know? You can email your comments to mim@maximpact.org or send them to us at:

Maximum Impact Ministries
P.O. Box 3128
Syracuse, NY 13220
USA

OTHER BOOKS BY ABRAHAM JOHN

Seven Kinds of Believers
Why All Believers Are Not Blessed Equally

Overcoming the Spirit of Poverty
Discovering and Fulfilling Your Purpose

Recognizing God's Timing for Your Life
Discerning God's Timing and Purpose Through Your Daily
Circumstances

Keys To Passing Your Spiritual Tests
Unlocking the Secrets to Your Spiritual Promotion

TO ORDER THESE BOOKS VISIT WWW.MAXIMPACT.ORG